Sex Power Money

Sara Pascoe is a highly acclaimed comedian, writer and actor. Her extensive TV credits include the BBC solo stand-up special *LadsLadsLads*; BBC2's *Frankie Boyle's New World Order*, on which she is a weekly guest contributor; and *Comedians Giving Lectures* on Dave, which she hosts. She wrote and performed the BBC Radio 4 series *Modern Monkey* and the BBC2 short *Sara Pascoe vs Monogamy*, which was inspired by her first book, *Animal*.

@sarapascoe
sarapascoe.com

Further praise for *Sex Power Money*:

'Whip-smart and funny, Pascoe digests reams of research into an eye-opening journey through social, cultural and linguistic anthropology. She has an engaging, conversational style of writing and an intriguing supply of curious facts . . . A fascinating and cohesive exploration of the human condition.' *Herald*

'With an impressive amount of research, she covers paying for sex, pornography, the reality of men's more active sex drives, the changes when we're aroused, and the evolutionary forces behind our desire . . . [Pascoe is] inclusive and of course, funny.' *i*

---

by the same author

ANIMAL

Sara Pascoe

Sex Power Money

FABER & FABER

First published in 2019
by Faber & Faber Limited
Bloomsbury House
74–77 Great Russell Street
London WC1B 3DA
This paperback edition published in 2020

Typeset by Faber & Faber Limited
Printed and bound by CPI Group (UK) Ltd, Croydon, CR0 4YY

A CIP record for this book
is available from the British Library

ISBN 978-0-571-33600-5

For Arminda Ventura

<3

Contents

Sex Power Money Money Money

We see things not as they are, but as we are.

Anaïs Nin

Heart of Darkness

My mum has a new boyfriend. He's called Geoff. I'm listening as he explains: 'I didn't have to pay because I made her orgasm.' I'm nine.

Geoff looks at me and then at my mother. I don't know which of us he's trying to impress but he's proud.

Geoff is using the word 'prostitute' in the easy way people did back then. If you say 'prostitute' now someone in the vicinity will be quick to correct you. They'll explain how the term reduces a sex worker's humanity and encourages stigma. Geoff didn't know that and nor did I.

'She said she doesn't usually cum with customers, but because I made her cum, she couldn't accept any money off me.'

My mum had told me previously, in a private conversation, that Geoff had quite a small penis. And if you're wondering how that's relevant, ditto, mate, ditto.

After Geoff had gone home the next day, Mum explained to me that prostitutes never orgasmed with their clients, they just pretended because of the fragile male ego. She told me that there was no way a prostitute wouldn't charge because they were excellent businesswomen and this was their livelihood.

I apologise that my mum is saying 'prostitute' as well. She's in the past when people didn't think about what they were saying. She would absolutely say 'sex worker' nowadays.

But sometimes 'sex worker' isn't the correct language either. If a person has been trafficked, if they are a child, if they are unable to give consent – they ain't working. We have to be careful with language because it creates the world. I recently heard a true crime podcast describe a woman being kidnapped and 'forced into sex work'. I'm sure you're aware that you can't be 'forced' to 'work' – that is slavery, and when sex is involved, that's rape.

I've been asked to keep the introduction 'light' so *shruggy winky emoji*.

Twenty-eight years later, I heard a comedian talking about PunterNet. 'It's TripAdvisor for prostitutes,' she joked, then missed her bus home thanks to the queue waiting to tell her: 'We call them sex workers now.' I went on PunterNet when I got home. It was mostly men discussing the parking restrictions around sex workers' houses. These men are breaking the law by paying for sex, but they're only worried about traffic wardens.

PunterNet's main page is basic and white ~~like your dad~~ with blue and black writing. There are no images. I felt safe to browse. There are reviews and message threads. I read a man's complaint about a woman's body odour and wanted to correct his spelling mistakes. I read a review that bemoaned that a woman 'didn't smile enough'. I thought this was funny. Men sometimes tell women to smile in the street or in a shop queue. Being told to smile has never made anyone want to. Do the men who say it know how much it pisses women off, is that why they do it?

I know it's not 'all men' who do this, but it only takes a few busy men to mean it happens on a daily/weekly basis to 'all women'.

Men don't tell other men to smile, they'd get punched. Telling another man to smile would insult his status, it would suggest that he's there to please you. That he's decorative. Telling a woman to smile does the same thing, but men aren't scared of women's punches.

HANG ON—

YES, sorry – women *can* be aggressors. YES, some women hit men. This is not a book about how women are always victims and men are always perpetrators.

When I was sixteen my mum had a different boyfriend. It was a complicated situation, he was married. Judge if you must; I certainly did. He would turn up at my house covered in what his wife had thrown at him, his shirts stained with food or smeared with condiments. The marks of her fingers on his face and neck. My mum would be kind to him, which disgusted me, obviously. His wife was a policewoman. She tracked his car. She broke into our house. She dragged him out of bed and beat him in front of my mum and sister. The people who are brutal and scary are created by more than biology.

So what I should've said above is: men aren't *automatically* scared of women's punches.

The result of evolution is that women *in general* are *on average* smaller and weaker than men, but it feels very sexist to say it. Like I'm criticising my own gender. Like I'm ignoring all the big strong women in the world and all the tiny men. No 'rule' about men and women is actually a 'rule'. It also sounds transphobic, or if not 'phobic' then at least trans-ignorant. Discussing sex and biology means stamping with large, insensitive boots over the fragile flower that is individual human experience. There will be a lot of caveats in this book. And one tiny bloke.

Me?

Yup.

Going back to Mr Complaints on PunterNet, he's whinging, 'She didn't smile at me once,' and I think he's pathetic. He knows this woman does not want to have sex with him. He knows that for *absolute definite* because he is having to PAY HER to do it. This could not be clearer. He knows this woman doesn't want to have sex with him and yet he expects her to look cheerful about it? I am laughing nastily to myself, thinking, 'You can pay her to have sex with you, but you can't pay her not to hate you.' Do these men live in a fantasy world where they're Richard Gere in *Pretty Woman*? Have they tricked themselves into believing that despite being paying customers they deserve to be desired?

I tried to relate this to my life. Sex work is so called by people who recognise it as a form of labour like any other. 'Sex work is work is work,' activists and allies repeat and reiterate. It was Gertrude Stein who wrote 'Rose is a rose is a rose' but it was easier for her because no one disagreed and criminalised roses, making their already difficult life harder. The parallel I found is that I go for massages. A form of physical labour, provided by a stranger's body. I pay people to touch me. It's weird for me to assess it like that. I think about the interactions I have with professionals I pay to touch me; they ask me what I want from the experience, they speak softly and treat me considerately. How would I respond if they did not follow this code of conduct? If they shouted, if they put loud rap music on instead of goaty panpipes? But I realise that while I understand consumer complaints, I cannot allow them from people paying for sex. I cannot correlate those things. In fact I worry that 'sex work is work' has made the people who buy sex feel even more entitled.

As hard as I try to understand the punters' point of view, they remain psychopaths to me. Unempathetic, selfish. They're all Geoffs, stupid, self-satisfying Geoffs. Have a wank, I think. Stop wanking in other people. This is a problem. I'm trying to write a book about how evolution moulded human sexuality – my starting point can't be 'male sexuality is essentially abusive' or 'straight men should all be in prison', although they are both things I have said when drunk. Researching this book, I've realised I am deeply prejudiced. Writing this book, I am attempting to confront that.

In my naivety, I have always wondered how anybody could be *aroused* by having sex with someone who didn't fancy them. All the sex I have had in my life AND I'VE DONE IT LOADS I've needed the other person to *want* to have sex with me. If you said, 'Sara, look over there, it's Idris Elba. He doesn't want to have sex with you. He thinks you are gross and smelly, but he *will* have sex with you if you pay him £80,' I wouldn't do it. Being desired is unequivocally connected to my arousal. The bad sex I've had, usually it's because I've felt the person didn't like me.

When I began researching this book three years ago, I didn't understand that some men become aroused *because* the other person doesn't want to have sex with them. There are delusional Geoffs who believe they're truly desired even in a transactional sex situation and there are also cruel Geoffs. Pain, discomfort or unwillingness turns them on. It makes them feel powerful.

The next post I read on PunterNet was titled 'WARN-ING: TRAFFICKED'. It detailed a location, described a woman. Approximate age, assumed race. 'Give this one a miss.' The language was blokey and informal. The man believed the woman was not there willingly. 'She could not speak English' – matter of fact, not a complaint – 'she cried throughout.' I reread the sentence hoping I had misunderstood.

'Throughout'.

He had done it. Finished. A weeping woman who couldn't speak his language. Why did he consider this a 'bad service' rather than the violation of a human being? Why was he writing on a message board rather than reporting it to the police? Paying someone downstairs does not mean what he did upstairs wasn't assault.

There are so many news reports of trafficking, a multitude of books telling the distressing stories of survivors. Why don't these Geoffs care about that? How can any person buying sex be sure the encounter is willing? Do they reckon that as a 'customer' it isn't their responsibility? Do they think money negates rape?

I'm supposed to be keeping this light.

My original premise, the provocation that led to my writing this book, was: what if, for some men, sexual excitement lessens empathy? Could that be true? There's an old proverb, 'A stiff prick hath no conscience,' and I wish I could feel what it's like to have an erection, if it does create a passionate mania that reduces the attached person's humanity. But I have to rely on neuroscientific studies and anecdotal evidence. I read a brain study that showed people are less disgusted when aroused. The evidence suggested that when people are turned on they do stuff they'd never agree to usually! This spoke to my personal experience of doing gross sexual stuff; it was true but I'd never consciously noted it. The study showed that activity in certain brain areas changed as the person neared orgasm. What if this also affects empathy? Later I explore the experiments on arousal and empathy and the existing evidence that supports and challenges my theory. I'll also investigate whether sexual psychopathy might have evolved to aid reproductive success in the chapter 'OH GOD MEN ARE HARDWIRED FOR RAPE'.

Don't get flustered, that was clickbait. Please cease freeloading the introduction and buy my book.

In October 2016 a video was leaked of the future president of the United States having a braggy conversation/admitting to the assault of women a decade or so before. We all know this recording off by heart. Trump says, 'I don't even wait. And when you're a star, they let you do it. You can do anything. Grab them by the pussy. You can do anything.'

I'm embarrassed to admit I believed his presidential hopes were over. In the 1980s Labour leader Neil Kinnock's political ambitions went down on Brighton beach when he did. If you're too young to remember this, you can watch it on YouTube. Kinnock was walking hand in hand with his wife when the sea surprised him and he tripped up trying to keep his shoes dry. 'That's it,' said the nation. 'You can't be leader, you can't even stay upright on pebbles.' When some American voters continued to respect Donald Trump, I realised I did not understand people very well. Or at all.

The discussions about what Trump had said were fascinating. Lots of people claimed it was 'banter', 'men's talk', 'locker-room'. What I'm expected to understand is that men in groups sometimes talk in a *special* way about women. It's not supposed to be taken seriously, which is why they keep it secret. This is difficult for me to investigate: if I go to a locker room to hear men talking about women when women aren't around then I'm around, being a woman, and the 'banter' stops. The men revert back to being considerate humans telling me to 'cheer up and smile'.

I need to know why men behave differently in all-male groups.

We're just having a laugh—

Why do stag dos go to strip clubs?

Same—

Why are there so many sexual assault cases involving groups of sportsmen?

Bitches after their money.

EXCUS—

I'm winding you up.

The thing is, I LOVE joking, it's my profession. There's great difficulty in proving someone 'meant' what they claim was a joke. Jokes are usually monstrous. We laugh when intentions are clear, we laugh because we know it's pretence and grotesquerie. Yet even when joking, people lose their jobs for saying the sort of thing Trump did. But Trump wasn't in a telemarketing or admin role which he could be fired from. No one told him, 'We can't allow that attitude in customer service – you're dealing directly with the public,' because he had no one to answer to. Grabbing women reflected how powerful he was. 'You can do anything,' he locker-roomed about his own authoritative position.

I was reminded of the *Ghostbusters* film, when one of the ghosts begins absorbing the other ghosts, sucking them inside him and becoming bigger and stronger and unbeatable. That was Trump. Rather than highlighting his unsuitability for democratic office, every uncaring comment he made built him up further.

Humans can't help but make quick, instinctual judgements about each other alongside our intellectual contemplations. Voters lost respect for Kinnock because he was overcome by gravity; because of his fallibility, because he seemed weak and jumpy at the foamy sea. Voters did *not* lose respect for Trump, because by being contemptible, sexist and cruel he seemed authoritative, a man who can grab women by their genitals without consequences. Trump perfectly personifies how a perceived dominance over women benefits a man's social position.

While people marched and tweeted and signed petitions about this new president over the subsequent months, I admitted to myself that a fear of male sexuality had made me sexist. That by late adolescence I thought of the male libido as a monster inside them, dormant and sleeping in some, shackled by the civilising mores of society in others.

That's sexist.

I said it was sexist. And while I was trying to work through this, become more reasonable and unbiased, the Harvey Weinstein stories started breaking. Woman after woman told the media what happened to them, and the journalists inserted 'alleged' because they didn't want to go to prison before he did. The world has many types of sex offenders. What appeared relevant about Weinstein was that it was his *position* that allowed him to coerce, manipulate, assault, maul and rape. Allegedly. It was his powerful status that made his victims vulnerable.

I had a further revelation when the women who appeared to be friends with Weinstein, photographed smiling next to him at parties, were criticised. 'They must have known,' said the journalists; 'why did they not stop him?' Yes, Meryl Streep, this is in fact YOUR fault. Millions of rapes and assaults* every year and you've been selfishly dancing in *Mamma Mia!* instead of preventing them.

I am talking about this drunk in a cab with my friend Roisin. We're debating the British comedy industry's own allegeds. People don't want to speak out because they'll lose work, perhaps their whole career. People do not want to go to the police about the crimes committed against them because they are worried about everyone knowing, forever being a victim. The people who commit these crimes are always in powerful positions; they are the owners, managers, promoters, or the established and successful. Bill Cosby wasn't drugging and assaulting Roseanne Barr. Kevin Spacey wasn't molesting Sir Ian McKellen.** These people prey on their inferiors. No one is abusing up.

All predators have allies who say, 'I can't imagine that of him, he's such a good bloke.' People can't help but presume the victim is lying, because it's never happened to them. Weinstein is the perfect example – he didn't do it to *everyone*. The men who do this discriminate. They often have women in their life they respect: wife, daughters, Meryl Streeps.

---

* Not all committed by Harvey Weinstein.
** Sean the lawyer has asked me to point out that Weinstein and Spacey are yet to go to trial and have both protested their innocence.

These women are 'in tribe', protected. I drunkenly try to explain my theory to Roisin and when I get home I write a Post-it in eyeliner: 'IN TRIBE WOMeN = SAFE. OUTSIDE WOOMEN = PREY'.

Human empathy has always relied on familiarity or in-tribeness and regularly fails when it comes to 'the other'. I will argue that this has been moulded by evolution. 'In tribe' women's fertility and attractiveness is owned and defended, while unfamiliar women are desired in exploitative ways. A perfect example is the kind of man who enjoys strip clubs but would be devastated if his daughters became strippers.

So stripping is exploitation?

Not especially and not necessarily; but as a transactional sexual behaviour stripping can be objectifying. It's performative fantasy created by removing the 'real' person and replacing them with someone who wishes to wiggle and serve. It is often an interaction without empathy, and lust without empathy can be dangerous.

I wanted to understand what men like Weinstein are getting off on. I found research about the effect of social status on the brain and learned that neurotransmitters like serotonin are released when we feel superior. This means a chemical that influences our happiness and wellbeing is boosted by dominance. Perhaps that makes complete sense to you, seems obvious? It feels good to be respected and terrible to be lowly. In the 'Sex Power Biology' section I'll outline some of the hormones and chemicals involved in human mating and bonding. We'll then get into the politically incorrect terrain of considering power and sex from an evolutionary perspective.

Gaining sexual pleasure from dominating another is known as sadism, named after a French philosopher called the Marquis de Sade. De Sade was a violent predator and has many modern apologists. I angrily wrote a lot of this book about him, then cut it all. What remained significant was something Angela Carter insisted in *The Sadeian Woman*: that all sex is an exchange of power. A matter-of-fact theory that does not reflect my experience. No sex that I'm having feels like a power exchange. My sex is friendly and fun and between equals. As I explore transactional sex for the 'Sex Power Money Money Money' chapters of this book, I realise that the power dynamic within sex is more than topping or bottoming. If people want to have sex with each other for no other reason than sex itself, where is the power being traded? To be an exchange there must be inequality to begin with. Usually economic. This is true of marriage in societies where women do not have independent income; it is true of any partnership with a financial dependant. It is explicitly demonstrated by sugar-daddying, sex-for-rent and other forms of sex work. But I've become more interested in the less explicit forms – a kiss-and-tell scenario for instance. Or the cultural expectations that a man should pay for a woman's dinner, or that a woman should feel obliged to sleep with a man who's bought a lot of drinks.

I saw a quote from the film *Scarface* on a men's rights message board: 'When you get the money, you get the power. Then when you get the power, then you get the women.' I should've got Tony Montana to write the foreword because that's my basic premise. Montana is not a respected intellectual but as I researched the relationship between status and sexual access in human beings, I found evidence supporting his proclamation. There are studies that show heterosexual women prefer men with expensive cars and designer clothes; that they find the same men more attractive when adorned with symbols of wealth. This relationship between power and attraction appears gendered; the studies did NOT find that heterosexual men prefer powerful women. Beautiful porn star Stormy Daniels had an affair with unattractive tycoon Donald Trump. No porn star has been wooed by Angela Merkel.*

To my surprise I found many straight women do believe it's 'fair' and 'right' that a man provide for them, that gestures of generosity are expected. I battled with this because I find it such a repulsive attribute, though as we'll discover, it reflects evolutionary logic.

I'll be honest, a lot of evolutionary logic has made me want to puke. I've written this book with the knowledge that all animals, including ourselves, behave in ways which maximise our chances of reproductive success. There are no morals, there is no intellectual debate, there is only the replication of genes, the spreading of traits. But I recognise why it's not a trendy approach for understanding modern behaviour. I understand why feminists and MRAs alike consider biological sex differences reductive and unhelpful.

Why?

Because people don't identify as animals! People would like to believe they're modern intellectuals making choices

---

* I'm so aware of the months that will pass between my writing this and it being published. So many ways to be out of date, but I will be happy to be proved wrong on this point if it's revealed that Merkel has been banging away with a multitude of young studs.

rather than bald apes responding to instinctual drives. We see stupid cows standing in fields without Netflix, we see dogs unashamedly sniffing each other's butts and we think we're something special. And we are. Giraffes have long necks, fish can breathe under water and humans have consciousness and the ability to reason. But that doesn't make us immune to natural forces and we shouldn't ignore our biology.

People talk about 'rape culture' and 'a culture of sexism', but I'm going to argue these things are not created by societies but remnants of forces going much further back. This book is my attempt to persuade you that an evolutionary approach can occasionally make the most baffling human behaviours less mysterious – from the popularity of pornography and our preoccupation with penis size, through to the stigma around selling sex. Biology is not a complete answer to who we are, but along with our childhood memories and Tony Montana quotes, it has the power to influence us.

Sex
Power
Biology

Achilles of the Groin

In the playground of primary school I learned that a kick between the legs would topple any male-bodied person. What incredible luck, I'd found boys' Achilles heel and it was in their pants. I enjoyed a kicking spree of several days, mad on the power of it. I laughed to see the Goliaths of my year writhing on the floor. Once a boy called Wesley kicked my groin in retaliation and we stared at each other, waiting, but my legs stayed strong. I did not topple. It was only MY kick that could work this magic and crumple lads like toilet paper.

At the weekend my aunty Jools asked, 'How's school?' and I bragged. I shared my secrets: the element of surprise, straight leg, run away laughing.

'You must never ever do that.' She was angry with me. Jools was a child-adult and never told me off. She let us eat humbugs for breakfast and pretended to believe Baileys was a milkshake. I sulked while she explained that when boys are hurt between the legs it sends shooting pains all through their body, up to their brain. The pain is so large they can't think, they lose control of their body and emotions. She made me promise to never do it again, because it wasn't fair. 'Even in a fight, gentlemen don't go for the goolies,' Jools instructed, and I apologised. I learned something important that day, the word 'goolies'.

Three decades later, and Donald Trump had moved into politics. Amongst the debates and speeches there was schoolyardy name-calling. Critics of Trump disagreed with his opinions, what he said and (when imitating a journalist with cerebral palsy) how he said it. But while attempting to undermine him, some dissenters aimed for his penis. Here's an example: in 2016 Marco Rubio entertains at a rally, first by saying Donald Trump has the hands of a much shorter man, then asking suggestively, 'You know what they say about men with small hands?'

Men's hands (and feet) have been referenced facetiously as indicators of penis size ever since I've been alive. When did this start? I don't know. Perhaps one of you can skim-read the Bible and let me know if there's a parable about Jesus being kind to a paltry-fingered man. I do know that contemporary data suggest some correlation between digit ratio (difference in length between second and fourth finger) and penis size, but it's not definitive 'small hands = small willy' evidence.

When my friend Hannah had her son the midwife complimented his willy. Do you think that's appropriate? The baby was several seconds old when a medical professional anointed him 'one for the ladies'. I wish I'd been there – I'd have shouted 'Heteronormative!' at her. Then I'd have run up and down the ward shouting at everyone. Reproduction is *so* heteronormative.

This happened in my family too, my uncle boasted to me about my young cousin being 'well hung'. What was I supposed to say? 'Congratulations on Stefan's todger, I'll get him lube for his sixteenth so he doesn't hurt anyone.'

If parents celebrate their kid's penis size, if a midwife expects to please parents by praising a baby's phallus, then it's clear the male organ has significance. It represents more than its biological function, it says something about masculinity and status – which must be difficult with such a small mouth.

Marco Rubio's question, 'You know what they say about men with small hands?' seemed rhetorical, but then, after pausing for laughter, he answered: 'You can't trust them!' I've checked and there are in fact zero studies relating a man's hand size to trustworthiness. Interestingly I did find two experiments (one from the University of California, Berkeley, and one from the University of Cologne) that found participants became less honest and reliable with an increase in status and power. That bears thinking about as regards all politicians, doesn't it? I've sent Rubio a LinkedIn request with updated speech suggestions: 'You know what they say about men with big power? Trustworthiness decreases.' He can get that printed on a tea towel or something. A consolation for losing is that he's probably a better man for it.

I've wondered whether I would care if someone said I had small hands, and I wouldn't. This is absolutely a masculine vs feminine thing. Men want big hands and women want small hands, even though we use them for all the same stuff: petting cats, masturbating, keying our enemy's car.

Oddly Donald Trump was more offended at being called small-handed than untrustworthy. At his next public address he asked everyone to look at his titchy, pussy-grabbing hands and declared, 'If they're small, something else must be small. I guarantee you there's no problem. I guarantee you.' It's so surreal. A man reassuring American voters that, if elected, he will provide an unproblematic presidential penis.

Trump's defensiveness reminded me that one of the many euphemisms for male genitalia is 'manhood'. That word can be used in an absolutely literal way about the male anatomy: 'Sara was running towards me and I grabbed a bin lid to protect my manhood'; or it can be metaphorical: 'After Rubio's comments Donald Trump used a public address to defend his manhood.' This word reveals the unsubtle connection between perceived masculinity and penis size. If you want even less subtlety, there's another presidential example. Lyndon B. Johnson named his penis 'Jumbo' and there are numerous reports of him waggling it in the men's toilets and asking people, 'Have you ever seen anything as big as this?' More perplexingly, there's a famous story of Johnson being grilled by journalists about the Vietnam war. Someone asked why US troops were even there. 'This is why,' Johnson exclaimed, freeing Jumbo from his zipped prison and presenting him like an answer.

Male genitals are symbolic. We say that people have balls, big balls, balls of steel if they are brave and great. We describe striving, go-getting people as ballsy. 'Big Dick Energy' fell onto the internet one day and we all instantly knew what it referred to – confidence, assurance, strength. I wonder what would happen if a presidential candidate shrugged off an attempt to belittle him via penis size? 'Sure, I've got a tiny wang,' he says in my imagination, 'but I've got big ideas about how to prevent homelessness and improve education/free the market and lower tax.'* Would people find it impossible to respect this man, and if so, why?

Is a man's whole being underwritten by his genitals? Do men consider their penises as representations of 'self'? 'My penis . . . why, I've never really thought about it,' said no

* Delete as appropriate for your political leaning.

man ever. You're all preoccupied or proud, AND WE'RE GOING TO FIND OUT WHY.

The first instance of our genitals dictating who—

Dick-tating?

No thank you, dictating who we are is when they're used to identify our biological sex at birth or even earlier. All of us were assigned a gender in utero or shortly afterwards, based on our genital formation. If you had a penis you were considered male. Someone wrote that in a file about you, told your mother. At birth, a doctor looked between your legs in the earliest moments of your life and announced you: 'boy'.

I used to believe the only difference between boys and girls was what we had in our underwear. When I was referred to as 'a girl' I understood that as 'a child without a willy'. By the time I started secondary school I'd also heard some confusing stuff about 'penis envy', because my dad was studying Freud, and 'bleeding from the site of a torn-off organ', because my mum liked quoting Germaine Greer. I was informed, explicitly and implicitly, that there were two kinds of human: the haves and have-nots. And unless you're reading this in a distant genderless future, so were you.

In the broadest sense *Homo sapiens* is composed of two phenotypes, two biological sexes. There are arguably many more sexes: people with extra chromosomes, solo chromosomes, intersex genitalia, etc. But for most intents and purposes humans are divided in two, and this is due to how we reproduce. We're split into As and Bs because that's how Cs are made.

A + B = C. Reproduction. Or in Ikea terms, plank + legs = table.

In our species the two types are referred to as 'man' and 'woman', and together they make 'babies', which are ~~a great drain on the resources of our planet~~ lovely. But reproduction doesn't *need* two types – there are plenty of hermaphrodite species like snails, slugs and some insects and fish that can make Cs by themselves if they want. My fantasy is to be like one of those self-fertilising frogs in *Jurassic Park*. I'd have daughters that were all the same as me, with exactly my genes. Then I could show them to my parents and say, 'See, it *was* my childhood, they're fine.' I'd prove nurture over nature – a perfect experiment. I realise that being genetically identical to your mother would come with its own set of issues. My daughters would look at me and see their aged future. I'd be a decaying premonition. When they grew old themselves they'd see MY FACE in the mirror, the horror! It'd be like a very long, very creepy episode of *Quantum Leap*, which is why I've decided against having kids via hermaphrodite gene replication.

Also, did you know mushrooms have thirty-six thousand sexes? It's incredible but, as this book isn't about the interrelation of economics, autonomy and sex in mushrooms, not especially relevant.

The reason most animals are As and Bs is because having two phenotypes ensures the jumbling of DNA with each coupling. Asexual reproduction makes evolution much, much slower. In Ikea terms, dual-sexed breeding gives the possibility of moving around the bits and pieces; you can make mutant tables with legs on the top or with doors and drawers attached to them. Being asexual means following the instructions very closely every time. If my clone children had clone children who had clone children who had clone children* and so on for thousands of years, then yes, planet Earth would be populated entirely with good-looking cool people, but we'd also be less healthy. With a lesser spread of genes, we'd be more vulnerable to viruses, unable to adapt to difficult terrains, new food sources, etc. There is resilience in variation.

The two biological types of human begin their lives looking the same. At a genetic and chromosomal level we differ, but we're all samey little bean people in the womb until around nine weeks old. What happens next is really fun. Foetuses with Y chromosomes begin to develop differently to those without. The female body is the default setting, but where there's a Y chromosome, increased testosterone causes the sex organs to unravel externally. I shall now describe this process in the most poetic way I can . . .

We all begin our lives with gonads in our abdomen. If you're thinking, 'Wow, that's so gross, imagine having goolies inside you,' spare some sympathy for us double Xs whose gonads stay right there and become ovaries. At eight weeks old everyone's external genitals look like this:

1. Anus
2. Labioscrotal folds
3. Legs
4. Genital tuber
5. Urogenital folds
6. Urethral groove

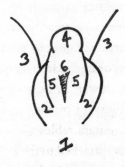

* If the whole world was me, who would be in the audience, hmmm? Another reason I decided against it.

I know 4 looks pretty penisy but the correct term is 'genital tuber'. The urogenital folds surround it, there's a urethral groove in the middle and some labioscrotal folds on either side. Spoiler alert: they're called labioscrotal because they can become labia *or* scrotum. Told you this was fun.

At eleven weeks the testes of the male foetus should be creating dihydrotestosterone (DHT), which causes the genital tuber to elongate and form the phallus, with the urogenital folds fusing underneath to enclose an area called 'the spongy urethra'. The urethral groove becomes the urethra, which you'd probably guessed. The labioscrotal folds drop the 'labio', stop folding and start bagging into scrotal sacks. Anti-Mullerian hormone is released and prevents the growth of the Mullerian duct system that would otherwise form an internal genital tract (vagina and friends). At around eight months' gestation the testes descend to the scrotum and congratulations, it's biologically male. In Ikea terms, the table has a penis and testicles.

Without the flush of DHT, spurred instead by oestrogen, the urogenital folds of a female foetus will develop into labia minora. The genital tuber becomes the clitoris,* while the labioscrotal folds forget 'scrotal' and flower into labia majora bracketing the vagina. Congratulations, it might one day present *Loose Women*.

Anyone who hears a baby has arrived asks, 'What is it?'

---

* You may well have heard that the clitoris has the same amount of nerve endings as a penis, and now you can understand exactly how. Biologically, a penis is a ballooned, blown-up clit. Or if you prefer, the clit is a minuscule, diddy penis. Either way, they respond very differently to touch and heterosexual people must remember to be gentle/grip it harder.

And everyone knows what the 'it' refers to. No one is asking about race or star sign, no one is checking, 'Is it the son of God again?' The first thing we want to know about a baby is its sex. From the first breath it's the most significant, most defining feature of a person. And unavoidably, biology is considered conclusive of gender. There's a brilliant bit in Juno Dawson's book where she admits to asking people the sex of their baby, even though she knows from personal experience (she's trans) that what a baby 'is' cannot always be ascertained by its sexual anatomy. But it's super hard not to ask – try it next time someone announces they've had a kid, deliberately don't ask, 'Boy or girl?' Feel the pull of wanting to, feel their needing to tell you. If you REALLY want the details, try asking the physiologically truthful, 'Does it have a penis?' Now lecture the people backing away from you about how gender is a construct and mushrooms have thirty-six thousand sexes and all babies look alike with their nappies on.

The Penis in Our Mind

Parents don't like to have their baby wrong-sexed. They correct you if you 'he' a 'she', get insulted. People adorn their babies with signifiers to avoid embarrassment. Bald, Church-illesque girls get pink bows velcroed round their skull. Pretty baby boys are dressed in manly sky blue, their soft blankets illustrated with sharks and dinosaurs to show that this sleepy idiot means business. He might drink from boobies and cry all the time, but he's a predator.

This initially seems illogical. If we have two sexes for reproductive purposes, to mix up genes, why would we care about the maleness or femaleness of a person so many years before they're fit for breeding? Parents shouldn't give a toss about the perceived gender of their babies – they're not putting them on Tinder.

There are a variety of studies demonstrating that parents, teachers, caregivers and strangers all change their treatment of children – even using different language towards them – based on perceived gender. My favourite one involves an adjustable ramp and babies just shy of a year old. Mothers were asked to estimate how steep a ramp their child would be able to crawl down. The ramp was then cranked to that position and the kid either proved their mother correct or ~~rolled to their death~~ didn't. The results of the experiment showed that mothers tended to overestimate their sons' ability – 'Oh yeah, make it vertical, he's Spider-Man' – and underestimate their daughters' – 'Let's leave it flat – she'll still fall off!' In both instances the mothers' gender bias was found to have no basis in fact. There was no sex difference in the ramp-crawling ability of babies at this age. How do we process this? Does it mean that from the word go parents are subconsciously pushing their sons to achieve more than their daughters? Or could it be that parents are subconsciously more coddling and protective of girls?

Either way, what I'm trying to convince you is that the genitalia you were born with affects more than your reproductive potential. There are ramifications in every area of your life. Let's have a little Darwin refresher to help us dissect why.

Charles Darwin was a Victorian scientist who loved finches and hated the idea of getting married. He was an Aquarius, his middle name was Robert and, more significantly, he was the first person to officially propose the theory of evolution. While we call it a 'theory', evolution has been accepted as fact by the scientific community for 150 years. You'll be familiar with 'natural selection' and 'sexual selection' as forces within evolution that shape all the beasties on our planet. Natural selection refers to how certain aspects of body or behaviour aid a creature's survival, and sexual selection signifies the aspects of body or behaviour that make him or her more ~~fuckable~~ sexually attractive. Both are important for the passing on of genes: to breed you must, firstly, be alive, and, secondly, desired.*

The relationship between natural selection and parenting is instantly clear. Mummies and daddies teach their children about the dangers of the world so that they don't drown or

---

* THIRDLY, there is a third way to continue genes and that is forced copulation in animals (rape in humans). This is a mating strategy and I have subconsciously omitted it.

set themselves on fire. Childhood is a learning stage, from eating and hygiene to sharing with others, crossing the road, keeping fit and not getting into strangers' cars. Parents protect and nurture their offspring when they are very small, then later bestow the skills and survival tools they'll need to look after themselves.

Parents are conscious of this process. They're aware of wanting their children to be safe; more than that, to *flourish*. We've all heard our breeding friends* exclaim how they 'want the best' for their kids. A phrase reeking of survival of the fittest: it is THE BEST they want. Life is competitive and people can't help but want their children to win. This makes sound evolutionary sense, but I believe it's also why a child's sex dictates how they're spoken to, how they're treated and what is expected of them.

A good way of surviving, aka not dying, is to avoid being killed by one of your own species. You'll be aware from GCSE history and the *News at Ten* that human beings kill each other. Are you also aware that this is gendered behaviour? Men are much more likely to be killed than women.** In every country in the world men make up over 80 per cent of murder victims, even without including the casualties of war. But men are also the aggressors, making up 88 per cent of murderers and a whopping 98 per cent of mass murderers. It's a completely male-dominated industry. Whenever a woman does break through she's referred to as a 'female murderer', which she finds very patronising. Makes her want to work even harder at killing people, until she gets some respect.

---

* An oxymoron, we all know you lose your friends when they breed.
** I should specify cis women here. Trans women are experiencing a very, very high murder rate.

If you want to passionately argue that this male-on-male killing is created by culture then I will watch your TED talk, but I'm unlikely to be convinced. Throughout our evolution males have competed brutally with each other for resources and mates, and only the successful shared the genes for physical dominance with their sons and grandsons. This (mostly) historical violence remains crucially relevant to modern parenting.

While most mums and dads don't *encourage* aggression in their sons – don't pack hammers in their lunch boxes or practise bare-knuckle boxing in the garden – male children are still to some extent conditioned to be 'strong'. Boys are taught and told to toughen up and suppress emotion, dissuaded from playing with 'effeminate' toys. It has been proven in studies that children themselves police this behaviour from a surprisingly young age, three or four.

One of my cousins was born camp. He was the kitschiest, queenliest, most brilliantly gay baby and boy, and continues to be now that he's an out young man. As he grew up, all the adults around him, teachers, parents and other relatives, attempted to kind of push the gay back in. They confiscated prized items, banned dressing up and tried, and failed, to coerce him into masculinity. I have to stress, I come from an arty family. We are not military officers and lumberjacks, we're painters and cruise ship entertainers. I want to say, 'We're not homophobic,' but there *is* an element of homophobia to that kind of behaviour, isn't there?

What I didn't understand, as a child myself, was that the grown-ups believed they were protecting my cousin by encouraging him to conform. I'm not saying they were right, but from childhood onwards, a male's safety requires social respect. Softness can lead to vulnerability. Standing out from the crowd can make a boy a target. I KNOW THIS IS NOT POLITICALLY CORRECT OR NICE. I know we're all beautiful, unique individuals shining like diamonds. I'm not attempting to excuse the behaviour described above. I'm trying to comprehend where it comes from.

The way I see it, if natural selection is about survival traits, and if being perceived as STRONG increases a male's chance of survival by making him less vulnerable to attack from other males, then thousands of generations will have compounded our expectations for a set of masculine behaviours that are virtually irrelevant now that most of us are not hunter–gathering. Strength protects men from other men. This is why we see boys yanked away from gentleness and communicating their emotions. Experiments have found that male children are less nurtured than girls, read to less, cuddled less after they hurt themselves. I would say how sad this makes me, except I'm a tough guy: rugby, bashing stuff, Jeremy Clarkson.

Enough of this girly gossiping, let's return to the biological ramifications of the penis.

Invention of Daddy

Here is an incontestable fact: the biological possibilities of our body have ramifications.

Mothering and fathering require different skills and advertisements. All of our ancestors, before there were any constructs of gender or condoms, had to behave in certain ways for their genes to be carried into the future. We are the proof that they did so. Here we all are with their survivor genetics. And the hangover of sexed behaviour expectations.

So once upon a time, between five and seven million years ago, our species diverged from chimpanzees. Over millennia several *Homo sapiens* species responded to environmental challenges with physical adaptations. They moved away from tree-dwelling onto the flat plain and began walking upright. Then over hundreds of generations our skeletons developed and became better at travelling long distances and running to escape or hunt. Our hips became smaller and more robust to support the upper body helping to conserve energy and regulate body temperature.* And here is where it gets precarious. While the selective pressure for effective and cost-efficient movement was drastically narrowing our bipedal birth canal, *sapiens* females still had the

---

* Being more compact means the body can stay warm using fewer calories. It's why people who have evolved in harsher climates like the Arctic are shorter and squatter, while people on the equator are lither and leggier.

excruciating job of pushing children through it.

To clarify, the hips of human women were shaped by *conflicting* evolutionary pressures: on the one hand the need for movement and thermo-regulation; on the other childbirth. The genes of uncatchable, calorie-conserving mega-hunters cannot be shared with future generations if there's nowhere for their babies to come out. A human female's hips needed to be small, yet expansive, like some bony Mary Poppins bag.

Tragically for the female perineum, as human hips got smaller, our brains got bigger. In fact, over the last five million years our brains TREBLED in size. Correspondingly our skulls got much bigger too. This caused a drastic alteration in human gestation time. If the *Homo sapiens* female gestated to the same point in development as other apes, she would be pregnant for two and a half years. If a human female gave birth to a two-and-a-half-year-old, she . . . well . . . that'd be like a Range Rover getting off a bus.* It would take the doors off, and half the side. Every birth would be murderous. And even if the child managed to survive their ~~matricide~~ nativity, without a mother to care for them they'd be unlikely to live very long.

What about their dad?

As *parents*, as caregivers, fathers haven't been invented yet.

Why didn't women evolve big enough hips?

Let's imagine a woman, Veronica. Her pelvis is strong enough to support the top half of her body but now wide

---

* Fun fact: my editor Laura is heavily pregnant and having to read and reread horrible sentences like this, and I won't lie, that's spurring me on.

enough to pass a baby human whose brain has developed to the same stage as a baby chimp's. She doesn't worry about dying in childbirth! She looks great in Levis' 501s! She can't walk! Veronica loves being a new mum but because she cannot forage or hunt or stand without falling over, she will starve and so will her son. Unless the predators get them first! Plus her boyfriend's dead because she sat on him, what a sad story.

The female body has a conundrum, so like any sensible person she writes in to a magazine problem page:

Dear Passage of Time,

I feel so trapped – my species' survival is increasingly dependent on our ability to run about and catch things to eat. This would be fine if we weren't also growing these head-computers that allow us to remember lots of things and socialise. How do I give birth without dying?

Yours sincerely, Slim Hips of Romford

The agony aunt that is evolution responds by having women give birth to smaller babies. As you'll be aware, modern humans gestate inside their mothers for nine months. The baby is then born before it's finished developing, while the bones of its skull are soft and holey to protect the mother. This evolutionary compromise is the result of trial and error – we're balancing on the edge of maximum survival potential for babies and mothers.

The brain is a very expensive attribute – not just in terms of the lives lost in difficult births* but in the number of

---

* Not you, Laura.

calories needed to power it. About 20 per cent of our metabolic energy is used by our brain tissue. To justify that consumption the brain *must* have been hugely advantageous for locating food. Its very existence proves it must have paid for itself. In fact scientists have found that increased social learning correlates with larger brain size in primates. This leads to the conclusion that our cerebral organ created the bonds, communication, memory and planning necessary to successfully hunt and forage on the African savannah.

Human babies are born well before their brain has finished developing. In their first weeks of life the brain grows by 1 per cent every day, slowing to 0.4 per cent a day by the age of three months. In total infants' brains grow by over 60 per cent in the first ninety days. Let's see what that looks like:*

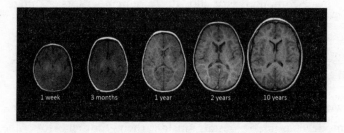

1 week   3 months   1 year   2 years   10 years

It's tremendous growth, and something that our species is unique in doing outside of the safe warm womb.

> You know what they say about people with big brains?

They hunt in groups, they can follow signs to water, they are able to intuit patterns that aid foraging and tracking animals . . .

* Not you, audio book.

You can't trust them!

Actually, you have to. Giving birth to babies that are so utterly dependent has moulded everything about our species. Unlike the young of other mammals, who are born ready to toddle around, ours can't even lift their silly, soft-boned heads up. Babies need regular feeding and constant protection; 24/7 supervision too or they'll choke or fall off something. They need regular cleaning because they can't control when they piss and shit.*

If you've had a child or been around someone with young children you'll already be aware of what a huge amount of energy, time and resources are required in preventing its unwitting suicide. Now imagine child-rearing four million years ago. There are no supermarkets or bottle sterilisers. You're a hunter–gatherer living with a tribe of around a hundred people. You'll have the necessary shelter – because you've built it or found it – but it's not safe to leave a baby in. There are animals that would eat it, another human might hurt it. It might smother itself in hay or something. The whole world is dangerous to a baby left alone even for a moment, that's why they cry all the time, as an alarm system.

They cry when they realise they're unattended, they cry if they wake up alone, they cry to demand the regular feeding necessary for growing their brain.

Let's consider the post-birth mother. She needs to eat a lot of calorific food to make breast milk, and she needs to hold and defend her child – all while she is healing. Have you seen what childbirth can do to a woman's body? She'll have tears,

---

* Feel free to cut and paste this into any 'Congratulations, you're pregnant!' cards.

bleeding. She might have a fistula, that's where the vaginal wall tears and—

Please stop.

As our physical evolution (big brain + small hips = earlier baby) made child-rearing increasingly difficult, our species evolved stronger familial bonds in response. A closely knit, helpful, supportive family increased our offspring's survival chances – hence the genes for ~~putting up with~~ caring about relations were selected for. When my sisters had my nieces, I was shocked by the force with which I loved them, how invested I felt. How defensive – the clichéd 'I would kill for them'.* That's how powerful the bonding emotions *have* to be, especially as babies are ~~loud and covered in piss~~ without immediately redeeming features.

As the brain grew and our species became more familial, our diets also changed. Six million years ago we are thought to have eaten like chimpanzees, mostly vegetation, with the occasional small animal. Meat comprises a very small amount, 2–3 per cent, of a chimp's diet. The increase in our brain's size and abilities meant we caught more meat, which in turn gave us more nutrients and fats for our cognitive equipment. The improvement in our communication made us deadly. We could talk to each other: 'Steve, catch it – it's over there,' or 'It's too late, Steve, I ate it.'

I mention the meat thing because alongside the team-work necessary to catch animals, we learned to co-operate in their consumption. With no means of preserving meat it

* It is worth noting that loving people often has an aggressive opposite. The more we love, the more we seek to protect, defend. Love has potential violence built in.

gets maggoty and poisonous quite quickly. Family groups would've shared diligently with each other and the extended tribe to the benefit of everyone. Human beings' social ties improve the quality of life for everyone in the group. Which brings us to the notion of paternity.

IT'S NOT A NOTION, SARA.

No need to scale a building in a Batman costume. Listen, the survival rate of human babies is directly correlated to how much care is taken of them. The more they are 'loved', the more likely they are to survive. Hence natural selection has favoured the most dutiful and attentive mothers, and the most closely bonded family groups. Alongside this, natural selection has favoured having an *extra* caregiver – a father.

Let's consider birds for a moment. Around 90 per cent of avian species are monogamous, and that's not due to cultural influence. It's not because the Bird Bible told them to marry and be faithful. It's simply because of their method of producing young.

Eggs must be incubated for chicks to grow and hatch. Birds use their body heat to do this. This means someone has to stay egg-sitting in the nest at all times. But riddle me this: how does the sitting, warming bird feed herself? She must have a partner to fetch her worms. If she starves and dies, her body warmth quickly disperses. A male bird's own genetic survival depends on his input; he can't replicate his genes if his progeny are in cold shells under the corpse of their mother.

If two birds collaborate to warm and feed, the chicks will hatch and then they'll need more than one pair of wings at their beak and call. The demands of rearing chicks create pair bonds between adult birds who reproduce. Birds are monogamous because their young require the input of two parents. This isn't romance, it's evolutionary necessity.

We should also clarify what biologists mean when they call a species 'monogamous'. It might not be what *you* mean by monogamy, and a bird could really break your heart. For biologists, 'monogamous' means that a pair share a nest/home, raise their young together and have selective (not exclusive) mating.

Should I emphasise the 'not exclusive'?

Being powerfully pair bonded, shared care of a brood – these things don't necessitate fidelity. Some amount of copulation outside of the pair bond may be of benefit to both sexes. THIS IS NOT 'CHEATING', it increases the chance of reproductive success – it is winning. No human lover will accept this excuse, by the way, and I. Have. Tried.

Only around 5 per cent of mammals are monogamous, it's much rarer than in birds. That's because, as you may have noticed, we don't lay eggs. We lay our young without shells. They gestate internally and are fed by lactation during early life. Most female mammals can do all this by themselves, they don't need no man, and yet you don't see them wiggling round and bragging about it like Destiny's Child. The only mammals who form pair bonds are those who need two parents for survival. And that's the story of how humans grew big brains and got dads.

Chemical Romance

It's believed humans' ancestors lived in groups co-operating socially for around thirty-five million years before they coupled up to care for their increasingly dependent babies. Millions of years of freedom, ruined. Obviously, the adaptation to dual parenting was very gradual, not one awful morning when men suddenly found themselves accountable for sexual consequences.* And before you blame this on nagging bitches, no one was *telling* men to babysit and wipe bums. Children who received the resources and protection of a male were more likely to survive and the genes of fatherly men were replicated in greater numbers. Over hundreds of generations males became more nurturing and increasingly bonded in two directions – towards their offspring and towards their partner. Over thousands of generations what we refer to as 'the nuclear family' was created within our social tribes.

So how does a behaviour trait evolve? In this case, genes responsible for the chemicals that bond people were selected for. As weird as it is to think about, what we call *love* isn't a magic, unknowable force but a very scientific assortment of neurotransmitters and hormones. That's all emotions are. What you *feel* is often controlled by tiny amounts of amino

---

* 'Sexual consequences' is the best way to refer to your friends' children.

acids. The most important chemical associated with all kinds of human attachment is oxytocin.

A bit of background: oxytocin was discovered in 1906 by Henry Dale, a pharmacologist, Nobel prize-winner and Gemini. Oxytocin can be a manual labourer, responsible for muscly jobs like the lactation process and contracting the womb for menstruation and childbirth. The hormone also has non-physical roles, emotional admin stuff. It makes you feel relaxed, soothed, connected.

Studies suggest that oxytocin initially motivated group living and was later hijacked for one-on-one bonding. It's so fascinating to think of a hormone working that way, initially creating bonds between family members and local friends, then over thousands of generations becoming the reason we fall in love with the people we sleep with. Sorry, I mean sometimes fall in love with the people we sleep with.

Oxytocin influences what we consider to be our 'rational', 'conscious' behaviour. A study conducted in 2007 found that people who sniffed an oxytocin spray were 80 per cent more generous in sharing money with a stranger than people who'd sniffed a placebo spray – you know what perfume to wear before meeting your bank manager. Make sure you give them a nice tight hug as well. Bodily contact will get their oxytocin flowing before you're thrown out of the building. Many studies have shown the link between oxytocin and empathy; in 2009 neuroeconomists Jorge Barraza and Paul Zak showed how watching an emotional video raised the oxytocin in people's blood by 47 per cent, and intranasal sprays have been shown to increase people's ability to read facial expressions – literally enabling better understanding of others. All this is so integral to how we live as a social species.

When we feel 'connected' and 'in tribe' we are kinder, more respectful, more thoughtful. If you've ever sung with a group or played team games you'll have felt the surges of *in-ness.* Playing with a team requires co-operation, perceptiveness – oxytocin. Scientists have proved that the more bonded a team feel to each other, the better they play.

Oxytocin is also why your mum likes you, playing a vital part in mother–infant attachment. Maternal bonding is thought to have developed first and subsequently those neural and molecular mechanisms were co-opted into partner bonds. ISN'T THAT CRAZY? Mum and baby became dating and romance. This means my boyfriend is like a son I have sex with!

I'm going to be sick.

He didn't like that analogy either.

While we're on the topic, sex increases the level of oxytocin in our bodies, with a huge spike when we orgasm. This creates a feeling of intimacy and closeness. I get overwhelmed with it sometimes, I feel so much love in my body it completely changes my mood, how I feel about the world.

More generous with your money?

Do *not* try to wank the bank manager.

Oxytocin also acts as a tranquilliser, making us sleepy and relaxed, because it counteracts the stress hormone cortisol. But the hormonal cocktail released while orgasming is different in male and female bodies. Males have a higher level of testosterone, which is thought to cancel out some of the intimate effect of oxytocin.

> That's why chicks wanna cuddle after sex but men don't?

That is a *cliché* and an unhealthy case of gender stereo-typing but also, yeah. It's something to bear in mind if your post-orgasmic mood is unlike your partner's. It can be very different from body to body, from day to day, and influenced by many things.

It's interesting to consider how powerfully chemicals can affect us. Emotions we attribute to our personality or a response to events are actually chemical compounds bobbing around in our bloodstream. Let's explore another one.

V Is for Vole

And vasopressin, which seems to produce the long-term attachment needed for raising children. At least it does in prairie voles.

I don't like animal experiments – partly for ethical reasons, but also because the findings are not directly applicable to us. But it's difficult to do lots of tests on people because of ~~political correctness gone mad~~ human rights. Every time I thought I'd found an interesting study about the effects of vasopressin on the human male, the third page would reveal this male lived on a prairie and enjoyed a diet of bulbs and tubers.

Some hot facts for you: vasopressin is made in the brain by the hypothalamus and along with your kidneys works as an antidiuretic to regulate the amount of water in your blood. The hormone is present in both sexes, but males produce more than females – at least in voles.

Voles have earned this focus because there are two kinds, genetically almost identical, but with very different mating strategies. Prairie voles are super devoted to each other and mate for life, cuddling and nestling and raising their pups together. If their partner dies, over 80 per cent never ~~celebrate by marrying someone younger~~ create a new pair bond. Montane voles, who look and behave the same in every other way, are not monogamous. The females raise offspring by themselves and the pups feed themselves by two weeks of age. Dad's nowhere to be seen.

It appears the voles' mating strategies have evolved in response to their environments. The prairie vole encounters a much harsher habitat with a meagre food supply, which results in a low vole population density. There aren't many mates around and so these voles can't be fussy. If a male vole were to remain free, single and playing the prairie, he would risk never finding a fertile female. Natural selection has favoured the males who 'settle down' with the ~~right vole~~ first female they find.

In biological terms, this is a trade-off. The prairie voles have evolved in a difficult environment to have 'high-quality, low-quantity offspring'. The vole parents have fewer pups and do more for them to increase their chances of surviving the godawful prairie. The montane voles, who enjoy a lusher landscape and plentiful food supply, can afford to be laissez-faire. They practise a 'low-quality, high-quantity' strategy, popping out pups and letting them fend for themselves because the environment is easier to survive in.

What is so interesting about human beings is that we deploy both strategies, sometimes dependent on economics or resources and sometimes in complete disregard of those factors. Our species demonstrates a flexibility, a sign of how well equipped we are for responding to environmental signals. If we were voles, all rich people would be swingers with hundreds of children and all struggling families would have deeply devoted parents and only one or two kids. Both my parents came from poor backgrounds, yet my dad is one of nine and my mum one of seven. Sometimes having many children can be a response to high infant mortality: having more children can increase the chance of some surviving even if resources are reduced. Also humans respond to our culture as well as the environment. Some religions encourage having many children, and both of my grandmothers were ~~rabbits~~ Catholic.

Another component to coupling up that's found in humans and voles alike – in all animals actually – is mate value. Taken straight from Darwin's theories, every potential mate can be assessed by what they are *offering*. Many factors may be taken into subconscious consideration, but mainly age, health and behaviour. Voles' compatibility will be decided by pheromones and fertility, with the prairie vole's only selective criterion being 'Were you there first?' This demonstrates what is called 'relative mate value'. The more partners an animal has to choose from, the more selective they're able to be. They can reject the sick and injured; they can opt for the fellow with the prettiest hair or the better nest.

In the majority of animals it's females who choose, while males must compete to impress them. Male peacocks have evolved beautiful plumage, bower birds build intricate nests, gorillas display size, strength and dominance. In fewer species, and only where the male has been lumbered with the larger parental investment, the females must compete to impress males. Seahorses are a good example, and poison arrow frogs. The dating game is always predicated on who gets stuck with the offspring.

And we know that this is not so simple with humans. With two parents each potentially investing a great deal of time, effort and resources into any young, both males and females must work to impress others with their mate value. However, it's worth remembering that what heterosexual humans are trying to demonstrate to each other is not the same. Women are not preoccupied with appearing strong and able to protect and provide. Men are not overly concerned with looking younger than they are while maintaining a small waist and curvy bottom. Judging mate value in humans is beautifully complex, and, as we'll be exploring later, very different for the sexes.

Research undertaken on voles has indicated the importance of oxytocin and vasopressin in creating their monogamy. In some outrageously cruel/informative experiments scientists gave male prairie voles a vasopressin blocker before they mated, which prevented them developing a partner preference. They then did the opposite – infused the males with vasopressin during a brief introduction to a female – and found they bonded even without sex. With female prairie voles, they found that administering oxytocin-blocking drugs stopped them developing a partner preference. It's a lab-based *Midsummer Night's Dream*, the scientists injecting potions and the voles waking up in or out of love . . . except all the characters are in cages and have their brains cut open at the end.

But guess what? In 2001, further studies found that some populations of prairie voles are NOT MONOGAMOUS, gasp. It seems they can be pretty flexible; if food becomes more plentiful and populations rise, mate value decreases and they don't need each other any more. Mr Vole can pack his stuff and get the hell out. This proves that nothing is ever as simple as genes or hormones and their receptors – these things are always working in concert with environmental factors. Animal species that rigidly refuse to respond to environmental changes die out – I'm looking at you, pandas.

Fish just need to learn to breathe plastic bottles and straws.

Exactly. With humans, the reason we are the most successful species of all time is because we are so responsive and adaptive. We're variable, flexible and sexy. It's worth repeating that nothing discovered about voles can be *directly* applied to humans, of course. We must look to human experiments for that. There's one that tested the blood levels of oxytocin and vasopressin in human men as they masturbated, and found that these hormones rose several-fold as orgasm approached. This supports the theory that human pair bonding has a chemical basis. And if the feelings of affection and closeness that facilitate monogamy are increased with sexual contact, this would at least partly explain why we have SO MUCH SEX.

Another unique trait in the sex lives of humans is the seeming pointlessness of much of it. The vast majority of creatures only mate when reproduction is possible. This is usually dictated by the female: her body signals that she's fertile, either through pheromones or physical changes; this arouses the male; they do it; baby animals are made. With our beloved prairie voles the female has her ovulation induced by the smell of male urine. It's a sure sign there's a male nearby and so her body gets ready for mating. The exact opposite of a human female getting a whiff of urinals in a nightclub and her vagina falling off in disgust.

An important thing for us to consider is that unlike most mammals, human females have evolved 'concealed ovulation'. Our bodies do not signal whether or not we are fertile in any reliable way. Males have no way of ascertaining if a female they copulate with will conceive or not. This has HUGE ramifications in our sexual behaviour, which we'll investigate further in the chapter 'Constant Sexual Signalling'. First, we must meet another of the chemicals underlying our sexuality, dopamine.

Addicted to Love

In order to get stuff, an animal has to want it. Animals need quite a lot of things to stay alive, so wanting stuff is pretty integral. Much of this *wanting* is created by dopamine, a neurotransmitter in the brain which sends signals between brain cells. These chemical communications are referred to as 'dopamine pathways' and are relevant to 'reward-motivated behaviour', which is a complicated way of saying, 'When we want things, we do things.'

Dopamine is released in amounts which affect how *much* we want something and how motivated we'll feel to get it. If we think of 'rewards' as the resources an animal needs to be evolutionarily successful, like food or sex, then the animal's desire should correspond to how *beneficial* the reward would be. People talk about 'dangling a carrot' as an incentive, which is stupid because no one wants a bloody carrot. I've got friends who give their children vegetables as treats and I judge those friends terribly. Humans need energy to fuel themselves and carrots only have a little bit of energy. We might eat them if they're right there on the plate but we're not going to run down to the shops especially. Doughnuts, though, doughnuts contain thousands of calories and lots of lovely fat and so we *really* want them. Think how long the energy in a doughnut would power you and it's obvious why they're far more appetising than carrots. If you're craving one now, that's dopamine, and if someone gave some to your kids, that was me.

It's important to clarify that dopamine is not released when a goal is achieved, but beforehand. The brain assesses how something might help our survival and gives us a little hit of dopamine in expectation. It's the *anticipation* of a goal being reached that stimulates the release of dopamine, hence the motivation. Dopamine acts as a subconscious incentive to human actions and behaviour because it makes us feel very nice indeed. It's referred to as the 'feel-good hormone' in pop science books and is available in large quantities via drugs like cocaine from the kids your mum won't let you play with. Dopamine can create bliss and euphoria at its best and a deep contentedness when being pro-social or altruistic. It also has a major function in romance.

When it comes to human pair bonding or 'falling in love', the deep longing and lust is created by reward circuitry in the brain called the mesolimbic pathway. Dopamine is made by the hypothalamus and then passes to the ventral tegmental area of the midbrain and the ventral striatum of basal ganglia in the forebrain. This is how the brain inspires reward-seeking behaviours: the more dopamine that is released into the circuit, the more motivated an animal is to achieve a reward.

An exciting/terrifying aspect of the mesolimbic pathway is that it works cyclically and can get us in a real tizzy. It can be greedy. Dopamine production can stimulate a need for even more dopamine, which results in a build-up of craving. In this way the pathway creates infatuation: the more we see the object of our desire, the more we *want* to see them. With this chemical reward our brain teaches us that THAT PERSON is VITAL for our survival, like sustenance; we become hungry for them. You'll have felt this, wanting to be around someone constantly, not being able to concentrate when they're nearby. First thought in the morning, last thought at night, hoping to bump into them and not leaving the very boring party in case they arrive later, dreaming about them, writing a poem about missing them although they've only popped to the toilet.

Falling in love is an obsessive behaviour, a compulsive need for another person. And while this sounds unhealthy expressed in those terms, evolution gave us this emotional machinery because we needed to be aggressively into each other for the survival of our species, for all those inept-baby reasons elucidated earlier.

We could argue that love is a socially acceptable form of addiction, because it's all the same procedures at work. Addictive behaviour is caused when the mesolimbic pathway sets up an obsessive desire for something that does not benefit survival, something that may in fact be hindering it. An easy example is food, an undoubted necessity for us all, but for some people the motivation to eat is never sated; everything eaten creates a desire to consume even more. Food addicts become very overweight, dangerously unhealthy and terribly misunderstood by society. The mesolimbic pathway can create the very definition of a vicious cycle. This brain circuitry that evolved to keep us alive and striving thousands of years before doughnuts were invented can become confused by the excesses possible in the modern world.

Oh, before we move on – an intriguing detail. An antidote to the withdrawal symptoms experienced by addicts is oxytocin, the bonding hormone we explored a few pages ago. Oxytocin can work as an antidote to craving. This is so interesting: if dopamine is creating our urges, needs, wants

– our desire – then oxytocin is sating it. This is why *being* with the person you love is so satisfying, while unrequited love is pure agitation. Our dopamine pathway is a powerful motivator to getting what we want, but when we can't get it, if we are fixated on something or someone impossible, then it can leave us anguished.

Which leads us nicely to another cause of male anguish, penis size.

Big Penises and What the Testicles Know

Humans have big brains and we have big penises too. Much bigger than they need to be and, proportionally, much larger than those belonging to the other apes. But unlike the brain, the benefits of a large penis are unclear. How has it assisted our species? We can only theorise.

A fun exercise for the male ego is to compare the human phallus with those of his ape bros. Gorillas are physically massive, twice the size of us, yet their penis is only about two and a half inches long when erect. While chimpanzees are our closest relatives, their penis is not at all close in length. The average human's is around six inches; for chimps it's only half that.

As clarified a few pages ago, for a trait to exist in modern humans it must have benefited us via natural selection (improving our chances of survival) or sexual selection (improving our chances of breeding). But there is a rogue third option, a kind of cop-out, shrugged-shoulders, we-don't-know area of biology. By-products. Some parts of our anatomy are believed to be surplus to requirements, neither aiding nor impeding our lives but remaining to baffle us thanks to the way we physically develop. The perfect example of a by-product is the male nipple. The female body requires nipples for feeding children, but as all bodies begin development along the same framework in utero (as we saw earlier) male bodies grow them too. Having nipples does men no harm, so they continue to sit on their chests stupidly, often hairily.

> You're saying the big male penis is a by-product? Because vaginas are roomy?

I am absolutely not. That would actually mean it was *sexually* selected because larger penises would perform better in larger vaginas. They'd be able to insert semen deeper, thus increasing the chances of fertilisation. In reality, the human vagina expands to accommodate whatever size penis is inserted, and there is no evidence that a larger penis improves the ability to conceive in humans. THERE IS NO EVIDENCE IT BENEFITS CONCEPTION. This is why it's a *mystery* . . . why have a big penis? If it doesn't aid conception, what the hell IS it doing?

We are going to explore all theories, but first let us descend a couple of inches to the testicles – a far less cryptic sexual organ. Our dicks are large, but our balls, not so much. Human testicles are a perfectly respectable medium size. Fascinatingly, this directly corresponds to how our species mates and bonds. All of the questions you might have about human sexuality – are we naturally monogamous? Is infidelity inevitable? To what extent did males dominate females in our evolution? Balls can tell us the answers . . .

Scientists can ascertain the promiscuity level of every species by the size of the male gonad. Isn't that exciting? For instance, gibbons are completely monogamous; they pair up, stay that way and consequently have very small testicles. Gorillas also have tiny testicles, but for the opposite reason – because one male has dominance over a group of females, his harem. What the gibbon and the gorilla have in common is that their sperm doesn't need to compete with that of any other male, because their females are not multi-partnering.

Small balls = small competition between males for females. Big balls = big competition. Chimpanzees have massive testicles because their females copulate with multiple males. A male's chances of impregnating a female are improved if he ejaculates more sperm. It's entirely logical: the more widely a female mates, the more sperm a male'll need to be in with a chance of fertilising her. Testicle size has evolved in response to female sexuality.

To put the sizing into perspective, if all apes were human-sized then gorillas' testes would resemble olives. So we know human females are more promiscuous than gorillas. Using the same system, a giant mouse lemur's testicles would be the size of grapefruits, so we know human women are positively frigid in comparison. Human testicles are medium-sized. We are not as promiscuous as chimpanzees and lemurs, but we aren't as faithful as gibbons; our mating strategy is somewhere in between. Our species pair-bonds deeply, but we also practise multi-partnering. Men's balls say something about the sexual behaviour of women—

They say, 'Stop sleeping with other men please.'

Well here's the thing, jealousy exists in our species because of our parental contribution. If a male is investing effort, energy and resources into his family it's imperative for him that the children are *his*. During our species' evolution, males who were not jealous and did not mate-guard, did not suspect anything was going on with the guy next door . . . those males were cuckolded. They were less genetically successful than dominating, controlling males and sneaky, philandering males. Our morality and modern-day ideas make it problematic to admit this, but being a possessive arsehole was of evolutionary benefit to men.

Consider this now: each pair of medium-sized human testes produces enough sperm to impregnate every fertile woman on the planet within a fortnight. If there was some disaster – perhaps a Zumba class got out of hand, took to the streets, committed a menocide and there's only one guy left, Kelvin, who was in the toilet and escaped the rampaging wiggling women – Kelvin would easily be able to continue humanity, he wouldn't want to, but he could! Wouldn't it make a great movie? Kelvin hates those bitches, yet he must get them pregnant. Even while they're trying to kill him, with Zumba.

I'm trying to demonstrate that there's a vast disparity in the male and female reproductive potential. A male could *potentially* have thousands of children in his lifetime, whereas a woman, she'd be very lucky to reach ten. An increase in partners doesn't increase the number of children the female body can produce, so why does she do it? To increase their quality. And for variety.

While the female of our species cannot spray her eggs about and have many ~~reasons I lost my friends~~ children, multi-partnering offers her the advantage of a range of genetic combinations for her offspring. If a woman breeds with one man, even if it's someone great like Prince Harry, then the offspring will be more limited in physical attributes, have similar responses to environmental challenges—

They'll all be pale and freckly.

They might all have the same congenital disease, the same weakness—

For Nazi regalia.

A woman who remains pair-bonded but has sexual encounters on the side is genetically spread-betting. If we take all morality and social conditioning out of the equation, it is the best mating strategy for females. She has the support and resources to raise her young, yet the opportunity to diversify and upgrade.

You're saying Meghan should put it about.

I sincerely believe she should kiss us all, it's her princessly duty.

Similarly for human males, the most effective mating strategy is to be pair-bonded but enjoy some extrapair copulations with other partners. This is something men have evolved to do, and the proof is in their competitive sperm.

Sperm Competition

As we've already established, any species that shares its females around has males pitted in direct competition to fertilise them. Over millions of years evolution has created a multitude of creative approaches to this problem. Let's start with a gross one: mating plugs. Guinea pigs can do this, and house mice. After ejaculation, the semen hardens inside the vagina, blocking the path for any subsequent suitors. It's disgusting but effective. There are subtler methods too. There's a desert ant whose sperm links up in groups so that it can swim faster towards the queen's egg, and an ingenious fruit fly whose semen contains mood-altering chemicals, so the female doesn't fancy any other guys!

It turns out that humans have a subtle method too. Human males can adjust the quality of their ejaculate. Not on purpose, not by thinking about it and squeezing really hard, but as an automatic response to certain situations. Studies have found that men released 'better' sperm when their partner returned from time away. After a separation of several days males were treating their partner to sperm at the top end of the motility range, especially if she'd been around other men. THIS IS HUGE. This means that the male body is subconsciously aware that its sperm *might* have to outswim some other dude's. He adds a little extra and makes sure the product is tiptop in order to improve his game. Further experiments on men in new relationships found that those who rated their partners as more attractive were ejaculating fitter, healthier sperm. How flattering. The male body is making assessments of mate value and potential competition, and the quality of semen can be adjusted accordingly. I love the idea of testicles talking to each other. 'Let's do our best today, she's been with Sexy Steve from work.'

The mechanics of the testes are amazing. Sperm production is most efficient at thirty-four degrees Celsius, a couple of degrees lower than body temperature. This is why male gonads dangle down between the legs, to keep cool. Storing spermatozoa like this ensures that they are dormant, preserved in chilly hibernation. When ejaculated inside the body of another person, the heat wakes them up. Now they can swim about and do their business with full energy, because they haven't wasted any doing laps in the balls. There is a special adjustment system in place to allow for changes in local temperature. The cremaster muscle can move the testicles up and down – nearer to the body if it's cold, further away if it's heating up – and it does this automatically, reflexively. The testes are dancing a little 'get the heat just right' boogie. Their sperm cannot compete if they've been frozen to death or burned alive.

In another example of incredible evolutionary design, the penis itself is a tool in the fight against rival sperm. We've already acknowledged how large it is for an ape our size, but it's also a unique and distinctive shape. A shape that is very important.

Whereas most ape penises are smooth, like a skinned banana, the human penis has a capped glans, like a banana with a hat on. For illustration please see overleaf, or any school graffiti.

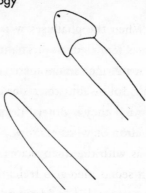

The human penis has this unusual headgear, and it's theorised that it works as a sperm displacement device. IT REMOVES RIVAL SPERM! Gordon G. Gallup sounds like something you might shout at a penis as encouragement, so it's fitting that the man dedicated himself to the study of this organ. Gallup claims the coronal ridge around the glans exists to remove the sperm of other men. Sperm can live for several days inside a woman's reproductive tract, so the ability to scrape out a gentleman caller's gentleman callers may have given our male ancestors a competitive advantage. Gallup oversaw some incredible experiments with prosthetic female genitals, latex phalluses and a pseudo-semen made from flour and water. I'm sure you can guess what he was up to, although the man in the sex shop may've been confused. The fake willies were all six inches. One was smooth, one had a ridge of 0.12 inches and another a ridge of 0.2 inches. Experimenters popped some fake semen in the fake female, thrust away with the fake male and measured which dildo displaced the most. The smooth one removed the least, around 35 per cent, but both ridged fellows got out over 90 per cent.

Even more interesting perhaps is that the experiments found that *deeper* thrusting resulted in more effective displacement. When the phalluses were entered only half-way, no fluid was removed. Shallow thrusting removed less semen and thus was ineffective sperm competition. Gallup et al. then did a follow-up: they surveyed two groups of students and found they reported deeper thrusting after a period of separation or when there was suspicion of female infidelity. Just as with the unconscious adjustment of ejaculate content, it seems men also feel an instinct to use their penis as a displacement device. My mind jumps straight to all the deep, aggressive thrusting in porn – a situation where the instinct for sperm competition would definitely be on high alert as you're watching a woman fucking someone else. I'm thinking about all the dirty talk that comes along with sex – it's all 'you're so deep', 'go at me hard'. Maybe I'll chuck in a 'your coronal ridge is right up there, mate' to complete the Your Sperm Is Competing Really Well triptych.

Then I got worried – surely the penis removes all of its own sperm too? But Gallup's theory explains that this is why the penis becomes sensitive immediately after ejaculation. It quickly loses rigidity and cannot keep thrusting, and shrivels its way out, leaving the semen behind. It has been argued that this is the reason for the male body's refractory period. Evolution has built in some resting time via temporary impotence so that Mr Penis doesn't go straight back in and dig up his newly sown seeds.

The idea that sperm competition may be deeply instinctual helped me understand some baffling products I saw online. There's a range of pills that claim to help men create more semen. Why? WHY? I stared at my computer; why would anyone want more of the sticky annoying bit? I clicked on a product called Yummy Cum which promises you'll produce super tasty spunk. While I understand the generous intention to improve one's flavour, what is attractive about *more*? I wondered if they were preying on insecurity caused by porn. Are some teens fretting about not spraying enough on their beloved's face? Unfortunately, because I clicked on one ad, all my pop-ups are semen-enhancing drugs now. There's one called Semenax, 'clinically proven' to provide 'massive loads of your own semen'. Volume Pills promise 'up to 500 per cent more cum', which is surely, surely 499 per cent too much. I'm no semen prude, but be reasonable, you're not decorating a room with it. When I first encountered these products, they didn't make sense to me. But if sperm competition has made men feel that a larger load relates to being an effective competitor, then perhaps there's a subconscious pleasure in making more of a mess.

Alongside deep thrusting, the amount of *time* spent thrusting is significant. According to Jared Diamond, author of *Why Is Sex Fun?*, the average human copulation is around four minutes long. So the answer is 'cos you can get it finished in an ad break'. It's also fun to find out that four minutes is far longer than sex needs to be. It has been proved in experiments that lengthy sex is not necessary for conception and does not increase the *likelihood* of conception. Chimp intercourse lasts about fifteen seconds and they're not facing extinction. Could our species' thrusty sessions be about sperm removal? Getting that ridge deep inside and having a good clear-out? Of course, as we've already discussed, some of the chemicals released during sex promote bonding between couples, so that four-minute session could be about feeling nice and close to each other. It's probably a combination of both.

Remarkably, sexual stamina is also connected to status. The reason I say this is because newly sexual men, young men, inexperienced men ejaculate quicker. Heightened excitement can be quite difficult to control. Evolutionary psychologists theorise that this is because sex was quite a dangerous thing for our ancestors to do. Focused upon your partner, naked and aroused, sex makes people vulnerable. That's why we hide away to do it and do it in the dark (mostly) and in secret (most of us). Fear inhibits the sexual response in most people. If there's danger around, a person needs to be alert and defensive, not balls deep and oblivious. Stress hormones can even affect a man's ability to get an erection. In nature this is a sensible mechanism, preventing him from forgetting himself in sexual abandon when he needs to be alert to protect himself. In the modern world, where people get stressed about the HR department and the price of ham, this mechanism seems unhelpful, but it's actually very clever.

So apparently lower-status human males might have an inbuilt, easily triggered system to get this vulnerable sex time over quickly. A speedy ejaculation can still impregnate someone, but there's less chance of a high-status male interrupting and fighting for the female. While a prehistoric male would have to be alert to predators and other dangers, a stronger man would've been the scariest threat. We mustn't assume that all sperm competition evolved via female-initiated consensual sex. Even though it's grim to contemplate, male competition would often have taken place in the bodies of raped women. Men get aroused by seeing sex, which we will be analysing shortly. The reason we evolved to hide our sex was to avoid the provocation of other males and their unwanted interference.

Interference is a polite way of putting it.

Regarding intercourse duration, I've been wondering if status ramifications are why there's kudos for men who can last ages. Maybe it subconsciously signals 'I'm alpha,' 'I'm not scared of big animals or other tribesmen,' 'I can go as long as the Bayeux Tapestry.' Maybe that's why fast ejaculation is embarrassing, feels diminishing . . . a reflection of masculinity? And that's what seems odd about this machismo: all this thrusting for hours and lakes of semen – where is the female pleasure? Is this the Conundrum of Heterosexuality™? The reason there's so often a disconnect between sex that would be enjoyable for the female (clitoral stimulation) versus what is enjoyed by the male (mindless thrusting)? The men of our species have been in competition for millions of years and the battlefields were often women's bodies. Does this mean male sexuality will always have an awareness of other men inextricably within it? Are males jostling for social position even in the privacy of the bedroom, and is that why porn looks the way it does? When I ask lots of questions do you hear them in Carrie from *Sex and the City*'s voiceover?

We're shortly going to be investigating pornography and its relation to sperm competition. But in order to comprehend why porn has such a powerful effect on our arousal system there are some other aspects of the human body that need your attention first.

Constant Sexual Signalling

I briefly mentioned concealed ovulation a few pages ago, but now I want to delve into the reasons we may have evolved to be so secretive about our fertile period, and the consequences for human sexuality.

Some primates, such as baboons and bonobos, have visual signals of fertility; their bottoms swell up and become infused with colour, yelling to local males, 'Woohoo, over here, ripe ova.' Other animals are less attention-seeking, relying on pheromones emitted from their skin or in urine. In addition to this, the majority of female animals are ONLY receptive to mating when in their fertile period, or oestrus. Any non-fertile sex is a waste of their time and any male trying his luck during this period will be refused. Sometimes politely, sometimes with a kick or headbutt.

How intriguing then that human beings have evolved to do the opposite. Technically, human females can be receptive to sex twenty-four hours a day, 365 days of the year. It doesn't always work like that, we get in bad moods and need to sleep sometimes, but technically we are constantly sexually available, regardless of what our ovaries are up to. Now I'd initially believed that our concealed ovulation meant that we didn't exhibit any fertility signals, closed and dormant like old volcanoes. 'How clever, human females,' I thought, 'keeping all our insides secret so that we can choose our partners and express our personal sexuality,' and I WAS WRONG.

Yes, there is no physical indication that a human is in oestrus. That is because, from adolescence onwards, the female body maintains a CONSTANT STATE of fertility signalling. Our breasts and bums don't swell up to say 'Hey, I'm fertile, come on over' on a cyclical basis. Instead they *stay* swollen up, saying that All. The. Time.

See, the great thing about signalling ovulation like a female baboon is that when she *isn't* fertile, the male baboons leave her alone. Sure, they'll hang out as friends, but she is not going to get continually pestered. The human female is not so lucky. Walking down a path, sitting in a Costa, waiting for the bus – a woman's life can be an assault course of avoiding male attention.

I've encountered this as much as any city-dwelling woman, but as for the reason it happens – I'd never really got past 'men are pigs'.

NOT ALL MEN.

Sure, but it only takes a very small fraction of you to do all the work for the rest. I know there are gradients, some men think they are being friendly or 'complimentary'. Not all the approaches are predatory, some are a mere nuisance. But I've never taken the time to wonder what causes the men to do it.

Here is my ground-breaking, personal-first attempt to see it from their point of view. If you're a straight man and the shape of women's bodies makes you *feel* stuff – you didn't choose that either. It happens automatically, instinctively. I'm not excusing any of the creepy stalkers, bus rubbers or unsolicited dick pic-ers; that *is* a choice, I still blame them. But I used to resent men for their *thoughts*. I wanted to exist in the world as a person, sexless in both meanings of the word.

I wanted sex to be something I could switch on, like a light, for a few relevant people, something that only I was in control of. When some man online or in real life attempts to flirt, I feel enraged. HOW ARE YOU SEEING SEX WHEN I AM HIDING IT? It feels important to acknowledge that we cannot control what people see.

We have another Conundrum of Heterosexuality™: 'can't say anything these days', '#MeToo has gone too far', 'can't even have a cuddle at work'. Many ~~old men~~ people are worried about the growing respect for bodily autonomy. 'How will anyone get together if you're not allowed to go up to someone and pinch their arse?' It's the vital question of our age. All of our grandparents met when Grandad shouted 'nice tits' out of a passing vehicle. What will we do now? How will any of us find love without the groping hands of a stranger letting us know it's real?

My initial reaction to the people who say this stuff is hard to navigate is to roll my eyes, it's too easy. But that isn't fair of me. It *isn't* easy if you don't understand the basis of what you're doing wrong, and it's exacerbated by the media, who are *very* good at picking up on stories which suggest #MeToo is out of control and oversensitive. Much attention is given to hysterical, OTT situations undermining the rest. Here's an example from a couple of years ago. A lawyer got upset with a man over a message on LinkedIn. The man posted under her photo 'stunning picture!!!' which is too many exclamation marks, but has he committed any other crime?

The man prefaced his comment by saying he knew it was probably un-PC, and he followed it by saying it would win a 'best photo on LinkedIn' competition and that he was always interested in connecting with people in his field of work. It wasn't predatory, or at least I am not reading it that way. It wasn't particularly flirty even. It was a compliment. The woman, Charlotte Proudman, replied saying his message was misogynistic and offensive.

Does that perplex you? It seems like an overreaction, eh? Misogyny is HATRED of women. This dude doesn't hate them, he thinks there should be a LinkedIn photo competition, like Miss World with headhunting and fax numbers.

I sympathised a little bit. There is no invisibility for women. Proudman wanted her photo to say 'lawyer' and resented the response 'attractive woman'. Our species does not have a set of triggered physical signals to create sexual interest, and that has resulted in constant sexual interest. Or at least awareness. And this means there is no downtime – no time off for us to just *exist*.

Until menopause.

throws self off cliff

Considering this from a straight male perspective I realise that it's true for men too. We live in massive societies, not small tribes, and even without the internet and billboards, even just with the human beings surrounding your average man there is a deluge of sexiness. It might be mainly or entirely inadvertent, but nature has sculpted men to be attracted by it like moths to light—

#METOO WANTS TO BURN OUR WINGS OFF

If you say so. The most important lesson of adulthood might be that just because you *feel* something, that doesn't mean someone *intended* you to feel it. That applies to both the women in LinkedIn photos and the men making comments.

We know that other female primates indicate fertility with tumescence, swellings and pinkness around their rump, but did you know that humans might once have had red bums too? We evolved out of it. The anthropologist Bogusław Pawłowski suggested that bipedalism may have extinguished our fiery loins because significant areas would have been hidden from sight unless we bent over. It's a curious theory and I like the guy's name, he sounds like an evil dog. I'd also like to *reverse* the theory and argue that women learned to walk upright cos they were fed up of guys looking at their fanny.

And men stood up to chase them?

Science is so easy. An interesting aside from this: studies have found men judge women as more attractive when they're dressed in red or against a red background. Is this an archaic response hardwired by our ancestors' blood-suffused labia?

I think you just ruined a Chris de Burgh song.

Thank you. Scientists then reverse-tested this idea: if heterosexual men find red sexy, then women would be more likely to wear that colour when they are fertile.

WOMEN DON'T KNOW WHEN THEY'RE FERTILE.

Stop shouting, subconsciously. Scientists theorise that women, while not consciously being aware of their oestrus, demonstrate behaviours signifying that their body *is* going through it.

Andrew Elliot and Daniela Niesta at the University of Rochester, New York, surveyed a hundred American women in 2008. They asked participants what colour top they had on and when their last period was, and then ~~got slapped for asking personal questions~~ calculated how likely participants were to be ovulating. They found 40 per cent of the 'likely fertile' group were wearing red or pink versus only 7 per cent of the rest, which is CRAZY but needs to be replicated with more people before I'll be completely convinced.

It isn't just visible changes that are absent in human sexuality. We don't release pheromones either. Or rather, we *might*, but our noses and brains aren't very good at noticing and responding to them any more. Pheromones are airborne hormones that allow animals to convey physiological information to each other: 'I'm scared,' 'I'm ovulating,' 'I'm your brother.'

Worst Christmas card ever.

Humans may have some faint pheromonal stuff going on. Scientists are still attempting to confirm this. There's a famous study that found strippers made more in tips during their oestrus phase. It's the kind of thing we want to be true: an echo of something ancient, useful to our prehistoric ancestors, now earning a woman in perspex heels more coin. The experiment had the dancers register how much money they made each day as well as tracking their cycle. Some of the participants were on hormonal contraception and did not see a rise in tips, while the women ovulating saw their cash increase on fertile days. There were only eighteen women in the study, so it's far too small to extrapolate anything meaningful from it. Reading it, I also questioned if the increase in tips was proof that male customers could subconsciously smell pheromones, or if the women *behaved* in different ways, were flirtier or friendlier when ovulating? Or wearing red?!

I'm absolutely better at my job during the middle of my cycle, which has nothing to do with feeling or looking sexy and everything to do with not being angrily depressed. If you'd like to find out more about my horrible personality and menstrual cycle, read my first book, *Animal*!

Although women can't pinpoint when they're ovulating without technical aids, scientists have found behavioural differences that might increase a female's chance of reproductive success during that time. Studies have found that ovulating women pay more attention to grooming and dressing, are more likely to have a one-night stand, more likely to have sex without using a condom, and if married are more likely to 'cheat'. There was also the astonishing discovery that heterosexual women are attracted to more masculine men while ovulating.

What does 'more masculine' mean?

The scientists defined 'more masculine' characteristics as 'strong chin, brow and jaw', which are facial indicators of higher testosterone, and 'broad shoulders, muscly', which indicate higher testosterone in the body. In one study fertile women chose the 'masculine type' 15 per cent more often than those in the unfertile group.

Hmm.

Don't sulk.

You'd be sulking if I said men preferred big bouncy boobs.

It is for that exact reason I've sulked my entire life.
Experiments involving sweaty T-shirts are popular with

scientists seeking to discover the invisible processes that attract us to certain partners. It's been found that people are drawn to those whose immunological profile (the major histocompatibility complex or MHC) is genetically different from their own, which is incredibly sensible, because offspring born of parents with differing MHC will be equipped with a more varied and thus more effective immune system.

Relevant to what we're considering, several sweaty T-shirt studies have found that men prefer the smell of ovulating women – their odours were rated more pleasant – and, even more astonishingly, that men's testosterone levels were raised by sniffing the sweat of women mid-cycle, but not at other times. It's an exciting area of science that needs more study to illuminate what hints the female body might be giving out, and what the possible effects might be on the male body, all happening beneath our notice.

A few other species have concealed ovulation – dolphins, grey langurs and vervet monkeys – but the difference is that they're all promiscuous. They don't form pair bonds to raise their young. The females have multiple partners, and no one knows or cares who's the daddy. It is theorised that concealed ovulation reduces aggression in these species; the males don't fight and kill each other over access to fertile females, because they don't know that they are. This is almost certainly a factor in human evolution too. Constant sexual signalling is the price we pay for increased male survival. Another advantage is reduced infanticide because paternity is in doubt. A male animal is less predisposed to kill young that could share his genes. How lovely of him.

Homo sapiens lost the explicit signalling of our fecund period either because it wasn't reproductively useful, or because of the advantages of having it hidden. One possible benefit, which would have powerfully shaped the social aspect of our species, is that if multiple males have mated with a female, they might *all* be willing to contribute resources and protection to the child. This means more food and increased safety, both for mothers and for their young. This theory allows that tribes composed of several families might actually be more invested in each other's success if there was some genetic overlap. So go on, shag your next-door neighbour, it's good for the whole street.

There's a paper from 1979 arguing that hidden oestrus would've motivated a change in male behaviour. Anthropologists Richard Alexander and Katherine Noonan suggest that our species started out as promiscuous as our chimp and bonobo relatives, a system that creates much 'wasted' mating. I am sure everyone enjoyed themselves, but from an evolutionary perspective, it was a waste of time and energy. A male who stayed with one female and copulated throughout her cycle would've been more successful in replicating his genes. Rather than hopping from female to female with no guarantee of who's fertile, through-the-month mating would guarantee that there was definitely a window of fertility at some point. Thus the monogamy trait was selected for, and males became devoted. But let us not overly romanticise this pairing up millions of years ago. While a human male exhibits bonding behaviours – I've seen you pushing prams in the park and crying at your wives' funerals – that is not the end of male sexuality, though, is it?

IS IT?

Sex and Chickens

There's an apocryphal story of President Calvin Coolidge and his wife being shown around a barnyard by a farmer. As the couple admire a hen coop the farmer points to the rooster and proudly announces, 'He can go twelve times a day.'

'Tell that to my husband,' quips Mrs Coolidge.

The First Lady shows with her sauce that even the most powerful man in the world can be undermined when it comes to his own virility. Hang on, though, because her husband has a comeback:

'Same hen every time?'

'Oh no, no,' the farmer says, shaking his head, 'different hens.'

'Tell that to my wife!' Coolidge wins. One–nil to men. Straight women go for a cry behind the pigpen.

The Coolidge effect is a term used by biologists, zoologists and anthropologists to describe a renewed interest in sexual activity when an unfamiliar female is introduced. Like we were discussing earlier, in our species and many others, males' ability to procreate is limited only by how many females they have access to. While the human male might be deeply pair-bonded, this does not switch off his appreciation for sexual cues from other directions. Especially new ones, novel ones. And this is why porn is such a successful arousal tool for men.

An ex-boyfriend of mine had a consuming relationship with pornography that I only found out about several months into our relationship. He had fancied me at the start but, like microwaving popcorn, after a noisy beginning there was a sudden drop-off. Sex went from daily to monthly and I dealt with it very badly. Culturally we're all familiar with a sexually frustrated male. He can be found in sitcoms and movies hilariously dealing with 'blue balls' or badgering a partner. There aren't many examples of horny, rejected women.

I tried to communicate my feelings by crying hysterically. It's an unhelpful paradox that a person is at their *least* sexy when sexually frustrated. It's particularly difficult to seduce someone when you've snot running down your face. I also knew that Nicholas was still masturbating. He had a sex drive, it was just motoring in the opposite direction. I found this impossible to process – I was right there, in my pants and weeping, why didn't he want me? It was still early in the relationship, the microwave hadn't pinged, yet it'd got to the point where he wouldn't kiss me on the mouth in case it 'gave me ideas'.

One night we got drunk and Nicholas told me the reason he didn't have long-term relationships was because of porn. Because after a couple of months with someone it wasn't exciting. He'd watch porn and masturbate, thinking, 'This is the real stuff, this is the *real* sexy feeling.' Nicholas looked sad, and I was supposed to understand and be kind to him. He was brave, being vulnerable – telling me the truth of what he was going through.

I was very angry with the truth. I was jealous. The world was set up unfairly, so that I, singular woman with one vagina and tiny breasts, was having to compete with the hundreds of thousands of people that high-speed internet could produce. I was losing, I had lost. The truth was my deepest fear: I am insufficient.

The Coolidge effect uses the sex lives of chickens to illuminate an accepted certainty about humans: that while females will be content with one stud, males, if unchecked, will do it with anything that moves. I do not want to believe that men are more sexual than women, but some evidence supports the argument that they are. Sometimes I hate evidence.

There's a study that I think about often, conducted by Russell Clark and Elaine Hatfield on American university campuses in 1989. They employed stooges to approach students of the opposite gender and ask one of these questions:

a) Would you go out with me tonight?

b) Would you come over to my apartment tonight?

c) Would you go to bed with me tonight?

The results of the first question didn't show much gender discrepancy; 50 per cent of males said yes versus 56 per cent of females. Women were slightly more likely to agree to a date than males. But the other propositions found a vast divergence. A whopping 69 per cent of men agreed to visit a stranger's apartment compared to 7 per cent of women. I know you can do your own maths, but that's 62 per cent more men. The huge ramification here is that a man's more likely to agree to come round your house than go on a date with you. For question c, 75 per cent of men agreed to sex. Just like that. Come on a date? Erm . . . Come round my house? I'll think about it. Wanna have sex? COUNT ME IN.

Can you guess how many of the female students agreed to the sex question? Zero. Big fat none. A difference of 75 per cent. Three quarters of men versus no women. This is massive, undeniable. It reinforces the cultural stereotypes of men as free-roaming cads, while women are uptight prudes requiring wining and dining.

Studies like the one above are used as evidence that we've evolved sexual strategies reflecting the amount of 'parental investment' incumbent upon us. Males have a teeny input; four minutes, a few thrusts and a dribble of sperm can result in their genetic success. A female must grow any offspring inside her body, then breastfeed for years afterwards. This is costly and demanding, not to mention gross. We learned earlier that it's more difficult to raise a baby human than any other ape. This means that selection pressures have moved a female human's behaviour away from the freer, looser promiscuity of her chimp and bonobo relatives. Evolutionary psychologists suggest that the children of sexually prodigious, unattached women millions of years ago were less likely to survive because they lacked male parental input. Sexual exclusivity and carefulness were rewarded with genetic success, which is a bit depressing. This doesn't match our modern values; we have contraception and babysitters and believe in personal sexual expression. Evolution is being pretty uncool here.

Do we believe that men are by nature more promiscuous than women? Research has consistently found that, compared to straight men, homosexual men have more partners and more sex with strangers. This is taken to be a true reflection of male sexuality without us frigid females slowing you down. It's a strong argument that women limit men's sexual potential, impede you with our big 'NO' signs and 'Take me to dinner first' banners.

Who ruins the world? Girls.

This is hard enough for me to process without you mis-quoting Beyoncé. Also, there's more to this than mere sexual inclination, as we shall see.

Sex and Danger

What if this isn't simply about sex drive?

To use a vehicular analogy, if male drivers were whizzing around at hundreds of miles per hour in their cars, while females were tootling about at 30 mph, our first assumption would be MEN LIKE DRIVING FAST WOMEN SLOW BORING BEEPBEEP GET OFF THE ROAD. But what if I gave you more information, if I said all the males' cars were reinforced? They're made of stronger steel and full of airbags. Whereas the females' cars, they're tin cans, fragile, with no seat belts. Could you still make the same conjecture? We'd probably have to agree that the women were driving slowly because their cars were precarious. Some women might really, really wish they could drive fast, but just couldn't take the risk.

I believe it's exactly the same with shagging. Throughout our evolution, women have not been free to follow our loins' desire, not just because of pregnancy risks and parental investment, but because being alone with a man can be unsafe.

If a female student says no to an offer of sex or visiting a stranger's apartment, it's not automatically a reflection of low libido, but an assessment of danger. Males are bigger and stronger than females; in scientific terms, humans have a body-size dimorphism of around 1.1 in the male's favour. This isn't accidental, it's the result of male competition. In species where males compete for females the strongest are more likely to win and share their big genes with the next generation. This worldwide physical advantage has historically been used to justify the superiority of men, justify why they should be respected and obeyed, and paid more in virtually all vocations.* But if you flip this around, the reason women are smaller and weaker is that men weren't worth fighting over.

Hold my bag while I victory-lap.

The sex difference in size and strength means that men have not evolved to be wary of women in the way we are of you. Sorry, I'm sure you personally are absolutely lovely, but we're talking hundreds of centuries of pre-civilised barbarism here; a few years of liberalism and a hashtag is not going to reverse it. The results of the Clark and Hatfield study do not prove that women don't enjoy sex or fancy new men, they prove that even the women who would like some sex, please, dare not take the risk. Zero per cent. ZERO women said yes. We do not have zero sex drive – I think we're predisposed to be wary of male sexuality.

I can't ascertain how much of my personal fear of men was learned. I read about phobias being learned from parents. That if a mum screams when she sees a spider, that makes her children jump and become scared also. It only needs to happen a couple of times for a spider–fear response to be conditioned. I won't say my mum demonised men because she'll read this and say I've cock-blocked her. So let's just say I was told a great deal about the evils committed by spiders, particularly spiders who preyed on little girls, and warned never to marry a musician spider because they lie.

---

* Although not in our main area of interest, porn.

Early in my adolescence it only took a couple of ... infractions, and I was changed. From eleven or twelve I did not want to be alone with a man, not even my dad, who never ever encroached upon me, but I feared him and felt guilty about it. Every man was a potential threat. I know how extreme that sounds and how unfair to most men. The reason I began with Anaïs Nin's words, 'We see things not as they are but as *we* are,' is because I understand men in general through a lens tainted by a few. I know why men shout at me on Twitter and write me angry emails about feminism – it's because they want to be understood as individuals, not as representative of a gender. And I laugh, of course, because that's all that feminism is asking for, for everyone. My fear is not your personal fault, and I was never saying it was.

It's been theorised that while terror of spiders is irrational in a country like England, we all evolved in countries and habitats where arachnids were deadly poisonous, and that's why we have a tendency to dislike them. All it takes is a little trigger, like our mother screaming or being assaulted by one on the way to school, and suddenly we're phobic. Is it the same with fear of men? Does their size and strength advantage – their *potential* to be deadly – live deep in my genes?

This is really sexist.

They used to be more dangerous, you know, in ancestral times. Any strange man would have been threatening. Tribes fought each other, raped each other, there were no courts or legal punishments. Perhaps the past is restraining some women's sexuality? Maybe without all that we'd be uninhibited and agree to shag more strangers we met in the campus car park?

I want that to be true, but there's evidence that suggests it's more complicated.

If it was simply fear of male violence that is hampering the heterosexual lady libido then homosexual women should be enjoying the same sexual variety as gay men. Lots of partners, more hook-ups, less boring commitment. Except they aren't. Studies measuring novelty in relationships and sex lives have found lesbians have even fewer one-night stands and fewer sexual partners than tedious old straight people do. Studies have also found that gay women orgasm more reliably during sex than straight women.

Signifying what?

I just wanted to mention that in case it looked like I was using stats to denigrate lesbian love-making – they are clearly excellent at it. Although, interestingly, women are more likely to orgasm when they feel 'safe', and what could be safer than sex with the people who comprise only 10 per cent of murderers?

It cannot purely be prehistoric fear that constrains female sexuality. The disparity between male and female parental investment cannot be discounted as affecting our sexual decision making. Men, technically, can have consequenceless sex; the male body cannot get pregnant. No amount of sex with any number of partners will get him up the duff and dependent on others for food. For the female-bodied person, pre-contraception, all sex has a potential five-year drain on her body and resources. That's if she doesn't die pushing a baby's big head out of her small body.

Broody?

It's fair to say that selectivity has become a female necessity. There are many things to assess in a potential sex partner. Personal safety is one thing, genes and health another. Our bodies cannot forget the connection between sex and babies, even though we can control that in modern times. Our bodies cannot un-know the toll of parental investment.

We'll be investigating later how our species' lack of paternity certainty has led to stigma about sex work. We still have to discuss the complex relationship between men and their penis size, and before we delve into the topic of pornography, I want to signpost one thing. It is a basic human instinct to be private and secretive about sex. Across all cultures. Yet all the other animals do it outside without caring who sees them. Couldn't give a shit. No shame, no underpants. But us *Homo sapiens* have a deep-seated desire to hide, to be embarrassed.

What about exhibitionists?

Yes. Some people get off on doing the exact opposite. We'll be investigating how human sexuality holds within its rules a million contradictions. Individuals have perverted idiosyncrasies, but in general, humans have sex in private. It's likely this evolved alongside our deep pair bonds. Our coupledom developed by excluding others. In other apes high-status males dominate fertility: in gorillas an alpha male maintains a harem of females; in chimps the lower-status males have to be sneaky or must settle for females with a low mate value. In humans, we couple up and avoid fights by doing our sexy stuff at home.

There are social rules we all abide by; unconcealed sexual performance is so rare we consider it a sign of mental impairment. You tell your doctor, 'Aunty Sheila tried to wank off her husband on the bus this morning,' and your doctor will reply, 'I'm afraid Aunty Sheila needs a brain scan.'

The reason I want to remind you of this before the next section is SEEING SEX TURNS US ON. We hide it from each other not because it's dirty or immoral but because it's arousing. In hunter–gatherer societies, pre-religion and getting sacked from work, the reason we evolved to conceal our sex was that *other people might want to join in*. And if they are stronger than you, you might not be able to stop them.

We have sex in private for our safety and for paternity certainty and all that stuff. But our sensitivity to sexual cues, the fact that we get aroused by seeing sex – that's older than the pair-bonded bit of us, it's our fundamental animal root. While we've learned a lot so far about the ancient mechanisms that have shaped some of our emotional behaviour, we are going to push this further. I want to understand why porn has become such an important part of the modern world; I want to know why some people become consumed and obsessed with it while others remain blasé. We're going to use representations of the penis in porn to try and understand what it *means*. WHY IS THE PENIS SO IMPORTANT TO YOU PEOPLE?

Let's learn about porn.

Sex
Power
Porn

Dirty Daubings

Waw chica waw waw, please come in and fix the washing machine.

Tens of thousands of years ago *Homo sapiens* began making images of bodies. We don't know how erotic early people found the images, whether these figures were nude to inspire lust or purely because no one had any clothes on. We don't know the *intentions* of the artists because they didn't do TED talks and Q&As explaining '*this* piece represents the death of my mother. Although she lives on in my mind. And in Chelmsford.' What I'm trying to say is that olden-days artists weren't pretentious arseholes, they just did their little pictures and died. We can't know what was considered aesthetically arousing by these ancient people. We only have their dusty artefacts and our modern ideas.

The earliest human-made image is arguably a vulva. The word 'arguably' doesn't flatter anyone, does it? Some poor woman 'flashing the pink' thirty-seven thousand years ago would be rightfully insulted by recent historians' doubt. Ditto the sculptor who carved it on the wall of a French cave: 'Zut alors! Dis defo is le voolva.' I apologise for that accent; I don't know if they had cultural stereotypes back then. I don't know if France was even a thing that long ago. Either way this is our first evidence of human art, and it's a fanny (probably). If you want to see this engraving search 'Abri Castanet female genitalia' on your computer. And do it on your boss's time, this image is absolutely SFW in that it doesn't really look like a vulva. I've drawn it for you as well – I'm sure thirty-seven thousand years means it's out of copyright:

So that's what we are starting with. It could be a prehistoric premonition of a doughnut, it could be the invention of the sideways smile emoji, it could be a masturbatory aid or a feminist self-portrait. I'll never know, and nor will you. Aren't mysteries fun?

Moving along, the oldest known example of *figurative* art is a tiny female nude known as the Venus of Hohle Fels. She is more than thirty-five thousand years old (there's no age limit on glamour modelling), carved from ivory, and has 'pronounced breasts and genitals'. In your ~~face~~ vagina, cave vagina.

For a younger woman, check out the Venus of Willendorf, who is a mere twenty-five thousand years old. She has massive stony boobs and a head like the handle of a table tennis bat.

There are tons of artefacts depicting the naked human form and lots of pervy daubings on walls and rocks which prove how long our species has delighted in its own image. As our forebears became more sophisticated in the visual arts, they used those skills to depict sex more accurately. There are plates from Mesopotamia that couldn't be used pre-watershed nowadays, and vases from ancient Greece that would get you banned from your pottery evening class. Because there's fucking on them.

The oldest image of human sex was found in a cave near Bethlehem. A carved couple wrapped around each other, it's called Ain Sakhri. The lovers are thought to be around eleven thousand years old. The extra fun is that whatever angle you look at them from their pairing resembles ~~the baby Jesus~~ a penis . . . apparently. I think a lot of ancient erotic art was made by people who hadn't seen genitals. Or only seen them after they'd been run over. If this was meant to be a penis it's gone terribly wrong. I mean, it's two people, so it has two heads. If you turn it on its side, it looks more phallic. But then doesn't everything?

Moving into more recent times, three thousand years ago the enticingly named Turin Erotic Papyrus was produced in Egypt. It's less than ten inches long. One third of it is pictures of animals doing human jobs and the rest is explicit and occasionally ambitious sex positions. Basically, the entire internet painted on plant material during the Ramesside period.

One art historian described the men on the papyrus as 'scruffy, balding, short, and paunchy . . . with exaggeratedly large genitalia', while the women are 'nubile' and 'gorgeous'. So far, so modern pornography – not that the papyrus *is* porn. Images of nudity and sex don't become pornographic until – well, aha, there is the riddle.

What is over two thousand years old but only became porn around two hundred years ago?

The Invention of Porn

Once upon a time (AD 79) there was a place called Pompeii in a place called Italy in a place called The World. All the people in Pompeii were living their normal lives near a volcano called Vesuvius when it suddenly ejaculated red-hot dangerous lava onto everyone. The liquid stone covered people wherever they were and whatever they were doing – making dinner, washing the dog or, ironically, contemplating suicide. The lava cooled, and the city of Pompeii was encased in rock and ash and hidden until 1748. The archaeologists who dug it up saw how saucy the ancient artwork of Pompeii was and were shocked and appalled. This is the historical equivalent of your mum coming into your room and finding you wanking, except you're a million Pompeiians and your mum is a volcano and this analogy doesn't work.

The art from Pompeii depicted all the sex positions. There were illustrations of oral sex and sodomy. There were statues with massive phalluses and mosaics of bestiality and gods swapping hand jobs, and while you might be thinking:

Finally, an art collection that isn't boring.

the Victorians decided these items must NEVER be seen by the innocent eyes of Mr and Mrs Public. They set up A SECRET MUSEUM that only everybody knew about. No one was allowed in except the most ~~perverted~~ qualified experts. It was opened in 1821, the door was bricked up by

1849 and the time in between was taken up with discussing obscenity and decency.

It is actually, *actually* fascinating that one historical period's public decorations become another culture's *verboten*. In Pompeii there were these street penises which poked out from buildings above street level. For some reason ancient Italians liked some of their buildings to have willies. Were they totems? Reminders of legends and myth? Or somewhere high to hang your cloak? We can't know for sure until you finish that time machine.

Along Oxford Street in London there are statues above shops of Britannia or boats and stuff. Tourists walk around and don't even notice until I shout, 'Look up and respect our sculptures.' Imagine if in two thousand years these statues were in museum prison because billowing robes and flags are mistrusted . . . it's equally silly. The human body hasn't changed a jot but these two civilisations drastically differ in their response to it. For the Pompeiians, a big stone willy was beautiful or funny or lucky. For British Victorians it was PORNOGRAPHIC.

Porne is a Greek word referring to a female slave, literally meaning a woman purchased for the purpose of prostitution; the poor bastards. I hate history so much. I'm not being anti-sex work by the way, I'm being anti-sexual slavery. Fun fact about me, I hate sexual slavery. There you go.

Porneion was an ancient Greek brothel. The *graphy* bit simply means 'to write'. Now you know where the word 'pornography' came from and why my script for *Sesame Street* was rejected. Today's episode was brought to you by the letter P and the systematic abuse of women by the patriarchy.

This new word, 'pornography', began to be used around the mid-nineteenth century. In 1857 it appeared in a medical dictionary as 'a description of prostitutes or of prostitution'. A slightly more modern definition was introduced by Webster's dictionary in 1864: 'licentious painting employed to decorate the walls of rooms sacred to bacchanalian orgies, examples of which exist in Pompeii'.

Today we use the word 'pornography' to describe explicit imagery or writing in general. The word can be used negatively. People say something is 'pornographic' when it's rude, dirty, crude. When people talk about *using* pornography, they mean something sexy, something that arouses them. Crucially, when we label something as 'pornography', we mean that its *intention* is to turn people on. That's why it was created. There's a level of explicitness implied by the word. My friend Tom* once gave up porn and started wanking to his female friends' holiday photos on Facebook. I don't know if you find that problematic, but you couldn't say beach bikini shots were porn, even though they were being used as a masturbatory aid.

The Roman artworks hidden away during Victoria's reign had been used for domestic decoration during Emperor Vespasian's. The frescos had been shame-free and visible to all, the paintings hung as proudly as the Priapus they depicted. They were not created as pornography, but seen centuries later they became it. So here is something to remember: for all of us – each individual and every cultural group – some of what we consider to be pornography is subjective.

---

* In case you're wondering, Tom *is* his real name. Careful what you tell me, friends, I'm writing a book.

One Man's Porn Is a Young Woman's Bottom

Whatever the dictionaries of our times may contain, we all define what is licentious differently. A Hollywood block-buster considered by censors to be suitable for twelve-year-olds may be simultaneously objectionable to an American Muslim. If I saw a poster of a naked woman in the street, legs apart, pulling at her bum cheeks to display her genitals – I'm sorry to tell you I'd be affronted. I'd consider it hugely inappropriate for a public place. But that same reaction might be triggered by someone wearing a two-piece swimsuit in parts of India, or a mini-skirt in an Italian cathedral. I was once shouted at by nuns on bikes in Milan because of a whorish, arm-revealing vest.

We discussed the constant sexual signalling of the post-pubescent female body in previous pages, and this is compounded by the fact that we all sometimes interpret certain things as sexual signals, regardless of whether or not they were intended that way. This makes life complicated.

A few years ago I was queuing up with a boyfriend to see a show. He was getting tetchy, because of the waiting, I thought, but then I realised the focus of his mood was in front of us.

He gestured with his eyes to a child's bottom.

I say 'child' but she was about thirteen or fourteen, so maybe that's not fair. Sorry if you were imagining a bum in a nappy. Ahead of us in the queue was a young woman. My boyfriend shook his head and asked, 'How can people let their kids go out like that?' in a way that implied that they shouldn't.

The 'kid' was wearing denim shorts, the very skimpy type that Topshop sold circa 2013. They only covered between half and three quarters of the wearer's bum cheeks, depending on your age and the pull of gravity where you were standing. For slim women under twenty-two, these shorts displayed the sweet smile of the lower buttock edge. They were fashionable. I'd been at the Reading, Leeds and Latitude festivals that year and seen clouds of teens in crop tops and tiny denim. I hadn't thought to judge any parents. But then teenage girls' bodies don't give me a hard-on.

'Someone should tell her.' My boyfriend was angry. I got angry too. My Feminist Issue Alarm was going off. This alarm is easily activated and will ruin adverts, politics and trips to the cinema. The soon-to-be-ex-boyfriend and I were now arguing. My point of view: why should this young woman consider HIM when putting clothes on her body? She wasn't dressing for men twice her age, but for herself. His point of view, fiercely supplied: 'She should know the effect her body has on men.'

Should she?

Boys with heterosexual feelings know how female bodies affect them, because they *feel* the effects. They understand as soon as the feelings start. At some point during their adolescence they learn that female attractiveness = an engorgement in their penis. Cause and effect.

The owners of female bodies can't feel what they're provoking. They get told. This may be through the sophisticated flirting techniques of men shouting on the street, a touchy-feely friend of their mum, teachers complimenting their development and boys groping them during PE at school. Or they might be educated in a more explicit way. My friend Justin has a thirteen-year-old daughter, and he was telling me she's allowed to wear lipstick inside the house, but not when going out. His daughter loves a bright red shade borrowed from her mum and doesn't understand why she can't keep it on to go to the shops. Her mum asked her if she knew what 'sexualisation' meant and then explained it. She told her that with lipstick on, she looked like she wanted to be considered as sexy, even though she was only wearing it to have fun or be pretty. I have a problem with this definition, and

BRRING BRRRING

I have an even BIGGER problem with a world where male reactions restrict female behaviour. Should teenage girls have their lives shaped by a hypothetical male response?

Another friend, Mark, praised his daughters' school for contacting parents before the disco. They sent a letter saying, 'We all know boys' hormones are going crazy,' and asked that parents 'ensure girls have shoulders and midriffs covered to avoid unfortunate incidents'. Why stop at a midriff, why not pop them all in burkas and ban dance music like the Taliban?

Because that would ruin the disco.

Why should a twelve-year-old getting dressed for a school party endure an argument with her mum about what she's allowed to wear? Why are boys' feelings a girl's responsibility? This is treating the male response as unavoidable: the problem is schoolgirls' hemlines. Why aren't they checking that the boys aren't dressing too provocatively for girls, or for their gay classmates?

You're being silly.

I'm not. Boys with homosexual feelings go through the same process as their heterosexual peers except the bodies that excite theirs are male. But lads don't learn, either implicitly *or* explicitly, 'my body is attractive to gay men'. I can't imagine a young man being told not to dress a certain way because a homosexual person might find them sexy. In those instances, the *target* of the attraction would never be blamed. Responsibility would rest with the feeler of feelings. You'd never get a letter telling teenage boys to wear baggy trousers because some of the sixth-formers liked fresh-faced lads with cute bottoms.

There are fewer gay boys than straight ones but I don't think that's why schools don't write warnings about turning them on. I think it's because only heterosexual men's urges are consistently upheld as red-blooded, healthy, 'what can you do about it?' This entitlement has not been nurtured in gay men, not in the same way. So no male urges *are* unavoidable, are they? If homosexual boys are expected to control themselves then so should straight boys, schools and parents should be teaching them. Not that there is anything wrong with their feelings, but that they are not anybody else's fault. To quote a wise and much shared meme, 'we teach our daughters to avoid the men we allow our sons to become' *brain exploding emoji*.

In Istanbul in 2016 a woman on a bus was kicked in the head for wearing shorts. Her assailant, Abdullah Çakıroğlu, told police he would have been 'less aroused' if she'd worn trousers. A year later a Turkish student was slapped around the head by a man telling her she should be 'ashamed' of wearing shorts during Ramadan. There are no Turkish news stories of gay men attacking others for looking too enticing during religious holidays, I've checked.

What's happening is that someone doesn't enjoy what they're feeling, whether it's an erection during Ramadan or arousal provoked by a much younger person. The feelings make him feel ashamed and the focus of those feelings is blamed. Like how when a Victorian man spotted a tantalising fresco on public transport, he'd go over to kick it in the head, teach that fresco a lesson.

I've never experienced lust leading to aggression. That is not how my body works, I have never wanted to thump someone for turning me on. Does that mean my arousal is less powerful than a man's? Is it because the female body is so discreet about its engorgement? We are going to be exploring gender differences in visual arousal a bit later. I wonder if I do ever get aroused by what I *see*? I can appreciate the aesthetics of a toned body, but it doesn't *do* anything for me. Not speaking for all women here, I am sure it does for many. Otherwise they wouldn't sell all those porno mags to women – oh, wait.

Of course I have felt unwanted arousal. Embarrassing, shameful, sickening. I know what it is to hate yourself because of something you've thought. An unbidden evil mind-spider. We don't control our thoughts; whatever our sexual preferences, proclivities and relationship status, we will have to keep accepting this and forgiving ourselves. We're apes, that's not our fault.

It seems that arousal obfuscates sense. Victorians had sexy feelings when they saw the artworks from Pompeii and it disgusted them. They didn't see nudity, depictions of intercourse or even history but obscenity and pornography. It didn't matter what was intended by the creators – it mattered what was felt. The response ruled.

People's responses to pornography vary. With an instinct to be secretive about sex, the male's visible arousal can be humiliating and shameful. If I was to live that moment in the queue again with my ex, having had all this time to think about it, I would tell him about the Coolidge effect. How humans' sexuality evolved over time but that our genitals remain trip-wired to notice sexual signals. The male response to females, especially young females, is culturally difficult for us now. When we think about equal rights and mutual respect, we have to navigate between a young woman's right to dress as she wants and be left alone, and a man's freedom to notice his body's reactions without anger and hatred. You see delicious food, you get hungry; you don't punch the burger. You understand why that instinct exists. It's about survival. Rampant, unbridled sex was also our survival. Our species' varied, around-the-clock mating kept ourselves in babies even when the landscape was bleak and desolate, even while temperatures were too high or too low. Next time you get an unwanted boner you can think, 'Thanks for trying, evolutionary tactic, but the world is different now,' and go happily on your way.

Dirty Stories and Jazz Mags

Pompeii may have been flattened by Vesuvius, but human creativity continued to find inspiration in sexual intercourse. You'll have heard the argument that every new technology was advanced by demand for porn, and there's much truth to that. Around AD 1040 movable-type printing was invented in China, during the Song dynasty. Woodblock printing had been around for about eight hundred years, but now technology was improving and people could reconfigure all the words and letters and use them to write saucy stories about the adventures of boobies.

Then around 1450 Johannes Gutenberg revolutionised printing with his metal movable type. The Gutenberg printing press was used to make copies of a special religious book called the Bible. Between 150 and 180 copies of the Gutenberg Bible were printed in the first mass publication ever.* The Bible is not considered erotica even though it has loads of fornication in it. Mostly it's referred to as 'begetting' but there's some proper nasty stuff too. Top of my head – Lot's daughters all trying to get off with him, and two entire cities wanking and bumming so much they had to be destroyed. Some later non-religious books were even sexier and that's why all the perverts learned to read. Some notable pornographic literature includes poetry by the Earl of

---

* Don't get confused, Gutenberg didn't write it – God did.

Rochester, John Cleland's *Fanny Hill* and E. L. James's *Fifty Shades of Grey* trilogy. Now you know why libraries have those 'Please masturbate quietly' signs.

The next exciting stage in human creativity was photography. This advanced incrementally through the late 1700s into the early 1800s. The images captured began as blurry, smudgy shadows, but by 1838 Louis Daguerre took the first ever photograph with a 'recognisably human image' in it. The photo is mainly of houses, but down on the pavement you can see a tiny man having his tiny shoes shined by another tiny man, and everyone in that photo is currently dead.

As soon as cameras could take pictures of recognisably human people, the photographers started recognising that people should take their clothes off. At first, daguerreotypes of nude women were considered art rather than erotica, they were collector's items or painter's studies, but the realism meant that nudie photographs were a lot more sexually exciting than oil paintings. A painting of sex is imaginary; these photographs depicted real sex that people were *actually* having. Photos were super expensive at first because they were so difficult to produce, but as cameras improved a whole genre exploded like Vesuvius, spraying red-hot lifelike images all over the world.

During the 1880s Jack the Ripper was killing women but that's not relevant to mass-produced photography. Halftone printing was created and soon afterwards the world's first porn magazines were published in France. They were black and white and depicted softcore nudes and sex scenes. Then a chap called William Lazenby launched a series of erotic periodicals in the UK. His first was *The Pearl*, which you can find online – very exciting if you're into poems about girls using carrots as dildos. It's hard to imagine someone masturbating to a limerick – but I'm imagining it anyway. Into the twentieth century and *Vanity Fair* was a far racier publication than its modern incarnation. By the 1930s porn consumers were enjoying Tijuana Bibles, which were cartoony sex booklets featuring celebrities and famous characters getting up to filthy stuff they normally wouldn't. Jump ahead to the 1950s and you land in *Playboy* magazine, founded by a man called Hugh Hefner who I presume you know about already, though I always got him confused with Howard Hughes or Jimmy Savile's mother's corpse.* Hefner rebranded pornography as a shameless, healthy part of masculinity. Just a bit of masturbatory fun for a 'boy' who wants to 'play' and likes his women to be hutch-based pets. This shift in how pornography was promoted successfully changed how it was perceived, and Hefner created a massive mainstream market. Over the next few decades that market grew as more and more publications competed for the sticky buck. While *Playboy* began with pictures of topless icons and pin-ups in their underwear, over the years magazines stripped people further:

1960s *Penthouse* magazine was the first to show models displaying their genitals.

1972 *Playboy* began to use completely nude models in its centrefolds.

1974 Larry Flynt launched *Hustler* magazine, which pushed the genre further – genitals were now photographed CLOSE UP!

---

* This might be too harsh, none of this is Jimmy Savile's mother's fault.

1982 *Hustler* did a scratch-and-sniff centrefold, which must have been technologically edgy at the time but now seems like the kind of thing Fred Flintstone might enjoy. Throughout the 1990s *Hustler* continued to become more explicit, publishing shots of penetration, lesbianism, group sex and fetishes.

As *Playboy* and *Penthouse* et al. grew increasingly likely to get you fired if found on your work desk, a new form of porn-lite became popular. A genre referred to as 'lads' mags' sprinkled articles about banter and alcoholism-as-a-lifestyle-choice between oily booby beauties' boobs. Magazines such as *Nuts*, *Loaded* and *FHM* have all gone bust now,* which they must have hated because 'bust' is a relatively polite way of referring to breasts. They'd have preferred to go 'jugs' or 'knockers' or 'TITS UP' – yes, that works. The market for photographs of semi-dressed or completely nude women has now diminished because ~~feminists' arguments were so persuasive~~ wizards worked out how to make photographs move and how to send them through the telephone wires. But did you know, before phone lines were used for the internet, they were used for phoning people . . .

* *Loaded* went online-only in 2015, and *FHM* is still published abroad.

Dirty Talk and Videos

Everyone knows the telephone was invented by Alexander Graham Bell. At school I was told that phones were an accident, that Bell had actually been trying to invent a hearing aid for his deaf fiancée. This is a super romantic part of history which I fact-checked so I could mention it and we'd all weep and wish we'd married inventors, but it's not true. Instead I found out Bell believed in eugenics and proposed that deaf people should be kept away from each other in case they bred. The moral, my friends, is that school is awful and we shouldn't go.

Phones become relevant to pornography production with the advent of smart phones on which we could view moving images, but first, sexy chat lines. These numbers would be advertised in the back of newspapers and magazines and connected the listener with some nice saucy talking.

The first advertisement for a chat line was in 1918. I don't know what it said, but I'd guess . . . 'The War Is Over, Now Release Your Soldiers'? 'Armistickle Your Fancy'? 'Kill Me So I Don't Have to Think of a Third One'? Later sex chat lines would sometimes be pre-recorded, but more often interactive so the caller could ask hot questions like 'What are you wearing?' and the sex phone operator would answer something sexy like 'Sexy pants.' It was usually a lie, but no one cared, they still had a great masturbate while running up their parents' phone bill. One of my friends from school had an older sister who ran a sex chat line from her bedroom. She earned more money the longer she kept the men on the phone, so she'd tell them disgusting things, e.g. pretending she wanted their penis in her mouth. We'd stare as she lay in tracksuit bottoms, smoking B&H, rolling her eyes and groaning. Carly earned more an hour than her mum did in a day. I thought she was the ultimate con artist. The callers thought her name was 'Diamanté' and that she could put her legs over her head, when in reality she was a twenty-stone lesbian who often ate raw potatoes.

The phone-sex industry was most in demand between the 1960s and 1990s, and while it's in decline today it still makes millions of pounds a year. Don't take my word for it, ask Cheap Phone Sex with Karen on 0908 1453050 or Hundreds of Scottish Guys NOW! on 0871 4000814.

The first spicy movie was released in 1896, after Thomas Edison and his colleague William Dickson invented the kinetoscope, an early type of projector. The film's title is *The Kiss* and it was scandalous at the time. There's only two minutes of footage left as the film has degraded (sauce goes mouldy) but those salacious 120 seconds show a male and a female face, side by side, kinda miming eating their dinner. It's a side-by-side almost-kiss, with lots of chewing. Look it up on YouTube, and make sure to scroll down for the disappointed comments. The Roman Catholic Church campaigned for *The Kiss* to be censored, which is cheeky bearing in mind they were still pushing the incest, sodomy and begatting-filled Bible.

Recording and projecting equipment became more sophisticated via the Lumière brothers and John Logie Baird. As film-making progressed, so did depictions of people having sex. By the 1920s 'stag' movies were popular in America. These were hardcore short films, usually without sound or colour and generally unedited, but no one seemed to mind. The equipment to project the reels was expensive and producing the films was illegal, so there was little money to be made. That is, until the 1960s, the so-called 'Golden Age of Pornography', when porn began to be shown on 'loops', 8 mm or 16 mm films that played continuously. A man called Reuben Sturman created coin-operated peep booths screening these loops, and boy did he make a lot of cash ($1 million a day) and pay very little tax.*

X-rated cinemas screening porno films opened in Europe and the US throughout the 1960s. But by the late 1970s affordable VCRs became available and people could watch other people having sex in the privacy of their own home.

I knew nothing about any of this. I hadn't heard of any of these Golden Age films, but apparently these are the most noteworthy and highest-grossing:

1971 *Boys in the Sand* was the first and only gay hardcore film to have mainstream success and remains the only adult flick ever to be reviewed by the *New York Times* – well done, guys. The title is a parody of *The Boys in the Band*, a movie released the year before. Porn films have continued to parody mainstream movie titles and I could list some for you but I'm not two chapters of Ron Jeremy's autobiography.** *Boys in*

---

* I can't help judging this guy. Let's all pay our taxes and be proud to contribute, yeah? Note to selves: Sturman died in prison, a place that wouldn't exist without taxes.

** If that sounds bitchy *you* read Ron Jeremy's book and see how you feel about his contribution to literature. TREES DIED. Big beautiful trees were chopped down so that he could write about his big woody penis, pausing only to list the times he has kissed his own penis.†

† I'm not being fair. He also lists the famous people he has met and the aforementioned movie-porno puns.

the Sand was the first triple-X film to credit its director and actors. I haven't seen it, but it sounds lovely and summery, featuring men having sex, oral sex, interracial sex and using sex toys at the poolside and by the beach.

1972 *Behind the Green Door* sounds like a song a Teletubby might sing, but this film is not for kids. It was the first hardcore movie widely released in the United States. It involves a woman called Gloria (played by Marilyn Chambers) who is kidnapped, massaged, spreadeagled and given oral sex in front of some priestesses. Then there is some multi-partner trapeze sex and – no spoilers, I won't give away the ending in case you're planning to see it. The film took over $1 million in theatrical releases, and $25 million from its video release.

1972 *Deep Throat* is the highest-grossing porn film ever. There are many ways I could humorously misconstrue the word 'grossing' here but I won't, if you wanted that kind of grossing you'd be reading Ron Jeremy's autobiography.*

I haven't seen *Deep Throat* (I haven't seen any of these films, but I *am* enjoying the blurbs). It stars Linda Lovelace as a character called Linda Lovelace, who has a clitoris in her throat rather than with her genitals. This means that to gain satisfaction she has to swallow penises deep into her – you guessed it – throat. I have a lot of problems with the science of this. Firstly, surely just having a sandwich would be nice and stimulating for this neck-clit . . . why does it need to be a penis? Also, any fans of the female anatomy will know that while the tip of the clitoris is nestled just above the vagina, the organ continues iceberg-like ~~destroying the *Titanic*~~ beneath the groin to a length of about four inches. This *Deep Throat*

---

* I'm sorry, I seem to have really taken against this man.

character would suffocate. It's unrealistic. But apparently no one cared how biologically unlikely the plot was; the film played for thirty-nine weeks in New York, took $600 million and became a cultural phenomenon, a symbol of sexual revolution and a feminist discussion point. People argued that *Deep Throat* was a fantastic exploration of female sexual pleasure because Linda was getting really satisfied by all the dicks in her gob. Pretty handy for the men that satisfying Linda involved something that was so great for them rather than, you know, stimulating an actual clitoris. Maybe I'll write a sequel where men have penises for fingers and they like pressing them on – naaaah, you'd just touch your own dick with your finger penises, wouldn't you, you greedy bastards?

Linda Lovelace is a very interesting woman. Years after making porn, she revealed that she'd not been willing and made claims of rape, domestic violence and coercion. She was embraced by anti-porn feminists as proof of how damaging the industry was to women. Lovelace later fell out with the feminists, claiming they were just as exploitative as the porn industry.

Didn't she have sex with a dog?

In a film, yes. In Ron Jeremy's autobiography he visits Linda's ex-husband,* the man she says abused her and forced her into doing these things. His dog was fathered by the dog Linda had sex with and he refers to it as 'Linda's son', and it's so horrible and full of hate towards her. These men laughing at her, believing her to have been denigrated by sex. Some people do believe women are denigrated by sex, even the

---

* Chuck Traynor. He died in 2002 and is unavailable for comment.

men who have had all the same sex, like Ron Jeremy. This sexism has cultural influences but it's also built on paternity certainty, as we'll explore later.

In 1973 Gerard Damiano, the writer/director of *Deep Throat*, released *The Devil in Miss Jones*. The movie begins with a lonely spinster in her thirties, hello my life, slitting her wrists in the bath, oh dear. Justine the spinster isn't allowed into heaven (cos she killed herself), so instead she does a deal with the devil. She's permitted to live her life again but this time having more sex. Justine does it with men and women, has threesomes, masturbates with a hose in the bath, slithers with a snake, uses a butt plug (in her butt, not the bath) and puts grapes in her vagina. When she dies again, she finds that Hell is an eternity spent with an impotent man. What a twist! No wonder this porn movie is one of the most successful of all time.

1976 *The Autobiography of a Flea*. This X-rated film was ground-breaking because it was the first to be directed by a woman, Sharon McKnight. It was also, I presume, the first porn movie to be told from the POV of a flea – no, you're not high, this is happening – living in a fourteen-year-old's pubic hair. This parasite-ridden child is seduced by a priest, and lots of people watched the movie and liked it apparently.

> Did you make that one up?

I wish.

1978 *Debbie Does Dallas* is arguably the most famous porn movie ever and is one of the most lucrative of all time. It was hugely successful and was released on video for home use. I remember it being talked about when I was at primary school, it was the punchline to jokes I didn't understand and very much part of the collective consciousness. There's a version of *Debbie Does Dallas* on YouTube that has all the sex scenes edited out . . . I'm not saying you should watch it, but I did. The full version is about a cheerleader called Debbie and her friends, who need to raise money so they can be cheerleaders. They perform sexual favours for teachers and other men in positions of lowly power. Then Debbie has full sex with her boss so that he'll pay for all the cheerleaders' expenses, but obviously I didn't see that bit. The version I saw was composed of short vignettes of men introducing themselves to cheerleaders, reaching out a hand and then, cut, next scene.

By the end of the 1970s advances in electronic equipment were changing how people could watch, obtain and make pornography FOREVER. There were two home video formats available to the keen consumer: the Betamax, released by Sony in 1975, and the VHS, released by JVC shortly afterwards. This 'format war' is often cited as an example of pornography fuelling technological advancement. I was lectured by a red-haired man at a party who said that Betamax had prohibited porn on their format. This meant that people who wanted to watch porn had to buy VHS recorders. Which meant they purchased their non-porn films on VHS too, so films were put onto VHS not Betamax and Betamax went out of business.

It's a great and salacious story that I believed (and repeated) but it's not true, FAKE NEWS everyone. Mr Redhead – a school teacher, I presume? The VHS was more affordable and that's why it won the format war. It was a war with one casualty, the Betamax, the oxymoronically named video player who died before we were all born.*

---

* If you remember Betamax, you go to bed *right now*.

Throughout the 1980s more and more people purchased VCRs and the films and programmes to watch on them. There was a boom market for video rental stores well into the 1990s, the most famous of which was Blockbuster Video, now more commonly referred to as 'what, who?' Most rental stores had whole sections devoted to adult movies and the industry increased exponentially. The US went from producing about a hundred porn features in 1976 to eight thousand releases in 1996. That's why now, everywhere you look, there's someone asking 'What's a VCR?' and being pointed to a corner of the Science Museum.

There were DVDs and Blu-rays, sure, they did their best. But nowadays no one is watching porn on a living-room TV after their partner has gone to bed. Instead people of every age are viewing hardcore sex on their phones, and it's all Alexander Graham Bell's fault. If only he'd stuck to practising eugenics on deaf people like he wanted.

Hotel Porn Party

We've been exploring pornography that existed before I was alive. I've outlined events and facts that are interesting or enlightening and I'm attempting to be unbiased. I'm not trying to build an argument, I'm saying, 'This happened and after that, so did this.' I've not mentioned any murderers who were inspired by the porn they watched, we're not venturing into filmed paedophilia or snuff, or the market for squish videos. Some things, once envisioned, flavour an intellectual discussion about pornography too strongly. Some truths of the industry can be so overwhelming they obliterate everything else.

It's the same with individuals – if I introduced you to a person and said, 'Here's Michael, he cooks homemade sausage rolls, he can speak four languages, he killed a man,' you wouldn't be focusing on how he rolls his pastry.

I've noticed with the discourse about pornography that both sides are blinkered. Imagine a debate about Hollywood where one side focuses on how many horses died during the filming of *Ben-Hur* and their opponents counter-argue that Angelina Jolie does a lot of charity work: neither extreme is representative. There's a whole spectrum of good and evil within all industries and pornography is no different. Our perception of what is good and evil is subjective, and that is why I now need to once again acknowledge my bias.

I was anti-porn for a long time.

The first time I ever saw hardcore pornography was in 2001, when I was nineteen. Doesn't that seem *old*? Don't I seem naive, like a nun or a Brontë sister? But I was an adult, I'd been having sex for a few years, stopping briefly to move out of home and get a job. I was working in a hotel near Nottingham as a backing singer for Robbie Williams's dad.* One night I was at a party hosted by a couple who worked in the kitchen. A few people were taking turns to smoke weed, sitting on the floor around their bed. We lived in hotel rooms, we had the same plastic mattresses and trouser presses and tiny televisions tuned to four special channels: Channel One showed the news, Channel Two local news, Channel Three showed the film *What Women Want*, starring Mel Gibson, on a purgatorial loop, and Channel Four was devoted to announcing all the crafts, events and sports the guests could take part in the next day.

What do women want?

Let me tell you. Mel Gibson does some great research into women: he puts on nail polish, speaks to his daughter (a woman), then electrocutes himself with a hairdryer. EUREKA, now he knows what women truly desire, all of them, every single one from sixteen to 105 years old, across every culture, race and religion in the world. What they *all* want is to be hounded by a man who looks like Mel Gibson until their life isn't worth living, he's ruined it, they might as well shag him.

---

* This is something I bring up on panel shows to make myself sound interesting. It'd be great if one quirky odd thing was enough – if that was your personality. I could have retired at twenty. 'I have my anecdote, now leave me alone.'

I was probably talking about this at the party, I was always referencing *What Women Want*. I sometimes quoted the guest activities channel too, but that's cos there was some low-level Orwellian shit going on.

looks around, lowers voice Our fourth channel always claimed there would be archery at 15.30 the next day if people requested it, but the archery never happened because *no one had ever asked for it*. The Events Team put archery on there so it *looked* like there was something for people to do. But no one ever wanted to do it. The Events Team had cleverly arranged it so they didn't *ever* have to do *anything*. This hotel specialised in holidays for older people, and it turns out the aged don't want sports and activities. They want a holiday that's exactly like a care home with the option of archery. They don't want to do archery, but they like to know they could if they wanted, which they don't. *puts cloak over head* Go now, mention this to no one.

'Anyone up for archery tomorrow?' was one of my witticisms. I'd said it three times already that night. I was uncomfortable cos I don't smoke drugs and was worried someone would offer me some and I'd take it because I need to be liked. Everyone else was chatting away, the TV was on behind me but I wasn't looking – I didn't need to watch *What Women Want*, this was a party! It took me a moment to realise that someone had changed the channel. The sounds being emitted from the TV were unfamiliar. There was muzak but not the tune from the 'archery tomorrow' doublethink . . . why would there be *squelching noises* on the news? I turned my head and was met by a flesh apocalypse.

THE *WERE* MORE CHANNELS! You must've had to pay for them, and look (or don't, I wished I hadn't),

I'd never seen penetration from that angle before. I had never seen a penis so large or furiously purple. I did not recognise what I saw on the screen as sex but as a butcher's window, a slimy massacre. I interpreted it as agony. A crime committed by a male who intended pain, a woman receiving vigorous punishment.

A lifetime later I can assure you that this was regular hardcore, a male-and-female couple performing doggy-style vaginal penetration. Quite tame compared to what I have seen while researching for this book – I've seen people fist themselves!

This is how lil' baby Sara went from never having seen porn to having seen two seconds of porn. I glimpsed a thrusting thrust and lowered my eyes like the Brontë sister I was. My reaction was physiologically and emotionally intense. I was embarrassed, face hot as I stared at the carpet, isolated, because everyone else was talking normally, not going bright red and having a breakdown.

I already knew I was prudish. I'd run away if there was kissing on *Neighbours* or *EastEnders*. I couldn't sit and watch people getting off with each other. I didn't know how I was supposed to feel about it, what facial expression I was supposed to pull. Interested: oh how intriguing, those characters are kissing. Impressed: wow, their tonguing technique is excellent. Precocious: all humanity is art.

Even now I'll skip forward through kissing or sex scenes in whatever I'm watching. I'M THIRTY-EIGHT but my brain responds, 'Uh-oh – this is private, I shouldn't be looking.' Unless there's fisting, of course, in which case I'm all eyes.

Earlier we considered the change in how humans mated, how we've evolved from multi-partnering into our current state of relationships and monogamy, with the occasional infidelity, and the need for privacy. I wonder if my lifelong aversion to kissing in films is related to our species having sex in private?

I feel the same about toilet stuff, I can't watch a character on the loo. Defecating in private is another universal, cross-cultural behaviour. When I see it in a programme, I get a disgust response as though it was *real*. How much of this is learned, or is it hardwired instincts about propriety? Thinking about this I've realised that so much of visual media is voyeurism – actors pretending they can't be seen, characters believing they're 'alone' – and I'm far too suggestible because I feel like a peeping Tom. Like I'm invading their privacy.

My reaction doesn't feel like a choice. Back in that hotel room I hated that they'd put a sex film on, I hated that it EXISTED. I wanted to lecture everyone about how penises should be respectful and kind to any orifice willing to admit them. My oratory would remind those present that a party was for moaning about our boss and asking 'Who's up for archery?' not for watching a woman be exploited.

Isn't that patronising?

To assume every woman in porn is exploited?

Yes.

That is what I believed then. It is a position of well-meaning ignorance. I worried that these women were unhappy people with no self-confidence and that we should 'protect' them, or 'save' them. Without having spoken to a single porn performer, without having read an interview or listened to anyone at all from that industry, I had a position I believed was 'informed' because of feminist literature. But actually I was prejudiced.

There is a fallacy that all women who work in porn are 'damaged', victims of abuse or addicted to drugs. This fallacy stems from a presumption that no one well-adjusted and perfectly sane would choose to have sex for money, would choose to have that sex filmed and publicly disseminated.

This kind of opinion demonstrates how we can believe we are being empathetic and kind, but in fact we are making women's lives more difficult. This wish to 'protect' women from 'exploitation' is built on our cultural morality that sex without love is bad, that there is something precious about sex which means anyone having it outside of a relationship is 'broken'. We don't view the men in porn that way, even though they're there too and BEING PAID EVEN LESS.

All because of the imbalance in parental investment. All because the female body can get pregnant and morality will not let us forget it, will not accept that sex is an activity performed by the body, like tennis or ju-jitsu. Actually some people *can* accept that and argue their case vehemently. I am trying so, so hard but cannot.

If sex is just an activity, can you do it with your parents, like tennis or ju-jitsu? No, because incest was selected against in our evolution. It causes genetic malfunction, it reduces the health and ability of offspring. We have a modern-day morality against incest that is built atop a deeply ingrained, evolved mating tactic, so—

SO, what I think I'm trying to say is that we have to decipher what is cultural conditioning and what might be deeper. We are quick to judge multi-partnering women because of the millions of years of evolution that reinforced pair bonding for the sake of offspring. Infidelity in our species is kept secret in order not to threaten those pair bonds. A porn actress is flagrantly violating two of our inbuilt 'rules' – sex in private *and* fidelity for paternity certainty – hence my unbidden unease about her profession.

I'm not saying I have any right to that unease; I'm trying to understand where it originates from. I can intellectualise and know she is doing a job. But I cannot feel the same about that job as I do about hairdressing or bus driving.

If the earliest female humans learned these survival tactics:

1) Be wary of men from new tribes
2) Pair with a male who can protect you
3) Only copulate hidden from view in order not to excite/incite unwanted males

then this would explain why contemporary women are concerned when they see women *not* practising these tactics. Do we subconsciously believe these women are behaving riskily and are in danger? And is that how we persuade ourselves that our negative treatment of porn actresses comes from a place of compassion rather than judgement?

Or jealousy.

That's what feminists get accused of. We're all so ugly and frumpy and no one would even rape us. I promise my opinion back in 2001 wasn't because the women in porn were all more beautiful than me, it was because I thought they were being hurt.

In the hotel room I had this strong reaction, and I believed I was right. But I didn't say anything because I knew everyone disagreed with me. It's like the story about the king* and the well. There's this place and it has a well, and someone, probably an imp or a wizard, poisons it. All the people of the kingdom drink the poison water and go doolally, start seeing dragons and fairies and saying stuff that doesn't make sense. The palace has its own water supply because of inequality, so the king never drinks well water. He has a filter tap and one of those fridges that can make its own ice cubes. The king is now isolated by his sanity. He knows everyone is mad, he's seen it happen. But the king's subjects, they all understand each other because they're living the same reality. The king *knows* that the sky is blue and he *knows* that the grass is green, but because he's outnumbered, he is wrong. Eventually the king decides to walk down to the well and have a drink so that he may see the same green sky and dragons as the people he owns. It's a great story; such a shame it doesn't pass the Bechdel test.

At the party, I was the ~~king~~ only person who felt uncomfortable about the porn. 'This is adulthood,' I thought. 'Being grown-up means watching people get stoned and not crying when they put on videos of aggressive sex.' I weighed up my options and announced to my colleagues that I had an uncle who was FBI and carried out random drug tests on family members. I had to go, the passive smoke would show up in my hair. I'm an exceptional liar.

We've all experienced this. We believe something so completely, are convinced of our own 'correctness', but we find ourselves alone or in a minority. I'm not a well-drinker, I don't pretend to agree with things – but also, and maybe I'm

* A male queen.

a coward, I don't tell other people what to do. I leave and write a book eighteen years later.

I went back to my room feeling nauseous and terrible. I didn't know how to express myself about the porn film. I didn't know what to say to my friends the next day. I thought I needed to stick up for women, but I had no idea how. This became irrelevant because the next day 9/11 happened and the events were so huge the mind couldn't comprehend them. It was a communal experience; everyone in the hotel gathered in the bar to watch Channel One together. Theoretical archery was cancelled. I didn't know what to feel about exploding planes and falling bodies and some people in the world hating other people because of where they lived or their religion or their governments. The guests were guessing what had happened, who was behind it. Some were blaming Israelis, Robbie Williams's dad said it was Scientologists, but I knew the truth – it was all pornography's fault.

This is how the mind creates narrative out of events and emotion. For me, 9/11 and porn became interconnected. It wasn't conscious. Images of planes crashing into towers combined with close-ups of penile penetration came to be symbolic of all the things that scare and confuse me.

Freudian.

So Freudian it's boring.

One Man's Porn Was My Bottom

In 2003 I had a boyfriend called James. He was my age, we'd met at school. He got emails every week from something called Anal Digest, which contained links to anal sex videos. I thought about the title a lot – was it a pun? Because the anus does digest, or at least it excretes after digestion. WAS IT A PUN? Did the staff at Anal Digest know what they were doing, or had they forgotten the two meanings of the word 'digest'? Surely a pun shrinks any boner? I never asked James what he thought about the name because he didn't know I checked his emails, it was one of *those* really healthy relationships.*

James never asked me to look at porn with him but was open about using it. He had posters of glamour models on his wall; he bought *FHM* and thought it was funny. He was softer and gentler than most of my other male friends; he once wrote a poem about an eagle. He regularly pestered me for anal sex, and I said no.

Over the time we were together, he did what I knew from my friends was common: he tried to get anal sex 'by

---

* Gonna flag some heavy sarcasm here cos if I don't someone will email me in six months that 'in their opinion it isn't actually healthy to snoop on a partner's correspondence'. After my last book I had some smashing messages from readers correcting my stupid jokes. My favourite was a short sentence that informed me angrily, 'ALBERT EINSTEIN DID NOT INVENT THE CAR.'

accident'. This is when someone attempts to put their penis in your butthole, coupled with some bad acting. I could tell what he was trying to do from the concentration on his face. His plan was to enter my bum so quickly I didn't notice, then by the time I realised I'd be too busy appreciating the incredible sensation to stop him.

James absolutely believed that if I would just let him put his penis in my rectum* I would really enjoy it. I absolutely didn't want to, I found the idea gross and distasteful. Linguistically, whenever any of our friends had talked about 'fucking someone up the arse' it was redolent of denigration. The ultimate in subjugation. I did. Not. Want. It.

At the beginning of our relationship this was a small conversation. James got me to watch a documentary about a couple trying anal together for the first time. They talked about their concerns, positions, techniques to make sure it didn't hurt the woman. They went off screen and tried it, and then talked jubilantly to the camera afterwards. Great, good for them, I still wasn't going to do it. James's friend Lauren was really into anal. He used her enthusiasm against me, as evidence – if she liked it so much, then I would too. But I didn't want to do it.

For his birthday we went to Amsterdam. I paid for it with my student loan cheque,** which was supposed to cover my university fees. James liked to smoke drugs and I liked to make him happy. The holiday was predictably rubbish because we ran out of money on the first day and the Anne Frank museum made me cry for forty-eight hours. Our last

---

* So many words for 'anus'. I haven't even used 'sphincter' yet.
** A cheque is an olden-days money promise which slowed down time as you waited for it to become cash.

day we floated in poisoned silence after bickering rows. I didn't want to go out. He went out on his own, while I had a bath and wondered how to pay for university. James returned that night, cheerful: we could make it all better. 'I've decided what I want for my birthday!' he exclaimed during the holiday I'd bought for his birthday. He emptied a plastic bag onto the bed. Some sachets of lube, rubber beads and a black dummy-shaped contraption. James waved his arm over his bum treasures like a magician's assistant.

I didn't shout. It's too horrible arguing on holiday because you're stuck with the bastard. I went for a walk. I tried positive thinking – 'At least Anne Frank didn't have a stupid boyfriend who wanted to put his dick in her arse' – but you can't pretend anyone who died the way she did was lucky. Anne didn't have time to get an awful boyfriend, a basic human right. Or maybe she was lesbian and was denied the chance to realise her sexual destiny, or maybe she was sexually fluid and would have written about it so clearly and comprehensively she'd have saved us decades of repression and stupidity? Poor Anne Frank, poor me from the past, poor us all really. I know you are thinking, 'At least you broke up with him as soon as you got home.'

You'd think.

I reflect now as a wizened thirty-eight-year-old and see lube-gate as a deal-breaker, a sign of mutual misunderstanding. We should have gazed together at the butt-opener nestling on the hotel bed and agreed: 'I don't think we're going to make each other happy.' If there are a million universes, a million dimensions inhabited by a million alter egos, I hope that in one of them I have a decent amount of self-esteem. In this universe, James and I stayed together for several years.

The second time I saw hardcore pornography was during my second year at university when I came home from a lecture and found James and my flatmates in bed together. They weren't having sex, the three men were sitting in a row on a single bed, a duvet over their laps and legs, watching a porno on a small square telly. They'd paused the video when they heard me come in, so what I saw on the screen was frozen. A young black woman naked and screaming. She had tears on her face. This was not an expression of feigned erotic joy.

This time I didn't quietly leave them with their well water, I had a tantrum none of the boys could understand. I did not express myself clearly because I couldn't. I was too frustrated. It was so unfair. How could I make sense of a world where nice men, people who felt bad if they trod on a snail, who stroked dogs outside shops, who played games with their nephews, who made soup from scratch if someone had flu – how could they also do *this*? I wasn't jealous, I wasn't 'insecure about my boobs' like James suggested. This wasn't prudery. The boys thought my problem with porn was that I had a rubbish body and couldn't compete with the woman they were watching. But I didn't want to compete, I wanted to protect her. Why weren't they concerned if the pain on the woman's face was real, why didn't they care?

Porn is pretend.

Yes, yes, absolutely, sometimes people are pretending. Sometimes they've agreed to be in pain for money. Sometimes the person gets sexual enjoyment out of pain, that does happen. But sometimes they are just in pain. Sometimes they've had boundaries pushed, they've been tricked, manipulated.

There is so little discernment in the people who watch porn about what they are watching.

Maybe I'm a silly prude who can't watch people kissing, but the other end of the spectrum is my ex-boyfriend not caring if a porn actor's tears were authentic.

My difficulty with James and my flatmates was: why do some men treat the women they know in a respectful, protective way and simultaneously treat others as objects? I felt they were watching abuse. Perhaps even rape —

That's about you.

YES, you're correct. We see things not as they are but as *we* are. I did not want to have anal sex while crying so I assumed that no one else wanted to either. Hence my difficulty in being objective about sex work. I get it wrong. I believe it must be so awful because it would be so awful for *me*.

It WAS awful for me, actually, because James did keep trying to put his penis where I didn't want it and he made me bleed and got aroused when I cried. So there you go: he was cruel, I blamed porn.

While researching this book I went into a school to watch the Great Men Initiative run a workshop with boys about pornography. A teacher prepped the male volunteers about the students by describing their religious and cultural backgrounds. 'We're doing this for the girls really,' she explained. The Year 10 and 11 girls had written an open letter to the headmistress. It said that they needed the teachers to talk to the boys about the porn they were watching. 'Plus we've had female students missing school,' the teacher added, 'because they're in hospital with anal injuries.'

Straight into the top ten Worst Sentences I've Ever Heard.

Perhaps the first thing that should be taught in sex education is that the anus is not a self-lubricating organ: 'Welcome to class, kids, sit your dry bumholes down.' The skin of the anus is delicate and full of nerve endings; thrusting can be dangerous. To prevent injuries and accidents we have to balance the fantasy fiction of porn with mundane information. No morality or value judgements, just neat packages of truth that equip people to make safe decisions. Even with all the explicit sex on the internet there is so much confusion. In one of the workshops I observed, a thirteen-year-old boy asked, 'Does anal sex hurt?' The workshop leader was embarrassed and said, 'You should ask a girl.' A different boy took over assuredly: 'If you get them horny enough you can do what you like.' There were murmurs of agreement among the students, the topic was changed and the question remained unanswered. After the children left, I brought it up with the workshop leader. 'It's a new session, we don't have all the answers yet,' he responded. But boys have bumholes, was my point. 'If he wants to know what it feels like to have something inside, he should experiment on his own body—'

'We can't tell children to put things in their anus,' the responsible man reminded me. And I suppose that's true. I suppose that's why no one wants untrained people like me giving sex education. 'Welcome to class, kids, sit your dry bumhole on this nice cucumber.'

But this is stuff I'm considering *now*. Before now was the past, and in the past is Adam.

More Boyfriends, More Porn

I hated staying over at Adam's flat cos he would fall asleep before me and there was nothing to do. Now I understand – the male body gets sleepy after sex. Men get a dose of the hormone prolactin after orgasm and this acts as a sedative. Prolactin is usually low in non-lactating individuals (it's the hormone that brings milk for babies) but it rises after sex and provides the sense of satiation, a pleasing 'there we go then' satisfaction. It's also related to the 'break' most men need between shags. Men with lower prolactin were found to need less recovery time, fancy that.

Wanna know another fun ~~fact~~ theory? This sex difference in post-coital response – the male quick to relax and fall into slumber, while the female remains alert, perfectly able to have more sex (and more orgasms BY THE WAY) – is theorised to be down to multi-partnering in our evolution. At least it gives the female the option, whereas the male gets stimulated, orgasms and is spent. A female has a cycle that can peak and trough many times without her needing to stop. This means that when dude number one is done, she could *technically* leave, ambling off somewhere else to have some more sex with a new partner. Great mating technique, females! More sperm competition for your offspring and, even better, partner number one doesn't know you've left because he's sleeping! It could be argued that is *why* men get sleepy, so they can't prevent women getting a second dose of D.

Another interesting detail that goes along with this concerns female vocalisation during sex. We make a lot more noise than men, something you will see manufactured in pornography. The women are always moaning and groaning, and this sound has been proved in studies to arouse men further. Even better, they found that women tend to make more noise when they want a man to speed up and finish. Isn't that clever – pretending to have a better time when you'd absolutely rather it was over and you could leave for the next guy, I mean, have some toast.

Back in 2008 I knew nothing about sex arousal cycles; I just thought Adam was lazy. One night I complained to him, said I would rather get a bus home than lie awake and bored for hours. Adam gave me his laptop and told me to watch something. He had lots of American comedy saved on there and blah blah blah, can you guess where this is going?

☐ YES you found his porn.
☐ NO, I've no idea what will happen when you find his porn.
☐ MAYBE people shouldn't share the electronic cupboard they keep porn in?

I sat on a sofa across from where Adam was already snoring and opened his computer. As I attached headphones, the desktop loaded, replete with just two icons. One was the browser Firefox chasing his tail. The other was a close-up of male genitals, squashed into a square and competing with the entire internet for my attention. That was it, not even a shortcut to iTunes. This was all that Adam needed at his fingertips, a host browser and a cube of testicles. Which one do you think I clicked?

☐ BALLS, you followed your heart and it led to a
  scrotum as always.
☐ FIREFOX was the one you didn't click on.

You're correct, otherwise this would be a boring story.
'Hey guys, a decade ago I saw a weird icon on my boy-
friend's computer, then I watched two hours of *Curb Your
Enthusiasm*, bye.'

I know it seems like I spent a lot of the early twenty-first
century spying on boyfriends. I'm not a snooper, promise.
Sure, I used to check James's emails, but that was a very long
time ago. Since then I've developed better boundaries, I've
learned to respect privacy. And secrecy. Now let me tell you
what was on my ex-boyfriend's Mac.

I clicked the testes and the computer began whirring, a
DVD started up. The title had the word 'tranny'* in it and
popped across the screen, followed by a person. Someone
with a penis and balls and augmented breasts was bending
over. The camera zoomed in and I quickly finger-pecked
ESCAPE CANCEL UNDO. The computer stopped whirring as the disc inside slowed and ejected itself. There was
some mild farce as I hurried the disc back in and it unhelpfully restarted. I did not have a useful thought.

I knew I was encroaching on Adam's private business. I
was expecting him to wake up and shout at me. I tried to
correct everything by doing what I should've done in the
first place. I clicked on Firefox and OH DEAR. The page
that loaded was the one that'd been visited most recently.

---

* I am quoting directly, even though this word is upsetting and
derogatory. There has been much discussion about whether I should
quote it, and I apologise if you believe I was wrong.

This website was a menu of sex workers and the services they offered. The agency or collective was called Shemale Escorts and Ladyboys.

These terms have historically been used in a catch-all, non-specific way to refer to people who might be transitioning, transitioned, transvestite, transsexual, a drag queen or even hermaphrodite. One of the things that has staggered me most in my research into pornography and sex work is that the language used about people can be reductive at best, hateful at worst. So much porn is racist and misogynist. People are called 'midgets', people are called 'horny sluts' or 'cum-buckets'. It's done to reduce empathy. Those terms turn a human into an object. A sexualised object that is easier to wank about. I found it surprising that people who in their everyday life wouldn't use racist or homophobic language would expect nothing less from the porn they consume. I AM SURPRISED ABOUT IT.

Back to Adam. I spent a long time looking at the made-up names and sexy headshots on Shemale Escorts and Ladyboys. I didn't know if Adam had been using these services, but I imagined how the transaction would play out. Had they come to his house? Did his flatmates know? Where did he find the money? I'd had to lend him a pound for a Pot Noodle that night, was that because he'd chosen 'Chantelle' over the weekly shop? I wondered coldly if he used a condom.

Then my ego took over and made it all about myself. I, like lots of people, fear I am not 'enough' of my gender. I'm a flat-chested woman. I have a big nose and fat hands and I'm not dainty or sweet. Adam's nickname for me was 'The Beast'. Did he fancy me because I am mannish? Did he pretend during sex that I had a male body? Was I disappointing, did he have to think about this porn and these sex workers to get an erection with me? I thought back over the months of our relationship, scanning for clues or oddities. It was pretty vanilla, he'd never asked me to bum him or called me David.

I slept on the sofa. And in the morning I was cold with Adam because I didn't know what to say. I didn't know where to start so I finished it, said I wanted to stop seeing him because I didn't think my feelings were right blahdiddyblah get out now before anyone is hurt. He was alright about it.

I tried to write stand-up on this a couple of years ago. I was sure I could find something funny in it, thought I could do a twist on the 'porn makes me insecure' sensibility with 'because I haven't got a penis'. But I couldn't, it never worked, partly because there was too much set-up with all the sleeping boyfriend and computer admin, and also because punchlines about gender and genitalia seem transphobic. It'd need to be written so sophisticatedly to make sure that sex workers and trans people weren't being denigrated, even accidentally. And you can't control what people laugh at. You could write a clever and intuitive piece about the word 'shemale' in sex work and some person would still laugh at the word itself and I'd have to stop them, and not letting people laugh is the exact opposite of my job.

It's occurred to me now that for people in the audience, the idea of a partner seeing what they've masturbated to is super uncomfortable. So maybe that's one of the reasons it didn't work? Nobody wants to be defined by what they watch. Someone might have a predilection for a type of pornography, might watch it on a weekly or daily basis, but keeps that compartmentalised away from the rest of their personality.

It's something I had just ignored until I wrote this book. I hadn't considered the role that porn plays in people's lives – and how isolating it can be.

Adam and I did talk about it a year later, when we got drunk together. He had a new girlfriend and I felt brave enough to tell him what I'd found and apologised for not being honest at the time. Adam was unembarrassed. He explained about his interest, how he'd been exploring it for years, especially the idea of meeting up with a sex worker and acting out his desires. I found everything he told me fascinating, now that my ego and emotions were removed and I could just listen. Adam was really turned on by pre-op trans women. He'd felt secure enough to tell his new girlfriend and was planning to pay an escort to have sex with him when he was home in Germany. He was excited about it.

Again, my feelings about this have changed. Gossiping with him as friends, I was so into it. THIS IS BEING ALIVE, I thought. Discussing bodies and fantasies, pushing the boundaries of sexuality, free from shame and morality and gender norms. I AM ONE OF THOSE PEOPLE WHO IS JUST REALLY COOL ABOUT SEX STUFF, I congratulated myself. Nothing human is alien to me.

Then, researching this book, I discovered that a high proportion of trans women have undertaken a form of sex work. Almost 11 per cent have participated at some point. We will be investigating the relationship between economics and choice in more detail later, but you see, what is important to understand is that trans people are twice as likely to live in extreme poverty as the rest of the population. This can be related to the expenses of treatment and counselling, as well as being ostracised by family and friends, or experiencing homelessness and unemployment after coming out. Being trans can lead to social exclusion for many women and this can make sex work an unwanted necessity—

Isn't that the same for some cis women?

Yes. For some people sex work can be their only option.

But it's still a choice.

Choice by its very definition requires more than one option. It's not a menu if it only says 'potato' on it. If society is unwelcoming and difficult for trans women, isn't that acting as a form of coercion? In episode five of the podcast *Sold in America* Noor Tagouri interviews a woman called Laya about her life experiences and she is incredibly eloquent on this subject, so listen to it if you want to think and learn about it some more.

I can't celebrate a rich white man like Adam buying sexual services from a woman who may have found sex work a necessity just because it transgresses social norms. Also, something I hadn't considered before reading the work of trans writers Juno Dawson, Juliet Jacques and Paris Lees is that men like Adam are fetishising these women, obsessed with certain aspects of their physicality. I don't feel like applauding him for living out his fantasy now, I feel squeamish.

But if it wasn't a potato menu? If it's grown adults making choices how dare I be squeamish?

The protective emotions I feel towards sex workers, especially those coerced by circumstances, may be justified in some instances . . . but the question that's striking me now is this: what worth do these emotions have? They can't be taken to the bank. They aren't paying anyone's rent. They aren't a solution.

Mind Rape

After this experience of chatting to Adam I thought I was porn-savvy. I didn't watch it, but I accepted it would be part of life for any man I loved. Even if you're having regular sex, madly in love and entrenched in monogamy, they'll still have urges and thoughts and fantasies about other people, and they'll masturbate. That's what modern people do – they wank to porn. They put porn on and have a wank. I mean, *I* didn't but my boyfriends did. I was still 'against' it, I worried about the mistreatment of vulnerable people – but I didn't lecture anyone about it. It's like being vegan at Christmas dinner, watching your family devour the charred corpses of a barnyard massacre, thinking, 'They seem so happy, who am I to ruin their fun?'

Don't take this out on Christmas dinner.

For a vegan, Christmas dinner *is* a potato menu.*

After Adam I grasped that porn was part of the world now, and it wasn't until I was in love with Nicholas that it caused a problem in my life again. I mentioned him earlier. He didn't want to sleep with me and I dealt with it very badly, because my insecurity outshouted compassion. He told me he was into ethical porn, produced by women, feminist. No one was

* And maybe carrots, which taste delicious and your mum can see you're enjoying them, so she reveals they're covered in butter.

being hurt. On one occasion, out of desperation, I said he could watch some while we had sex. It was quite horrible, he was inside me but his focus was on the screen. He asked me to look; a woman was licking another woman's bumhole. I *can* imagine how it might be enjoyable to watch people licking bumholes with someone you feel closely connected to. But that wasn't my experience.

Around the same time one of my friends told me her boyfriend was looking for a book deal. I was instantly jealous; all book deals are for me and everyone should stop stealing my stuff. 'What's his book about?' I asked anxiously in case it was an idea I wished I'd had. 'It's called *Mind Rape*,' she said. 'It's about how when men look at women, they imagine how they'd fuck them.'

'That's not true,' I insisted, because I absolutely believed that. How could that be true, how could men function like that? I said only very poorly men who needed professional help could feel that way. Men like Russell Brand, or Russell Brand. I cried for my friend, I felt so sorry for her. She had such an awful, broken boyfriend. She told me Geoff had said – HIS NAME WAS GEOFF, why are all Geoffs perverts? – that when he walked down the street, every woman he passed, every woman he saw on the tube or who served him in the shops, he would get images, snapshots of them being fucked; cocks in their mouths, cum on their faces. He undressed women mentally, *constantly*, without any choice in the matter. It was automatic. His mind turned real-world life into hardcore sex, like a soldier getting flashbacks or a hungry cartoon character seeing heads become roast chickens.

I described this to Nicholas when I got home. 'Can you believe it?' I asked. 'And she thought this was *all men*!'

'Only if you've been watching a lot of porn,' he shrugged.

Nicholas understood what Geoff was describing. Said it happened to him too. Said it could be very uncomfortable, shameful, made him hate himself. I was thrown. I'd acknowledged that my boyfriend had a myriad of sexual feelings that didn't include me. I'd accepted my lovers would all use porn. But I hadn't figured that porn might change their world view, might impose bare, brutal sex atop everyday street scenes.

If a man in the supermarket is visualising the woman behind the till giving a tit-wank, I don't want to exist in the same universe as him, let alone be holding his hand.

And so I realised I'd accepted nothing, I'd been hiding. I hadn't explored how porn affected the person I was in love with because the truth was that I hated that porn existed and I hated that people watched it. I was an uptight Brontë sister masquerading as sex-positive. John, my most recent ex, had to put up with me being incredibly nosy and paranoid about his predilections because I now believed that every man had a secret brain dungeon where women were punished.

Sex is the reason we exist, but now technology is altering what sex is. We have these ancestral desires and they've been hijacked, and I want to know the intricacies of how. Not the moralistic stuff, but what has been studied, what can be shown through evidence. Does online porn affect the people who watch it? Does it change what people are aroused by? Can it incite aggression, or make violent people worse? How does watching porn affect children?

On a personal level, I'm most fascinated about where a person and the porn they watch interconnect, where porn and real-life sex intersect; how it might motivate or limit sexual satisfaction; how it might relate to depression.

There is disagreement, but also a lot of research attempting to answer these questions. We'll have an open-minded sift through it, but first we must get up to date. We explored the history of sexual imagery up to the advent of VCRs and porn people could rent from Blockbuster. It's time to slide ourselves back in and press PLAY on a documentary called *How We All Got the Internet and the Internet Got All the Porn*.

An Internet History
(You Don't Need to Delete)

THEME TUNE is the Babylon Zoo song 'Spaceman', but only the really good fast bit at the beginning. As the song starts to slow down into the shit bit* the screen goes from black to all fuzzy, which signifies the olden days. People are throwing Frisbees and saying 'How you doin'?' so we realise it's the nineties. The people seem happy and carefree, but then a cloud casts a shadow in the shape of a laptop as we realise that everything is about to change.

Squiggly rewinding as we leap backwards through history, bumbags, big moustaches and . . . SCREECH, we stop. It's the sixties. While most people are screaming at the Beatles, a few dweebs are trying to make computers talk to each other. They use little wires and a lot of hard work. Thankfully 'Can't Buy Me Love' is playing in the background cos this is boring to watch. The sun rises on the summer of love, 1969, it's all recreational drugs and sleeping on haystacks, except for Charley Kline, the only person indoors with his clothes on. Kline sends the first ever message between computers. It is 'LO'. Kline talking-heads a funny story about how he was actually typing 'LOGIN' but the SRI system crashed. The interviewer laughs politely and pretends she knows what an SRI system is.

---

* The shit bit of the song 'Spaceman' by Babylon Zoo is the majority of the song 'Spaceman' by Babylon Zoo, but that beginning, holy macaroni. It was a time of great hope for music and what it could achieve, those twenty-nine seconds.

Quick ident of an old-fashioned computer monitor and dial-up modem noise.

The presenter is walking around a museum pointing at flared trousers and bell-bottoms. 'These would have been what the inventors were wearing,' she says. A calendar flicks through the years until we hit 1973. 'Disco Inferno' plays as a computer in London connects with a computer in Norway. Networking is now global. The term 'internet' is first used. The presenter gets this fact tattooed on her body.

Now Queen Elizabeth II is talking-heading. 'I sent my first email in 1976,' she says to the camera. The corgi on her lap yawns.

Words appear on the screen in neon writing: 'ARPANET', 'Transmission Control Protocol', 'Domain Name System'. 'There's a lot of jargon,' says the presenter in voiceover.

It's 1984 and George Orwell talking-heads: 'This was the year that William Gibson invented the term "cyberspace". You should really be speaking to him. I was dead by now.'

William Gibson says, 'George Orwell has always been jealous of me.'

Ident of a real mouse running across a mouse mat while a computer mouse watches.

'1985,' shouts the presenter from a clifftop, 'and the first domain name is registered.'

The presenter is standing holding hands with a hologram of Tim Berners Lee. '1990, and this guy –' the hologram dances and waves – 'invented HTML.'

'1991' flashes up on the screen in pink and the presenter lies on a waterbed. She turns towards the camera. 'This is the year CERN introduced the public to the World Wide Web.'

The Public is seated in a restaurant opposite the World Wide

Web. They both say 'How do you do?' and eat lasagne. The World Wide Web begins to explain how next year both audio and video files will be shared via computers and that people will start using the term 'surfing' about going online. 'Can't surf without water,' says the Public in a Yorkshire accent. The Web looks sad and misunderstood.

Ident of a computer mouse running across a desk while a real mouse watches.

The presenter climbs a fence and talks down the lens to us. She explains that by 1993 there were around six hundred websites, including ones for the White House and the UN. Yahoo! was born in 1994, Amazon, Craigslist and eBay in 1995.

The presenter double-takes as a rabbit runs past looking worriedly at his watch. The rabbit notices her and the camera crew. He jumps away, the presenter follows and begins falling down a really massive hole. Familiar internet brand names whizz past her face as she falls. Google whacks her between the eyes and leaves a mark that says '1998'.

The presenter wipes away her tears and speaks to camera. 'We're here, the year I got my first ever email address.'

The presenter climbs out of the hole and wipes soil from her burkini. She begins to grapevine while doing a tuneful rap about the technology available in 1998. We STOP the video because we can't bear white people culturally appropriating nostalgically.

The internet exists, we all use it. But when did people start using it for porn?

Who Wanked When?

I got my first email address in 1998. I remember signing up to Yahoo! and asking what the point of it was. My friend Ben told me it meant you could get messages from people on a computer. I didn't have a computer, nor did my friends, but now we could message each other whenever we were all in the computer room together. A computer room, a room with a computer in it. Now every room is the computer room, computers are so ubiquitous they've become invisible – I AM WRITING *THIS* ON A COMPUTER AND I HADN'T EVEN NOTICED.

I went along with it, like I do everything, because I am weak. My email address was Sarayellowhat, inspired by a children's book I hadn't read, and the fact I had yellow hair. I don't check that address any more so don't think you can crack the code and send me critiques of my rapping.

1998 was when I became aware of the internet as a thing, but I had no idea people were utilising this technology to access pornographic content. By the end of the nineties the market for internet porn was estimated to be worth between $750 million and $1 billion. That's a lot of people spending some of their money on porn or ~~Richard Branson~~* someone less litigious spending *all* of his.

---

* The lawyers said I can't insinuate that Mr Branson spent his entire fortune on porn in case he sues me. If he doesn't want people thinking he's a greedy porn hound, he shouldn't have grown that beard.

Figures estimating porn revenue are inexact because the people making the money often hide their income due to legal restrictions. Most banks and financial services refuse to create accounts for people and businesses who sell sex.

Estimating the profits of any other industry is as simple as a trip to Companies House. If I wanted to tell you what the building trade was worth in 1998 I could. The figures in porn are ~~curvy~~ much guessier. We must don our monocles and be wary. Ditto with statistics, there are millions out there, enough to support any argument. Too often porn stats are used for dramatic effect by the media. For instance, there was an arresting *Time* magazine cover in 1995. If you Google it you'll tremble to see the gaunt and gobsmacked young boy, his skin a pallid semen-blue. 'EXCLUSIVE', the magazine tells us; we lean in – we love capitalised words. 'A new study', we're informed, shows 'how pervasive and wild' this new pornography is. This cover is designed to trigger concern. It aims to convey that online porn is damaging children, whether we can be bothered to read the article or not.

The study was conducted by a research group at Carnegie Mellon University. They recorded online activity and claimed there was much more porn on the web than people realised, specifically that '83 per cent of images stored on Usenet were pornographic'. Usenet was a kind of bulletin board that preceded internet forums, with thousands and thousands of users, and from this statistic it was extrapolated that over 80 per cent of the internet was porn. The logic was that if three quarters of Usenet was pornographic images, so was three quarters of the rest of the internet. The statistic was 'sticky', easily requoted, shocking but believable. You may have heard such a figure yourself. Someone at university told me that *99 per cent* of the internet was porn and I believed him. Why wouldn't I? Statistics sound so correct and mathsy. Sex is a primal instinct, why wouldn't it dominate any new technology? The guy was wearing a Care Bears tie, how could he be wrong?

Do a little investigation into the Carnegie Mellon study and you'll find that the Usenet boards studied were specifically set up for selling porn to adults. To be clear, 83 per cent of images *in the porn image section* of Usenet were pornographic. That means 17 per cent of the images in the porn groups were not pornographic, and I'm sorry, that is far more intriguing. What were they? Cats? Birthday cakes? Counting the percentage of porn in an online porn shop and presenting the results as perilous for children is like counting the dildos in a sex shop, then screaming on a front page about Toys 'R' Us selling rubber cocks to kids.

Time magazine was forced to print a retraction, which was in small print and without an eye-catching cover image. Wrongness is much more fun than facts. Statistics that inflame emotions are far more likely to be repeated than those with boring qualifiers. We'll be seeing more examples of this later, don't worry. Don't worry about anything – except that 100 per cent of murderers and people with erectile dysfunction have watched porn.

I looked for a trustworthy graph showing the amount of people who were using the internet for porn in the 1990s and how that has increased until the present day. I wanted a clear idea of how quickly 'no one has the internet' became www.weallwatchporn.com. I'm certainly not representative of my generation, having to leave the room when *Neighbours* gets racy.

I was struggling to find reliable stats so I changed tack. I decided to email Ben from college. I hadn't spoken to him for twenty years but he was the person who got me electronic mailing in the first place. I was sure he'd appreciate this random missive asking if he knew about internet porn in 1998.

He replied so matter-of-factly, I couldn't believe it: 'Hey Sara. In answer, porn was available back then. My first sight of it was actually at fifteen when I visited my brother for his twenty-first. That was 1997. Take care.'

Ben didn't specify that he saw this 1997 porn *online*, so it's not of much use, and he didn't put any kisses at the end, which is mighty cold. But inspired by how willing he was to answer the question I decided to do a little non-scientific research and post on Facebook:*

Sara Pascoe
2 February 2018 · 🌐 ▼

HELLO, this might seem like a strange post, but anyone who is around the same age as me (36) can you remember whether at 17/18 years old (around 1998) you knew that porn was on the internet, or how to get it? Was it common knowledge yet? What age/year did everyone start using computers for porn? You can DM me if you want- i'd be very grateful!! xxx

👍❤️😄 37   75 comments 1 share

👍 Like   💬 Comment   ↗ Share

Notice the triple kiss, because I'm not a monster. You may also appreciate the thirty-seven 'likes' including my aunty Linda, and that *seventy-five* people commented – more

* A platform for sharing pictures and boring on about your kids that launched in 2004. I'm telling you this in case there is an environmental apocalypse and a paper copy of this book outlasts memory of social media.

participants than many studies I've seen quoted. I'm the new Alfred Kinsey.

Most of the replies are people bragging that by 1998 they knew all about internet porn. My friend **Aisling** has sweetly commented that she didn't know about it until her twenties, which makes me feel better about my ignorance. Me and Aisling have both been excluded from porny conversations because ~~we are so cool~~ we're prone to high-pitched sermonising at the first hint of female objectification.

I learned a lot from these replies. **Matt** says that in the late nineties he read magazines with a list of URLs in the back that linked to pictures of naked celebs. He says there wasn't an engine where you could simply search, you had to know how to find what you were looking for. By 1999 he remembers looking at videos that were more like gifs because of file sizes and the time they took to download.

Ed tells me (and nosy Aunty Linda) that in 1998 he was caught selling porn to boys in the year below at school. They'd plugged their phones into sockets around the school using dial-up to access images, and that was how the IT teacher worked out what was going on.

Spencer is ten years older than me so was a grown-up with a job in 1998. He worked in computing and had access to new technology. His porn was on floppy disks, which he complains meant very low resolution. He says there was porn online from the mid-nineties but it was slow to load. By the early 2000s it was all much quicker, he rejoices, before mentioning that his first computer had a pornographic game on it called 'MacPlaymate', described poetically by Spencer as 'you dropped items into a woman and she moaned louder and louder'.

I stare at that sentence for a long time. Women aren't shopping baskets, in my experience. I hadn't been researching pornographic computer games because, honestly, I didn't know they existed. Now I do. Someone helpfully tagged a YouTube link to Spencer's comment. There's a video on there that gives you a good look ~~into~~ at MacPlaymate. Here she is:

Once you've entered the game you've got a 'Toy Box' full of dildo things, a lube tube and two disembodied hands. You click and drag these items and place them creepily on the Playmate's body, while her breasts vibrate in the air like they can smell it. With the right combination of implements in/on her erogenous zones the Playmate will simulate increased arousal and eventually orgasm. So realistic! I love a pair of men's hands on me but only if they've been lopped off. 'Hey baby, let's go to bed, but can you steal from a Saudi Arabian merchant first?'

There are extra controls along the top: you can dress the woman in fetish gear or peekaboo underwear, provide her with a lesbian lover, print out your handiwork or PANIC. That's my favourite button. PANIC – 'I'm lubing a computer animation's eye.' PANIC – 'What if I find real-life boobs disappointing because they hardly pulsate at all?' PANIC – 'What if life is a matrix and I exist inside someone's Mac and all the sex I think I'm having is actually them clicking a dildo on me?'

You'd be able to see the dildo floating around?

Not if you've got lube in your eye. The instructions explain that the PANIC button is for those Playmating at work. When you press it the screen becomes an innocuous spreadsheet of Apple computer dealers. It's a really pleasing detail. Technology is great.

Back to my investigation of nineties porn. **Sarah** (who went to my school) says she knew stuff was on the internet, not because she'd looked but because porn sites 'popped up' all the time. She didn't seek any out until after university (2003), when she got her own computer. **Matthew** says a similar thing, that it was easy to stumble on sites, especially if you typed a URL incorrectly, e.g. 'hot male' instead of 'hotmail' – YEAH RIGHT, MATTHEW. He says that if 'very motivated' it was possible to download content overnight, but that you had to be relatively tech-savvy to find things and have patience with connections and quality.

JoJo is a couple of years older than me. In 1997 she went online with a Yahoo! site that was advertised as free, then earned her a £300 phone bill. The first word she ever searched was 'cock', which is hashtag on-brand for JoJo. The picture took twenty minutes to load, but she doesn't say if it was worth the suspense, or the three hundred quid. **Sean** explains he had 'fixed-medium porn' back then (magazines/ video tapes) rather than the internet; ditto for **Will**, who was working from 1997 but not using porn online until the early 2000s. **Eve** knew that people looked at sexy pictures on computers but also that they were slow to load. **Charlie** is younger than me. He says that in 1996 he was eleven and knew porn existed and what it looked like, but didn't start watching until university in 2003.

Joel says something interesting: apparently the regulations on porn had to catch up with technology, so 'whereas porn was hard to access, once you did there was more wrong 'un stuff about if you were a wrong 'un'. By 'wrong 'un stuff' I'm assuming he means illegal practices like assault and paedophilia. Perhaps such material was closer to the surface in the early internet days? **Howard** is my ex-boyfriend Nicholas's dad, so I'm really glad he's joining in. Howard says, 'I was aware of porn from about 1998 when NTL became a new broadband service and my friends at work said they'd been looking at it. Obviously it took an age for anything to load so it was not the most worthwhile activity.' Howard wanted a quick wank, not a tantric two-hour self-loving session, hurry up internet.

It's something I haven't considered before, but I guess the loading speed is an issue if the person masturbating has little privacy, if they're living with other people. Someone might wake up, walk in. I guess that's why people keep mentioning how slow it was, because for many people masturbatory material that appeared over an hour was tantalisingly un-useful.

Rachel has sent me a private message. She was stripping in the late 1990s and reckons she had a good awareness of the sex industry in general around then. She writes: 'In 1997 I don't remember internet porn being much of a thing. What I do remember around that time was chatrooms, and people doing dirty typing in there. Some of the women at the club where I worked used to pre-arrange phone sex with their customers for later that evening, so that was a thing. I don't remember any customers ever mentioning porn to us.'

There are lots more messages but most of them are un-original, we've heard it already. My friend **Nick** goes off-piste, writing that he used to print pictures of bodybuilders and use the pages as porn, then asks, 'Is this for material?' No. 1, Nick, what has your hard-on for bodybuilders got to do with the internet, and no. 2, why would I do stand-up about what gay teenagers get up to with their parents' printer? I'm a very intellectual act.

Mark throws a spanner of 'sexy Ceefax pages' into the mixture. Ceefax is, or rather was, a text information service on television. It started in 1974 and died in 2012. 'WTF, where?' I demanded, and Mark sent me a link to some pages from the nineties. It isn't porn, it's pixelated neon-coloured womanly outlines and ads for phone sex. You can find these with a Google search if you want. They all look far too Microsoft Paint to imagine anyone was actually aroused, but it draws comparison with that ancient probable vagina – give a human male any surface, any platform, and he will draw a nudie woman there.

Annelie says Literotica was available by the late nineties so I suppose we'd better find out what the merry hell that is.

I love literature and I love sex so I'm *very* excited by this mash-up. Literotica is a bright clunky page, all links, no images, and in a bulletin-board format, so potentially it hasn't changed much in the last two decades. There's the potential to live-chat with other users, links to stores selling sex toys and then a long list of erotic stories grouped by topic. The categories are what you'd expect for a porn site: 'anal', 'incest', one that I excitedly read as 'ferrets' but is actually 'fetish', which makes more sense. Some of the topic titles are intriguing: 'loving wives', 'mind control', 'non-human'. If I'm completely honest, all I want to do is explore this website for the rest of my life. I might submit an erotic missive about a comedian writing a book who gets sidetracked reading horny stories about obedient wives loving their alien husbands who have hypnotised them.

Sara tried to type facts but her hard nipples kept getting in the way.

Stop it.

Said the housewife softly to her alien master. His tentacles were getting slime on the curtains she'd made specially from her pubic hair.

The link I felt drawn to was titled 'How To'. This must be how Columbus felt when he arrived in America – some random navigation and suddenly a new-found land! Let's ~~slaughter natives~~ explore.

How to Cuckold

The 'How To' pages of Literotica are voluminous. Page after page of generous instructions: how to give oral pleasure, receive oral pleasure, female ejaculate, deep-throat, throw a swingers' party, have better orgasms, maintain your erection, write erotic fiction—

> You should read that one.

I should read them all! How to do phone sex, cross-dress, become a cuckold – *tyre screech*, stop the car. Become a cuckold?

I have to keep reminding myself: 'Never underestimate the immense extent of human sexuality.' Absolutely everything is sexy to someone. I must stop being surprised at what's arousing to people and save my astonishment for when Dad remembers my birthday.

We touched on cuckoldry earlier. The word itself is borrowed from bird behaviour. Cuckoos are famous for laying their eggs in other birds' nests.* The idiot non-cuckoos don't realise and warm the marauder egg alongside their own. It all ends in tragedy when the cuckoo baby is born, greedy and demanding, and either starves its adopted siblings or nudges them floorward to their death. Every single cuckoo

---

* They have that reality TV show: *The Only Way is Egg-sits*.†
† I hate myself.

has caused the death of smaller birds, yet the politicians stay quiet. When you gonna comment about the shameful cuckoos, Crooked Hillary Clinton?

Imagine someone left a child in *your* home and you didn't notice because your brain is so tiny, then while you're out working at the worm factory the fake child murders your existing children. *The Nest*, an eight-episode BBC drama airing this spring.*

In the human world a cuckold is a man whose wife has cheated on him, the inference being that the chump could be warming someone else's eggs, raising large, feathered children that are not biologically his. In evolutionary terms, this male loses three times over. If you understand that all animals are mere meat machines churning out smaller versions of themselves as repackaged genes, you'll realise how dire the cuckold's situation is.

Loss 1 The fool might not have biological offspring of his own (evolutionary loser) OR if he does he's effectively weakening them by delivering food and resources to the non-biological offspring. Parenting is a zero-sum game, there is a set amount of ~~love~~ resources. Any food or protection going to Jeremy is taken away from Sophie, and vice versa. This is where sibling rivalry comes from. Just by existing your brothers and sisters are potentially lowering your quality of life and survival chances. The bastards.

Loss 2 In evolutionary terms, unrelated humans are competitors. We compete for territory, for mates, for mangoes. A male providing sustenance for a non-biological son or daughter is helping his enemy. He unknowingly spends his

---

* BBC stands for the Bigger Better Cuckoo.

time and energy strengthening the genes of an unrelated opponent, thus working against himself.

It might seem contradictory to remember that people adopt children. We're not robots with evolutionary instructional manuals, we're conscious creatures and our social group is vitally important. We form bonds with unrelated people in order to survive and our emotional capability means we can deeply and dearly love children we're not related to. But the *conscious* aspect is important. If a parent finds out that a child is not 'theirs' – say a mix-up happened at the hospital and sixteen years later they're told the kid they've brought up is someone else's – that's devastating.* No one says, 'Don't worry about it, I'm attached to this one now.' Our relatedness is important.

When I was growing up, my mum had boyfriends, and my sisters and I drove them all away. She would tell us, 'It's so hard to meet someone when you've got three kids,' but she met them fine. It was when they came over and met US that the problems started. Again, I know that many men do become fathers to children they're not related to, but as a culture we don't necessarily expect it of them. We're very impressed if they do it, especially if they do it well. But occasionally they're viewed as schmucks, which brings us on to:

Loss 3 If people in the tribe or community know that a man has been cuckolded, he loses status. He himself may be blissfully unaware, raising a beloved family and living his best life, but his masculinity will be judged by those around him. For all male apes, a loss in status means an increase in danger.

---

* Always get a baby's ears pierced straight after birth. Then you can recognise it, and also it'll look nicer.

Human males do not have paternity certainty. Let us spend some time examining this, because the ramifications are huge. I've mentioned paternity certainty a few times already in regard to the stigma around female promiscuity, so what does it really mean?

In most mammals, it doesn't matter which male impregnated the female because there is no male parental investment. He has contributed his sperm and little else, he has nothing to protect and nothing to lose. If, as with humans, the male IS necessary for the child's survival, if he has to potter about getting food, keeping the nest safe, going out in the freezing cold to de-ice the car while his family wait inside in the warm, well, this man has a lot to lose. 'Who's the daddy?' is one of the most important questions in human nature.

So how does a male ensure that he is not cuckolded? Sperm goes in, time passes, baby comes out. He cannot see inside the lady, he cannot be sure that it is HIS sperm fertilising her, the only thing he *can* do is ensure that no other male gets near enough to become a threat. So he guards his mate. Not all sperm competition between males is fought in the female's reproductive tract, some of it is behavioural. Mate guarding, sticking around your female and warding off any other plucky gents, sounds like an effective strategy when we're thinking about ants or fruit flies. But when we think about humans it suddenly seems oppressive, abusive, an infraction of human rights.

One of the ugliest and sometimes most destructive human emotions is jealousy.

However we intellectualise it, sexual jealousy has deep roots in human psychology. This feeling evolved as an alarm system to protect our emotional investment, hyper-vigilant and often irrational. Love and jealousy co-exist, they support and strengthen each other. A pair bond without exclusivity doesn't seem un-sensible to us modern people; we've all had 'fuck buddies', read articles on polyamory, have friends on 3nder.* We know that love and lust take many forms and monogamy doesn't satisfy the needs of everyone. We're aware that most of the sex our horny species undertakes is not procreational; pair-bonded couples are a by-product, not the point. But we must also acknowledge that for pre-agricultural people reproducing was not a choice, and survival depended on parents who cared for each other and you.

There's a fascinating argument that jealousy is experienced differently by the sexes. In 1992 psychologist David Buss and colleagues proposed that men would be more jealous of a partner's *sexual* infidelity, while women's jealousy would be provoked by *emotional* infidelity. This was based on evolutionary principles: human females are fertilised internally, and males have no paternity certainty, thus males would resent and/or prevent their partner having sex with other men. A man who didn't care, who wasn't jealous – well, he'd be far more likely to be raising the children of other guys, spending his time and resources continuing the genes of some sneaky suitor, while his laid-back, 'let Marjorie express her sexual needs' genes were lost in the evolutionary cul-de-sac of non-reproduction. The very jealous men, those who mate-guarded, harangued and checked all Marjorie's text messages – they ensured that offspring were genetically theirs, they bred successfully, and many of

* It's an app for singles to meet up with couples, or couples to find singles who wanna join in. I know you knew that already, but just in case you lend this book to Grandma.

us have those unattractive and antisocial traits, making us unbearable to this very day.

To reverse the theory, the way women get pregnant means that they have complete maternity certainty and need never doubt their relation to the children they birth. Marjorie's partner having sex with other women doesn't affect this; her genes are in the children she is raising. She need not feel threatened by his sexual exploits, BUT affection for another woman might lead to him sharing his resources. Any food or protection going to this second woman is subtracted from Marjorie and her offspring. She's correct to worry about this. Her children become more vulnerable if they are less well provided for. Even worse, emotional attachment might lead to ~~my dad~~ this man abandoning Marge and the kids for his new family. We have a reversed situation: any prehistoric females who couldn't give a flying goose about Roger's close female friendships and obsession with his cousin Joan, those women were more likely to lose the resources and support necessary to raise their offspring to adulthood. We didn't inherit as many of their genes. We're descended from the watching-his-every-move, spreading-rumours-that-he's-impotent, accusing-him-of-flirting-with-his-mum, jealous bitches.

The Buss study tested sex differences in jealousy in three ways. Experiment one was self-reporting. 202 undergraduate students were asked:

Imagine that you discover the person with whom you've been seriously involved became interested in someone else. What would distress or upset you more?

  a) Imagining your partner forming a deep emotional attachment to that person

    b) Imagining your partner enjoying passionate sexual
       intercourse with that person

It's like a very short, traumatic version of those quizzes in women's magazines that let you know whether your personality matches your blood type or what handbag you'd be if you were made of leather. I bet men's magazines don't have quizzes. Is that sexist? Is *this* a quiz?

    a) No.
    b) No.
    c) No, quizzes give you a range of possible answers.
       This is a new thing I've just invented.

Participants chose whether emotional or sexual infidelity would hurt them more, and the results demonstrated a large gender difference. Almost 60 per cent of males were more upset about sex than emotion and over 80 per cent of women were more upset about emotion, than sex. The study isn't claiming that these people don't care about *both* kinds of infidelity, simply that for most of the men sex cheating was worse, and the opposite for women – but I'm a woman, and I would've answered B. Sexual infidelity makes me feel sick, I'm taunted by it, tortured with paranoid images. I've never had sweaty nightmares about my boyfriend writing someone with bigger boobs a poem.

How can anyone care more about *feelings* than fucking?

This is the difficulty when the results of some well-conducted experiment do not reflect one's own opinion or experience. Maybe I should ask my aunt if she was more bothered by my uncle shagging her friend Michelle or the love letters he sent her? Is that insensitive? Either way, she hasn't replied.

I want to know who these people who fear emotional infidelity are. Who *are* they? I bet they listen to ballads and cry at *EastEnders*. I bet they keep cards up all over the house even though their birthday was *weeks* ago.

A follow-up to the Buss experiment tested participants' physiological responses. They got fifty-five students, covered them with beepy machines and measured electrical activity on their skin while asking them to visualise, you guessed it, emotional or sexual infidelity. They found that men had a more pronounced reaction to the sexual scenario, women to the emotional scenario. I imagine it wasn't a pleasant morning for anyone, covered in electrodes, picturing their partner cheating.

These studies inspired a genre and since 1992 over a hundred experiments have investigated sex differences in jealousy. Meta-analysis has proved the 'men more bothered by sexual infidelity' hypothesis to be robust. But it's important to remember that this doesn't dictate anything about you and me, as individuals. Women and men do not fall into separate, distinct categories. Our sex alone does not dictate how and why we get jealous. We're shaped by environment, culture and conditioning. When studies examining gender differences don't reflect my experience I sigh to myself, 'Must be a man then, what with my masculine reaction,' rather than remembering that it's only ever a small sample being extrapolated from. Four out of ten males in the first survey answered that they were more worried about emotional infidelity. But the spectrum of human reactions gets lost when the results come back as MORE MEN THIS and MORE WOMEN THAT.

I became intrigued by an experiment I saw quoted in many books and articles often with a headline like: 'Male Brains

Respond to Jealousy in Centre for Sexual Aggression'. This centre sounds like a youth club that needs closing or every single comments section. But I looked the study up, because if there are neurological differences in the way genders react to jealousy, that's proof that those differences have been hardwired by evolution, isn't it?

a) Yes.

b) Yes. Oh, it's another one of these.

Maybe this paper will illuminate what's going on. It cost $35.99 for nine pages but I still bought it, there's nothing I won't do in the name of research (if it's tax-deductible). The title of the study is: 'Men and Women Show Distinct Brain Activations During Imagery of Sexual and Emotional Infidelity'.

In 2006 the neuroscientist Hidehiko Takahashi and colleagues popped people into an fMRI scanner, which magnetically measures brain activity, and asked them to read statements that were either neutral ('my girlfriend telephones her parents on the weekend'), sexual ('my girlfriend was naked with her ex-boyfriend in his bed') or emotional ('my girlfriend gave a gorgeous birthday present to her ex-boyfriend'). I really like the sound of this girlfriend, she's thoughtful and generous with her time, gifts and unclothed body. These were the 'jealousy conditions'.

Analysis of the brain scans showed that men 'demonstrated greater activation than women in the brain regions involved in sexual/aggressive behaviours such as the amygdala and hypothalamus. In contrast, women demonstrated greater activation in the posterior superior temporal sulcus.'

It's very tricky to simply accept studies like this one, because despite all the quoting in books and science journals, they only studied eleven men and eleven women. No one can extrapolate anything about human behaviour from such a small sample; it's dangerous to do so. Also no brain region has one pure function; there are not 'bits' that deal with one emotion or process. The brain is not a Sainsbury's with clearly defined aisles that you can navigate and say for certain, 'That's the dairy section,' 'There's the bakery.' It's all overlapping, at cross purposes, and we still know so little about it. The brain is a Lidl. Yes, it does sell milk and bread, but not where you'd expect, and you might not be able to see them in between the trumpets, microscopes and children's trampolines. When people are studied in an fMRI machine it is not as simple as 'bits' lighting up, bingo, sexual aggression. The brain is always active, and it's the scientists themselves deciding which parts have become *more* active, and this is not an exact science.

Studies like this *want* to find differences between the sexes because, in their demonstrated behaviour, men are more aggressive. DON'T HATE ME, I'm not saying *you* are, you're a sweet angel reading a lady book written by a lady, but you know the stats. Men are far more likely to be violent and domineering towards their romantic partners – married women are nine times more likely to be killed by their partner than a stranger. In fact, until the 1970s the 'Cuckold Defence' was a valid excuse for murder. If a man came home and found his wife in bed with someone and strangled her, the law was like, *shrug* 'What else can you do?'

Most women in shelters name jealousy as a prime reason for their partner's abuse. Beatings, invasions of privacy, restricting access to a phone, money and other freedoms – these are mate-guarding behaviours and in evolutionary terms can be linked to males' lack of paternity certainty. I made the mistake of reading a book about 'wife-beating' being an evolutionary tactic before going to speak to volunteers at Standing Together Against Domestic Violence. I excitedly told these women, who saw first-hand the effects of violence, what I'd been learning about mate guarding in apes: that from an evolutionary perspective, brutal or cruel abuse which dominates a partner is a way of ensuring paternity certainty and genetic survival. The book I'd read quoted studies on women who had escaped their abusers, saying that the very low self-confidence they had, plus the almost non-existent sex drive, proved that systematic abuse *worked*. These men didn't want their partners to look at other men, and after months and years of domineering and violent behaviour *they didn't*. It was the last thing on their minds; they only wanted to be safe.

I wish I'd just listened. They were staring. A woman politely but emotionally told me that people are not animals. Another explained that she had no interest in these kinds of theories while we live in a society that does little to support the vulnerable victims and their children.

When looking for evolutionary explanations it can seem like we're seeking to excuse behaviour, to justify it. But I do not think there is any excuse or justification. Evolutionary pressures are not a defence. I am sorry I was insensitive.

The Takahashi study was prompted by the hope that perpetrators could be better supported, and their violence prevented, if we understood the neurological processes. But there are many factors that influence human emotions and behaviour. Experience and environment must be considered alongside evolutionary theory, as sexed division is too reductive. The either/or choices of these 'emotional versus sexual jealousy' studies ignore the complicating factor that most people experience a combination of both. To be oblivious or unbothered by a bonded partner sharing any type of intimacy with others would have lowered the reproductive success of *any* of our ancestors.

To bring this back to porn – I read many of the 'How to Cuckold' pages of Literotica, written by men who were sexually excited about sharing their wife or girlfriend with other men. But from everything we've learned, cuckolding is something that *should* be the *opposite* of sexy. It would be anti-selective for humans to become aroused by something that would cost them genetic survival. Intentional cuckolding is a terrible reproductive strategy for men AND YET it's super hot to some of them. Isn't this a crazy aspect of human sexuality? Some people fancy dead bodies, some people attach sexually to objects, some people would rather wank to porn than have sex with an actual person, wouldn't they, Nicholas?

Human sexuality is much more than the conscious and unconscious desire to reproduce. It contains contradictory aberrations. If sex was all about reproduction, how could so many individuals be aroused by a practice that works against them? Why has our species evolved so many sexual practices that are unconnected with the continuation of the species? We've learned that we evolved to be private about our sex lives, yet some people remain exhibitionists who are most turned on by breaking that rule. We know humans evolved to be secretive about going to the toilet and be disgusted by excrement, yet some people will shit in a cup on the internet. No other animal expresses the range of behaviour that humans do. Dogs do mostly dog things; they all like walks and have a good sense of smell. Cats all like to sleep in patches of sunlight. All polar bears are united in wishing we hadn't melted away their habitat. Humans are everything. No spectrum has ever been so wide. We are, all at once, spectacularly stupid and incredible geniuses. The theory is that our early birth, because of our big brains, means that we are affected by environment more than any other animal. Our brain grows while we are outside of the womb, meaning we are shaped and individualised by external stimuli through our extended childhood.

With all human behaviours there is an inbuilt plasticity. We all recognise the weight of nurture in the nature/nurture combo that we inhabit. Kindness is shaped. What we enjoy as hobbies, what we like to eat can be magnificently different from culture to culture. How we speak is moulded by who spoke to us as children, and how. Sexual behaviour is no different. All of us went through critical learning stages. Some of us heard a balloon pop, felt a sexual thrill and now have a fetish. Some of us associated certain sex acts with fear because we misunderstood the plot of *Dirty Dancing*. Some of us have a guilt provided by religion that makes our orgasms incredibly powerful and then regrettable.

Let's think more about the multivariate possibilities for human arousal as we continue to consider the industry that it has created.

Outdoors Sex Survey

After gleaning so much from the Facebook responses to my question, I decided to ask some strangers in real life. I knew that my Facebook friends would be a similar age range and demographic to me, and I wanted diversity. Also, writing a book is lonely.

At a gig in Leicester Square I told the audience what I'd been researching. I couldn't effectively describe MacPlaymate with words. 'She's a cartoon lady who can put outfits on . . . she likes amputee hands on her . . . HER BOOBS CAN SMELL.' I tried showing images on my laptop but every way I turned it the woman was upside down and I seemed like a mum who can't use her own computer.*

At the end of my technologically challenged set I said, 'If anyone has any memories about internet porn, come tell me in the interval.' I had some stimulating chats. People seem very open to discussing porn and are free with their experiences and opinions. I've not met a single person who isn't worried or fascinated by this relatively new aspect of sexuality and sexual expression.**

---

* Mainly referring to *my* mum. She has two computers, one in front of the other because one broke and she bought one with a bigger screen to hide it. Also, she has six cats now. Which isn't relevant, but it *is* too many.
** A nice change from researching my last book, when NO ONE wanted to talk to me about child brides and rape law.

Some women in their early twenties told me their first experience with porn was boys at school making them watch '2 Girls 1 Cup'. 'Yuk, gross,' I said maturely, just like Alfred Kinsey would have done. They explained that by the time they had phones, aged eleven or twelve, they knew you could look at porn on them. A few minutes later, two girls (one conversation) came over and told me EXACTLY THE SAME THING. That they became aware of porn when boys at school made them watch '2 Girls 1 Cup'. 'It's not porn, it's a YouTube video,' one of them clarified.

'WHY were they making you?' I wanted to know.

'You had to watch it or they called you frigid.'

Both groups of women described this as a rite of passage. They didn't know each other, were from different parts of the UK, were a few years apart in age, yet repeated virtually the same story.

I've since wondered if kids in the late 2000s were all aware of '2 Girls 1 Cup' *because* it was on YouTube and easily accessible. There are always cultural tsunamis that come out of nowhere and hit us simultaneously: the ice bucket challenge, fidget spinners, a third example.

When I was at primary school there was a Tango advert where an orange blob man tapped people on the back, slapped them round the face and yelled informatively, 'You've been Tangoed.' This went whatever things went before they went viral. Crazy? Popular? It went crazy popular. The kids in my school did it all day long. We slapped and got slapped, and we loved it even though it hurt. We were unified by it for several cheek-smarting days. Then the advert got banned, orange blob man was elected President of the United States and the fun was over.

Twenty-five years later and I still have a powerful urge to tap and slap any time I'm in a queue. The instinct occurs to me daily. Things we see as children can have a lasting effect on us. Hence *why* people worry about children watching hardcore sex, hence why articles have been asking 'Can we protect our kids?' since ~~time immemorial~~ *Time* magazine.

I was ten years too old to have anyone make me watch '2 Girls 1 Cup'. I heard what it was about and that's why I didn't watch, because it sounded awful. Ditto *The Human Centipede* and the second series of *True Detective*. When it came out in 2007 I was doing reminiscence theatre in care homes. Our plays were about childhood after the war, women learning to drive, marriage in the 1950s. When *I'm* in a care home the theatre will be about getting Tangoed and slapping foreheads and yelling 'Spam!' Millennials' pensioner nostalgia will be 'Remember when that girl ate the other girl's poo then puked in her mouth?'

The responses to '2 Girls 1 Cup' weren't sexual. Most people found it disgusting. Kids showing it at school were trying to revolt each other, not inspire an orgy. But to those with particular tastes, it *was* erotic. I now know (I read the Wikipedia entry) that '2 Girls 1 Cup' is the trailer for a scat-fetish porno called *Hungry Bitches*. It's a genre that a subculture of people enjoy and another reminder of the huge spectrum of what pornography can be. It's also an interesting bookend. 2007 is a decade after I took my GCSEs and left school. Technology changed dramatically during those years. While I used to enjoy flicking through the dictionary looking for sexy words, by 2007 part of a young person's journey into cultural consciousness involved finding or being confronted by porn. In my documentary this will be illustrated beautifully:

A blonde child, dressed in an Amish outfit, or maybe an Elizabethan ruff. She looks around furtively, then opens a large leather-bound book. Her finger scans down the Ps until she finds it – Penetration! The girl gasps, giggles and faints. Fast-forward sounds, broadband wires wriggle across the screen like sensuous snakes, they vomit out smartphones and children pick them up from the grass and bite into them. 'Biblical symbolism,' says the presenter, while holding out a red apple with the Apple logo on it. The children behind her start pooping the words 'wifi password' and 'parental lock' onto the dictionary.

> Are your fingers made of lead? Cos that documentary is heavy-handed.

The reason I brought up the gig is because one of the people who came over to talk to me was an older man called Stefan. He was chatting away about the old dial-up speeds and accompanying frustrations, then announced, 'I always wished they would post the pictures upside down.' I thought he was trying to make me feel better about showing MacPlaymate the wrong way up, I didn't understand. He clarified: 'So you could see the good bits first and not waste time on the face.'

'Whoa,' I exclaimed, wasting more of his time by existing above the waist.

Stefan had meant his remark light-heartedly. He waited for me to laugh. I'm a comedian, I'm supposed to love jokes. He'd misjudged me as a crowd because onstage I'd been talking about pornography obscenely and without reserve. But I'm still one of those hardcore extremists who expects women to be treated like people and not bits of body.

Stefan walked away, a perfectly nice normal man. He'd come to my show to listen and engage; his comment wasn't intended to threaten or humiliate me, and it didn't. Images of people aren't people, are they? We don't empathise with a poster, a billboard, a centrefold. We didn't evolve to consider the feelings of inanimate objects; our ancestors didn't ask cave paintings what they wanted for dinner, didn't befriend the cloud that looked like a face. Maybe that's why although pornographic images depict real people, to the viewer that person is made object. The human body becomes 'bits'. A normal man at a gig can also be a butcher surveying a cow he's about to eviscerate – good meat and bad meat, useful and irrelevant.

He can't wank to a face.

And thank goodness, he doesn't have to. We have broadband now.

There is no neat graph detailing how the numbers of people using porn have risen. It's all unreliable estimates. All we can say for certain is that with the introduction of the first 'tube site' in 2006, the amount of people who had unthinkably easy access to an all-encompassing range of porn increased exponentially.

This moment would be pivotal in the documentary:

Same-sex and heterosexual couples hold hands while browsing in a vintage clothes shop. A shopkeeper stands behind a counter looking at a poster for the Beatles song 'Can't Buy Me Love'. A tannoy announces: 'It is 2006 and now there is YouTube but with porn on it.' The shoppers all start grabbing jackets and trousers off their hangers and running out of the store. 'Stop, stop,' yells the shopkeeper. 'We don't need to pay!'

shouts a tall woman. 'But it's my livelihood,' cries Samira. (She's the really good actress playing the shopkeeper.) A man pushes Samira out of the way – this is my friend Brett, who is appearing in the documentary as a favour. He looks at the Beatles poster, then ejaculates the words (this is done with CGI) 'Don't Buy Anything' over the song title. The Beatles all look sad (Photoshop) and I win best BAFTA in every category.

So can we tell what difference free porn makes to the lives of the people who watch it? Are their lives improved, destroyed? Is it true that people suddenly can't concentrate at work or have erectile dysfunction? More people are watching porn, but do they also explore more? Do they watch things they wouldn't have done if they'd had to type in their full name and credit card details? Is it the ease of access or the freeness that's changed things? Or more probably a combination of both? What I noticed in the recollections of nineties porn was that it was those good with computers who managed to utilise it. There was some capability involved. Now even the most illiterate person can open a search engine and watch as much hardcore fucking as they like. Even my mother could manage if she didn't have so many cats sitting on her.

Pornhub launched in 2007, fast becoming one of the most popular websites in the world. At the time of writing Alexa* ranks it as the thirty-third most visited site worldwide, just behind Google Hong Kong and one ahead of LinkedIn.**

---

* Alexa is a disembodied know-it-all who works for Amazon. Stefan wouldn't like her, she's all brain and no good bits.

** I still don't know what this website does or why Pete from university sends me biweekly emails asking to 'connect' on there. We only spoke to each other once when I told him Gemma Williams might have given him chlamydia, what's there to 'connect' about?

The people at Pornhub keep track of their users and regularly release figures about common search terms and trends which are useful for someone like me trying to get an insight. I wanted to ascertain how reliable these numbers are so I checked with my friend Mona, who's a statistician. She replied: 'I steer clear of stats where the source is a private company that has an interest in saying things are a certain way. Pornhub's stats are published by their own PR team. At a minimum they are not going to be disclosing when the stats aren't good for the company. Most likely, though, they're just a bit selective and exaggerated so anyone reading them should keep that in mind.'

With that in mind, here are Pornhub's (bragging, selective) stats. In 2007 they recorded around one million visits to their website every day. Ten years later that had apparently risen to seventy-five million daily visits. They can't all be Richard Branson, when would he have time to balloon? In their first year Pornhub uploaded 134 hours of content. By 2010 this had risen to over 22,000 hours. In 2012 it was up to 120,000. In 2016 it was over 476,000 hours . . . that's over FIFTY-FOUR YEARS' worth of content! If you laid the tape from all those films around the earth, you'd get in trouble for leaving porn all over the floor.

It's fair to say that this technology has changed the world. Is it changing us apes along with it?

Science of Masturbation

I could write a metaphorical short story about a man who consumes so much pornography that it piles up around him. Towering towers of video tapes, metres of genital posters, acres of gaping legs and mouths. As his collection grows the man masturbates in a smaller and smaller space each day. The more porn he uses, the less life he has until one day – SPLAT. The porn falls down. The man is killed. His body isn't found for months, but when it is, the weight of the tapes and magazines has squashed his head in such a way that his eyes have popped out.

He ogled himself to death!

It's so gross, and so perfect. It's a morality tale, a perfect analogy of what many of us believe to be the dangers of obsessive porn use. The user becomes shut off from the world, out of touch with reality, they ~~wank themselves to oblivion~~ find life is not worth living. I would love to write this story, especially the bit about the popped-out eyes – how perfect is that? He's been gawping and gawking, his eyes bulging more and more until they fly from his skull towards the boobies. That's my favourite bit.

But that man's death was a real thing that happened and was on the news.

Joji, fifty years old, Japanese, squished by his porn collection in 2016. He might have been a really funny man, very kind, brilliant at crosswords or a super good swimmer. But

I don't know anything about him, because his death is the kind that obliterates any life.* I think about old Joji, I wonder if he would chuckle at his ending. 'What a way to go!' he might quip, but in Japanese. Or maybe he would be deeply, deeply ashamed of what happened to him, this avoidable tragedy, stealing decades from his existence and telling the world he was a pervert?

People don't usually get physically hurt by their pornography. Your mum didn't get papercut to death by her copy of *Fifty Shades of Grey*. The internet doesn't weigh anything, so even the most compulsive porn watchers needn't fear a fatal collapse. But there remains much discussion about the non-physical dangers, the harmful effects of porn on mental health and relationships.

I've felt sick and sad through lots of my research into this topic, but my intention isn't to make you feel like that. I want to examine this intellectually where possible and explore the existing studies, so we have a full set of information to support our arguments. Let's dedicate our investigation to Joji. Could his life have been saved if he'd found a different hobby? Maybe if he'd played squash, he wouldn't have *got* squashed? I'm raising my keyboard to ya, Joji, this is for you.

The male body has an evolved need to masturbate. No matter what you might have heard from the NoFappers or the Catholic Church, men should masturbate. Even if men have regular sex, they'll feel masturbatory urges. Sometimes the more sex a man is having, the MORE he will feel inclined to masturbate. If a male-bodied person forgoes masturbation,

---

* Obviously all death obliterates life. I mean his type of death overshadows, that's the word I should have used.

their body will often emit nocturnally (wet dreams), which is something that the sleeping person cannot control.

You may know yourself that attempting not to masturbate, for religious or personal reasons, can require much focus and energy – that's because it is a necessary part of sperm production. The male body wants to do it because it *needs* to. It takes around three months for spermatogenesis to take place, but the little fellas can't stay in the balls forever. After four or five days they lose energy, become weary and ~~need walking sticks~~ have less chance of making a healthy baby (their whole *raison d'être*). By masturbating every few days a man keeps his sperm fresh and energetic, vital for sperm competition. New studies also suggest that masturbating reduces the chances of getting prostate cancer and lowers stress, so it's an all-round great way to spend your time.

PRIVATE TIME. PLEASE DO NOT DO IT ON THE BUS.

And with my 'kindly sex education teacher' face on, let me say that while all men vary, any amount of masturbation is normal. Some people do it several times a day, some people a couple of times a week, maybe some people only once or twice a month. There isn't an official 'average' wank rate, there's a spectrum that ranges from 'very little' to 'a lot' depending on the person. It can be influenced by hormones, stress levels, boredom, a sexy new receptionist at work. It might lessen in older age due to a drop in androgens (the viropause).

Even if you are trying to get someone pregnant the amount you wank will not affect your sperm count. The testicles produce 1,500 every second! It's only when self-pleasuring becomes 'compulsive' that it's a problem. But that's the same with any behaviour, like checking your phone or picking your nose.

Do men do it more than women?

If you believe culture – yes. Male masturbation is talked about as an inevitability and joked about in comedies with PG ratings. In general, I think we're more familiar and comfortable discussing men self-pleasuring. When I was at school boys were always going on about it, but there was only one conversation about female masturbation, when Vicky Thomas got caught fingering herself behind the cricket pavilion, and looking back, I think that was just a rumour. Vicky didn't even like cricket, but too late, she remains Sticky Cricky Vicky to this day.

Sex differences in masturbation have been investigated by scientists. In 1974 sex researchers Ibtihaj Arafat and Wayne Cotton found considerable disparity between male and female students, with the former being much more likely to masturbate, and to masturbate about three times more frequently. But interestingly, they also discovered women were twice as likely as men to be depressed after touching themselves.

This could be cultural rather than physiological, especially if there is more of a taboo around women touching themselves. A study of US teens published in 2010 found that more boys reported masturbation than girls (73.8 vs 48.1 per cent) and also found marked racial differences in frequency, which could reflect the effects of culture, religion, family guilt. Oh, my favourite thing is about Catholic priests: it's against the rules for them to masturbate, yet psychotherapist Richard Sipe discovered through probing interviews that of course they do. And yet again there was a sex difference. He reported that priests masturbated more than nuns. I mention this because while multiple studies find there are cultural differences in the frequency of male masturbation, the frequency of female masturbation is reliably lower.

So does that prove men have a higher sex drive than women? I HATE this assumption. I hate it because I feel like it's not representative of individual difference, that it minimises female sexuality. But it's undeniable that there is a divergence. And maybe it's the fault of a hormone that we've not really explored yet. Testosterone.

Testosterone

It gets referred to as 'the male hormone' but all bodies have it. In the female body it's made in the ovaries (indoor testicles) and the adrenal glands. In male bodies it's produced by the adrenal glands and the testes.

TED talk voice It's a 19-carbon steroid hormone made from cholesterol and it's largely responsible for the creation of what we consider 'male' attributes. During adolescence testosterone production ramps up to endow the male body with heightened sex characteristics. These include a deeper voice, facial hair, increased body hair, pubic hair, broadening of shoulders and face, and maturation of penis and testicles, becoming ready for reproduction. The body also becomes stronger as testosterone assists the building of bones and muscles. Male testosterone peaks in the late teens and begins to dwindle after the age of thirty.

That's why teenagers wank all the time?

I've never been a teenage boy, I don't know how it *feels* to have peak testosterone, but there are many pop-cultural representations of this being a very 'tossing off into a sock' time of life. And maybe apple pie if American movies are to be believed. 'Liver in a stiletto shoe', according to an unforgettable *Buzzfeed* article I read.

In men and women testosterone has been proven to promote sex drive. When it dwindles people find their libido decreases. There are illuminating descriptions from people transitioning. Male-to-female (MTF) people having testosterone (T) blockers describe feeling deadened, losing some spark and magic. And the opposite: I read blog posts from a female-to-male person who was aghast at how he was staring at and ogling women in the street all the time with the heightened sexual effects of T injections.

The male body produces about twenty times more testosterone than the female body. Due to the faster male metabolism, this results in a blood testosterone level that is seven or eight times higher than women's. But because the female foetus does not receive as much testosterone in utero, our bodies and brains remain much more sensitive to it, so a sharp rise will have a large effect. Women will notice a difference in their libido over the menstrual cycle partly due to peaking testosterone (although, bizarrely, this usually occurs after the peak of fertility).

When it comes to sex hormones, trans people are the Rosetta Stone, the only ones who have felt both levels of testosterone and who can compare its effect on arousal and desire. Us cis-genders cannot experience the libido of the other side, but it's utterly compelling to imagine. I'm sure you know the Greek myth of Tiresias. He was a shepherd's son who was out on a walk one day when he saw two snakes copulating. He hit them with a stick, we don't know why – jealousy? Boredom? Either way, Hera, goddess of women and marriage, saw him and it pissed her off. She struck him down with a sex change and Tiresias lived as a woman for seven years. During this time Hera was having an argument with her husband Zeus (the god who dresses up as a swan to rape people*) about who enjoys sex more, men or women. Do you have this kind of row with your partner? I think it's a sign that your lover's finding you selfish in bed when they start saying 'You're enjoying this more than me.' Either way, Tiresias's answer, having experienced intercourse in a male and a female body, was that men got only one tenth of the pleasure that women received. Rather than being pleased at being the ten-times-better-sex sex, Hera struck Tiresias blind in her fury. A bit like me when the results of a study don't reflect my opinion.

We discussed the Clark and Hatfield campus study before, and how the female students showed no interest in stranger sex, which I put down to the necessity of assessing danger rather than a reflection of low sex drive. The website Ashley Madison provided an unwitting insight into men's and women's sex lives on a more level playing field.

You may remember this being in the press back in 2015. Ashley Madison is a dating site for married people which was hacked – IDEAL for those of us interested in social study and terrible for those trying to have some spicy affairs in secret. The hack revealed the names of the site's users *and* the fact that Ashley Madison had been lying about how many women there were. Half of the ladies chatting away were actually bots – only 14 per cent of the genuine profiles belonged to women. That means 86 per cent of the real profiles were male, which is quite the imbalance. Online messaging is a lot safer than going home with a guy you meet in a car park – you can screen those you chat to and there is no obligation

* The legal department had no problem with me saying this even though Zeus is far more likely to strike me down than Richard Branson.

to meet in person – yet it appears almost all those inquisitive about extramarital sex on this forum were male.

How do we resolve this? We know, evolutionarily speaking, that extramarital affairs can benefit both sexes: males may have more offspring, females can find better genetic qualities and variation for theirs. We also understand that for females there are risks involved in meeting new men/strangers. They may also have more to lose if caught 'cheating'. From an evolutionary perspective, a female losing a male partner due to her infidelity would become vulnerable, her offspring less likely to survive and pass on her genes. Though we're all Strong Independent Women in the modern world, this may be echoed by our cautious behaviour.

Unintentional experiments like the Ashley Madison data breach make it seem that while *some* women are philanderers, they are far less numerous than the male equivalent.

Is that fair?

It allows for the individual – some women enjoy multi-partnering – but makes it less of a female trait *in general*. Could this be related to testosterone level? As well as influencing sex drive, this hormone has been proved in studies to be related to risk-taking behaviours. Heightened testosterone in adults and adolescents has been linked to reduced fear and lower sensitivity to punishment. That's why teenaged boys can be such daredevils – they're swimming in testosterone, while their brain has not fully matured to evaluate danger.

Testosterone plays an important role in human interaction. It can make a person more domineering, more fearless. It's easy to comprehend how such traits would have been beneficial to ancestral *Homo sapiens*. No leap in imagination is required to fathom that when living tribally, being in charge would have meant better quality of life. It makes absolute sense that being respected would result in security and safety. Testosterone is a biological component underlying power, and POWER* is a social dynamic we'll be paying more attention to from here on in.

The most fascinating study I read on testosterone was on the brain's reward system, the dopamine pathway that we discussed earlier. At the University of Cambridge, Michael Lombardo and colleagues tested the level of foetal testosterone in twenty-five boys, then gave them fMRI scans later in childhood. They found that the boys who had been subject to raised testosterone in the womb had an increased sensitivity in their brain's reward system later on. If the dopamine pathway motivates all animals towards the rewards that will benefit them, this study is evidence that heightened testosterone develops a brain that is EVEN MORE AWARE – which would have an evolutionary benefit.

But it might have a modern-day disadvantage. The dopamine pathway is linked to addictive behaviours. Having a more sensitive, goal-orientated brain may have helped our ancient ancestors forage longer, but might now lead to destructive, compulsive behaviours – like Joji enclosed and ultimately flattened by his porn collection.

The reason I find this intriguing is that stress can affect the testosterone levels of a pregnant woman. From a biological perspective, this makes perfect sense – a stressed mother indicates the environment is dangerous or difficult to navigate. Those stressors create hormones within her body that affect how her baby develops, preparing them for a more

---

* You remember, from the title.

precarious life by making extra certain they'll be driven by rewards.

STRESSED MUMS MAKE PORN ADDICTS.

Before you go writing headlines please remember that hormones and genes never predict behaviour; rather they interact with the environment to have an effect on us. An effect that may well be negligible. We are considering these biological attributes not as blueprints that build us, but as interesting considerations. A perspective rather than an answer.

I struggle with the idea that a loading of testosterone creates imbalance between males' and females' desire for sex and risk-taking behaviours because the maths doesn't make sense. If 86 per cent of affair-seekers are heterosexual males, who will they all have sex with? The 14 per cent that are women cannot get around them all, as hard as they might try. Nature has made a silly mistake? Or was this over-enthusiasm of the male necessary for sexual success?

I believe it is worth considering the pressures of social conditioning on sexual expression. I would argue that women have been the victims of social and moral obstructions to their sexuality for centuries because of paternity certainty, and this contributes to the numerical imbalance in studies of affairs and masturbation. But while male sexuality may not have encountered the same stigma and suppression, while the cad and philanderer have been tolerated and celebrated, men have had their share of anti-masturbatory taboos in western culture.

Anti-Fap

Let's start with all the old wives' tales that wanking will make you go blind, wanking will give you hairy palms, wanking leads to shrivelled, pale, wasted lads with no energy, confined to their bedroom. There's a whole heap of propaganda we've all absorbed without really noticing. Did you know cornflakes were invented as a way of quelling masturbatory urges?

Is that why there's a cock on the box?

LOL. John Harvey Kellogg was an American doctor who believed abstinence necessary for health. Kellogg thought exciting foods got people all stimulated and worked up, and that tasteless food was the antidote. He also advocated cutting into penises to prevent erections and putting carbolic acid on clitorises, so a legacy of boring breakfast is the least of his crimes.

The Christian church has a long history of inducing guilt and shame for natural bodily impulses. The word 'onanism' for masturbation comes from Onan in the Bible.* He is a minor character who appears in Genesis and gets killed by God because he spilled his semen on the floor (to be fair, he was trying not to get his sister-in-law pregnant). Any kind of 'wasting' of 'seed' has been interpreted by theologians

* Aka 'My name is God and *this* is My Story.'

as sinful. Masturbation is warned of as 'self-abuse' and a sin against the body. The Bible's main character, Jesus, tells people they mustn't have lusty thoughts, and his disciple Matthew says that adultery, one of the top ten sins, *includes* looking at a woman lustfully.

So porn is adultery?

Yes, if you're married to Matthew. I want to flag now, although it should have been stressed two thousand years ago, that what Jesus and Matt are preaching is impossible. The more you try not to think about sex, the more you'll think about it. Same with anything. Obsessing about NOT LOOKING actually makes it a lot harder not to look. Perhaps this is the root of all the guilt created by religions, we're doomed to failure.

The modern incarnation of the anti-masturbation movement is the NoFappers. 'Fap' is a slang term, an onomatopoeic description of a man's fist moving quickly up and down his penis. NoFappers are a wide community of men who have 'given up' porn and masturbation because of the negative effects they felt it was having on their lives. On the NoFap website or Reddit threads these symptoms are said to include poor concentration, insecurity, depression, general malaise and inability to connect with others, as well as sexual problems, being scared of women and unable to get an erection in 'real' life. It's immediately clear that for some people the amount of time spent watching porn and masturbating was a problem in itself – if you're masturbating for five or six hours a day, where is the room for anything else?

I must add that porn and 'fapping' seem inextricably linked. I have looked through as many threads as I could stomach, searching for anyone masturbating a lot who *didn't* use porn, and couldn't find anyone. There were no guys saying, 'My imagination is out of control, I can't help picturing sexy scenarios.' They all used porn. They all blame porn for the compulsion. The visual aspect of male sexuality is a vital element for us to now consider.

Making Eyes

Visual stimuli and arousal are undoubtedly connected, so let's think about the eye for a moment. Like the wings of birds, eyes have been used as evidence of 'Intelligent Design'. The ~~logic~~ narrative of Intelligent Design claims that the mechanics of living things are far too clever and intricately made to have been thrown together by a random process of cell mutations. Some complete genius must have planned us and put all the bits and pieces together. Someone called God.*

For Intelligent Design theorists, the most persuasive evidence against evolution is eyes and wings. How can *they* evolve gradually? You either have them and can see and fly, or you don't and can't. What use is some wing? What you gonna do with a bit of eye? You're not making any sense, evolution, get out and take your scrawny half-wings with you.**

If you fancy swinging by Fact Town (population: most of us), here we know that the eye did evolve gradually. Beginning with a single light-responsive cell, growing to a patch of cells, eyes have evolved unrelatedly in over fifty distinct ways in very different animals and insects.

Our eyes and the act of seeing are about much more than processing light. There is deep interplay with the brain.

* Bestselling author.
** The wings of sanitary towels – they *were* intelligently designed. You can have that one, God.

What we see will affect our emotions, our sense of safety and sometimes our level of arousal. When I first learned about the senses at school, I considered all this passing of information as being very superficial, e.g. the eye 'looks' and can 'see' a red rectangley thing. A messenger runs from the eyeball into the brain and shouts at all the brain, 'Anyone want a red rectangle?' And the memory says, 'I remember that thing, it's my school blazer!' Then the brain sends a messenger down to the hand telling it to pick up the blazer . . . you get the idea, and that idea is oversimplified.

Now I've learned more about the brain and the different ways it controls our bodily processes, I understand that a human being is an instinctual animal inside a conscious animal. Fear and arousal is not just a great band name, they predispose our deepest, most subconscious emotional needs.

Here's an example of this at work, something universal that'll surely have happened to you unless you're a robot. In a dark room have you ever seen something human-shaped and jolted with fear?

☐ Yes
☐ I have an instruction manual and no feelings

This startle response is easily triggered because our brains do not wait to have all the information before alerting our fight-or-flight circuitry. The visual cortex registers any abnormality as possible danger and, rather than waiting for our conscious mind to ascertain if it's an intruder or Henry the Hoover with a hat on, we react. Our glands provide the adrenaline we'd need in a worst-case scenario. Sugar is released from our cells to fuel fleeing or defending ourselves. This startle response might seem a touch histrionic, but it kept our ancient ancestors alive. Anyone dopey perished; their reactions were too slow. The shadow became a hungry wolf. The strange face wasn't Henry, it was the girl from *The Ring*, and now you can't continue your genes because she's eaten them.

Human beings have physiological reactions that bypass our rational selves.

Sexual arousal can be like that fear response. We don't consciously command it. We don't see things we intellectually recognise as sexy and instruct our genitals to react appropriately: 'Quickly, there's Nelly Furtado, get a boner!' The slightest shadow of sexual suggestion can send blood to the genitals. Studies show that vaginas lubricate and penises engorge in response to many things, even when we have no conscious desire to have sex. You may not need a scientist to tell you this, you may have noticed from your own experience of having a penis or a vulva and vagina that they have a life of their own. Twitching, saluting and responding to the world and people around you in a very different rhythm to your sane self. Like a sleeping dog raising his ear to a distant noise, 'Hello?' says our body. 'What's this?' 'This' for me today was an old man on the tube wearing the same aftershave as my ex. *puking emoji*

It's common to be surprised and/or ashamed by some of what arouses us because it diverges from what we *choose* to be aroused by. But the ability to *be* aroused is an animal behaviour that pre-dates our developed consciousness. Our reproductive system is trip-wired, it's excruciatingly sensitive because our ancestors who were reliably aroused had more children. We carry their 'getting horny at a stick that looks like a woman' genes.

It is these genes and instinctual responses, central to our survival, that are being hijacked by modern technology. You may not be a robot, but you still have buttons and pornography is *intended* to press them. Human beings are not intelligently designed but pornography is. And millennia of product testing and perfecting have already been undertaken. From cave vaginas to sexy pottery to Xhamster.*

The evolutionary biologist Stephen Jay Gould used the term 'spandrels' to describe characteristics which are a by-product of evolution, rather than being directly selected for. This applies perfectly to the human predilection for porn. Humans evolved an interest in naked people, in sexual signals, in seeking sexual pleasure. But those physiological systems which made us reproductively successful must now contend with the huge abundance of sexual stimuli that surround us on billboards and TV screens and Instagram and, of course in pornography.

Porn is like doughnuts. We didn't evolve around doughnuts, they played no part in the moulding of our species, but our predilection for fat and sugar means that they're delicious, irresistible, and some people eat too many of them. Some people eat so much food that it makes them dangerously ill . . . this is not a problem our prehistoric relatives had to contend with.

Is porn making us unhealthy too? That's certainly the opinion of NoFappers and some feminists, but their

* What is so wonderful about the publishing industry is that every person who proofread, edited or fact-checked this book suggested I add a footnote to explain that Xhamster is a porn site. It is the third or fourth most popular porn site in the world, but it turns out everyone at Faber & Faber is still masturbating to the imagery in Plath and Hughes.

approaches differ. The former focus on how porn affects the consumer, and we'll be analysing studies testing those effects later. Feminists are less concerned with the mental wellbeing and reliable erections of frequent porn users and much more worried about their view of women.

Let's critique your classic feminist anti-porn statement.

Susan Brownmiller stated in 1975 that porn depicts women as 'anonymous, panting playthings, adult toys, dehumanised objects to be used, abused, broken and discarded'. Gail Dines described the sex in porn as 'making hate to women'. Andrea Dworkin believed that the essential truth of pornography is that 'any violation of a woman's body can become sex for men'.

These are strong accusations and if you watch a lot of porn, I don't know how you feel about them. There's an accepted wisdom within second-wave feminism that anyone who watches a great deal of hardcore porn cannot help but have reduced respect for women, another theory we'll be examining further. But first let us query the usefulness of anti-porn sentiments that assume everyone watching it is heterosexual and a man.

Hard-on vs Wide-on

If you had to guess, having learned what we have about sex differences on dating websites and campus pick-ups, would you say that more men than women watch porn?

☐ Yes
☐ I said yes, I'm not an idiot.

You're correct! Using Pornhub's 2017 statistics I can tell you that 74 per cent of their users worldwide are male. That's a big discrepancy. Now, I would love to waste a few hours of your life telling you my *personal* theories about why women might be less interested in hardcore porn, from its focus on thrusty penetrative sex (unlikely to make most women cum) to our ability to create better fantasies in our minds, but the findings of this next experiment are a better use of our time.

In 2009 Meredith Chivers attached willing men and women to machines that measured their genital responses to visual stimuli. The subjects were shown homosexual, heterosexual and lesbian porn, solo masturbation and finally bonobo sex. With each video they had to rate how stimulated it made them feel, while their genital responses were also measured.

The results were quite surprising. Chivers found that men's physical arousal matched what they self-reported. Straight men got hard at straight porn and lesbian porn, homosexual men got hard at gay porn – this is called 'category-specific arousal'. The men knew what would turn them on, and it did! While we know that men can have unwanted, unpredictable erections – on buses, at job interviews, while asleep – the erection is still a reliable signal of direct arousal.

The female subjects in Chivers's study demonstrated genital responses to *all* the categories.

The women often reported that they didn't feel aroused. They said, 'No, the gay sex isn't turning me on; the bonobo sex leaves me dry.' Meanwhile, below the belt, they had increased blood flow; they were lubricating. The study found that women were not becoming significantly more aroused at the films they did like than the ones they didn't. They lubricated as much for the bonobo bonking as they did for the lesbians.

Theories about this are valuable to debate. It's been suggested that in a chicken-and-egg-type scenario, men may get 'turned on' by the feeling of a growing erection. It grows when you think about sex; when it grows, you think about sex. But this is not the case with vaginal engorgement.

We explored earlier how a female has much to consider about a male's 'fitness' and suitability before mating. It is argued that evolution has put the brakes on her mental arousal process so that she isn't blindsided. Never so horny that she forgets to consider her safety, and the health and resources of her mate. Perhaps this is the sexual reticence we saw reflected in Clark and Hatfield's university studies. I'm a woman, I consider myself a throbbing centre of vibrant sexuality – but I also would never go back to a stranger's flat. I hate being approached by men, I don't want to speak to them and I have never, ever wanted to sleep with one I've just met. I'm not saying that's true for all women, I'm not saying I'm representative. And actually, I hate this theory, 'maybe our bodies have slowed our sexual response so we can have better children'. It suggests we're frigid *and* maternal, yuck.

Another theory about the results is that the women *were* aroused, they just didn't admit it. The argument is that society's judgements towards sexual women have led to suppression. That biology has endowed women with a plastic and easily triggered arousal mechanism but we're in denial about it. So we shake our heads, 'I'm a good girl, I feel nothing,' even when we're engorging like crazy.

The theory I found most arresting was that vaginal lubrication might have evolved as a self-protection mechanism. Chivers postulated that 'ancestral women who did not show an automatic vaginal response to sexual cues may have been more likely to experience injuries that resulted in illness, infertility, or even death subsequent to unexpected or unwanted vaginal penetration, and thus would be less likely to have passed on this trait to their offspring'.

Of course we have to wonder about how much rape/ forced sex was involved throughout our species' development . . . it's not a pleasant thing to think about. In other animals, we know forced copulation is abundant, but when it's ducks or giraffes we call it a mating strategy. At what point did *Homo sapiens* become 'non-animal' enough for this mating strategy to become a socially unacceptable crime? Why has the civilising of humanity over the last few thousand years not wiped it out completely?

While it's very clever and useful in protecting us, I think it's annoying that the female genitals lubricate without their owners necessarily feeling aroused. This makes it easier for women to have unsatisfying love lives. We can have sex when we're not really into it, not turned on enough yet. This automatic lubrication might be preventing a revolution in how we understand female pleasure. Imagine if men had a pre-boner stage that was just rigid enough to get it in, but didn't feel particularly nice—

Like a shoe horn, but in my dick?

Thank you for understanding so perfectly. It's another example of a sex mismatch. The female body has a response to sexual stimuli that is not yet arousal, something that male-bodied people might not understand.

It preoccupies me that the male body's sexual response is less complicated because throughout prehistory they have had less to fear from female partners. Women have evolved to compute danger, and some men find that idea offensive.

When I'm on tour by myself I've had trouble with men offering me lifts or wanting to walk me back to my hotel, men who are expressing a wish to protect me or reassure me. They mean well but they don't understand that *they* are the danger. There was a man in Southend, he wanted to drive me home and I politely said no. He didn't understand why I wouldn't get in his car, why I wouldn't trust him. He said, 'I'm not a murderer,' which is exactly what a murderer would say. When I left the theatre he was waiting in his car in an alley, pulled out and followed me. He was so affronted, and I have to wonder if he knew how scary he was being?

If I'd got into his car and been assaulted the whole world would've said, 'Why'd you get in his car? You're so stupid.' And I'd say, 'Oh, he really promised I could trust him.' When bad things happen to women the crime is always examined for the victim's culpability. Why did she wear that? Walk that route? Not lock her door?

Even though it's only a minority of men who are violent or predatory, I don't know if men realise that girls are trained our entire lives to minimise the danger from you – and blamed if we don't. I think it's worth bearing in mind how much this might be shaping our sexual response.

When reading about porn, this thing about men being more 'visual' comes up repeatedly. What does that mean? Magnetic resonance imaging experiments have been conducted in search of sex differences between men's and women's brains. Researchers from Emory University in the US showed people sexual pictures and monitored their brain activity. They reported that men showed greater activation of the amygdala, a centre for emotion and motivation.

The results were used as evidence that images stimulated the men more. We've already debated how reliable it is to assess brain activity in this way; there's a huge amount of variation between brains and no study has ever found a clear, down-the-line gender divide. It's obvious why a 'men are more visual' argument is tempting, because then Pornhub's users being 74 per cent male makes complete sense. But why would evolution have made males more alert to the female body than vice versa?

Well I'll tell you. In response to the female human's concealed ovulation and constant sexual signalling the male human has had to become hypersensitive to the physical cues that signal fertility. WARNING – this is going to sound incredibly un-PC and shallow, but a flat stomach and pert breasts are visual signals that a woman has not already conceived. Thinness and youth are attractive not simply because of the fashion industry and glossy magazines, but because our ancestors used them as indicators of a woman being impregnatable. I'm very sorry, evolution did not care about body positivity and loving ourselves as we are, it only cared about sperm competition and getting everyone up the duff.

Breasts and bottoms are fetishised in our culture, and the biological explanation underlying this is that these fat deposits on a post-adolescent body are an assurance that this person's offspring will survive in times of difficulty and famine. The female body breaks down fat deposits to breastfeed her children, which is a) amazing and b) described more fully in my book *Animal*, which you should read if you haven't already.

The curves of a female body tell a story about that woman's health and fertility, a story which transfixes straight men. Evolution programmed them that way. The waist-to-hip ratio (WHR) has been confirmed by scientists as a reliable indicator of a woman's level of oestrogen. Women described as the most attractive in studies had a WHR of 0.7, and women with 0.7 WHR were found to conceive more easily. I find this phenomenal and infuriating in equal measure.

It is difficult to relate this to the modern world – we know a person's worth is not connected to the shape of their body – but the reason certain bodies are sexy is because they are appealing to the ancient breeders in us.

The reason that women might not need to be so visually aware of men is because men's fertility window is open for longer. While male fertility does decline with age, they do not have the brutal cut-off kindly served to women by the menopause. Men can father children into their old age, which means their youth is less of a factor in being an attractive mate. It is still a factor, women do assess health, youth and strength in a sexual partner, but in nature, in terms of genetic success those visual signals are less important in a male mate than in a female.

While I feel this is drastically, drastically unfair, we'll find balance in this inequality when exploring how important wealth and resources are in male courtship later in the section 'Ha Ha Ha, We're All Screwed' on dating.

It's worth noting that if you're a man who fancies men, or a woman attracted to women, you're still assessing all these things – youth, health, body shape. Even though we consciously know that same-sex mating cannot create children, the attraction is driven by entirely the same circuitry involved with lust and pair bonding. Writing this book I have wondered if it was concealed ovulation that freed human sexuality. When we evolved out of bright-bottom displays and signalled fertility, our species was no longer dependent on male- or female-specific cues for arousal. The sexuality that has sprawled since is much more fluid in all of us. Maybe we're *all* millennials now!?

Speaking of fluidity, it might interest you to learn that more and more women are watching pornography. According to Pornhub's statistics, in 2017 the most searched-for term was 'porn for women' and female users are growing across every territory (apart from Russia).

If we trust these numbers, though women still comprise a markedly lower percentage of porn consumers, the fact the figure is rising could be taken as evidence that culture affects sexual expression. That as we become more interested in, accepting and supportive of female sexuality, women themselves become less inhibited. Or it could reflect the fact that the more ubiquitous something becomes, the less shocking or shameful it seems.

That is a very sex-positive view. There are feminists who would counter-argue that the increase in women looking at porn is due to young women and girls feeling pressurised to perform a certain way for their partners. That they're watching it for instruction rather than as a source of genuine pleasure. Even if a woman was to say, 'Excuse me, feminism, but I really enjoy watching porn,' feminism might say, 'You just *think* you enjoy it because the patriarchy has won.'

I don't know how to disprove that. It's like when Freud used to tell people, 'You've got an Oedipus complex, you want to murder your father and marry your mother,' and they'd say, 'No I haven't,' and Freud would smoke a cigar and say, 'That's because you've repressed your desires, that means they are even deeper within you.'

We can all agree that human beings have a gross, weird and wide-ranging sexuality. What I'd like us to investigate now is whether the porn people watch is a reflection of what they're into . . . or whether it can CHANGE it?

You Are What You Watch

Humans can be sexually aroused by absolutely anything. From women eating excrement to your wife banging another guy, from ugly feet to popping balloons. Fetishes and pre-dilections are not new, but the fresh element, the unknown quantity, is the internet. If sexuality is a plastic, mouldable force – if it is nurture over nature – how worried should we be about the porn we've seen?

The first study I ever read about porn was conducted by behavioural psychologists Rachman and Hodgson in the late 1960s. They showed male participants photographs of old boots followed by pictures of nude women, all the while measuring their penile tumescence. After repeating this many times, they found the men were beginning to get increased blood flow, aka erections, when they saw the old boots. It's a sort of Pavlovian sexual conditioning. The men's bodies started to associate boots with sexual stimuli, the boots became sexual signals themselves . . . this suggests that porn can change what we get aroused by, doesn't it? The mind leaps; does this mean that stumbling on child porn will make you a paedophile? Does watching violent porn mean you'll need to strangle your lovers to get it up? This study confirms everything we worry about.

Let's address these worries one at a time.

Concern One: Porn encourages rapists. Probably the first thing I ever heard about porn and, having felt as I did as a young adult, I believed it without qualification. 'Men are so stupid,' I would've told you. 'They see women in porn pretending to like certain things and will go out and force other women to do them.' There are absolutely cases of rapists who have used pornography – or blamed pornography. Serial killer Ted Bundy said that his sadistic crimes were all the fault of violent porn. He claimed that he started with softcore magazines and was consumed to 'keep craving something harder, which gives you a greater sense of excitement, until you reach a point where the pornography only goes so far'.

That's the root of our anxiety about how porn might affect someone right there. He starts off a wholesome lad admiring the front cover of *Jugs* and ends up brutally murdering thirty women.

Rationally, we know that it's not common for a porn user to descend into murderous rampaging, purely because there are so many men watching porn and so few rampaging murderers. Just as horror movies or computer games might influence an impressionable few with destructive or fatal consequences, though it's a sorry outcome the films and games cannot themselves be blamed.

Some heartening statistics: if porn encouraged rape, then we'd expect rape rates to rise along with the availability of the internet. The 'Porn Up, Rape Down' study conducted at Northwestern University School of Law found that the incidence of reported rape *declined* by 85 per cent in the United States after technology made porn freely available. The author of the study, Anthony D'Amato, argues that porn has a cathartic effect and that its availability reduces the likelihood of rape rather than encouraging it. D'Amato found that states with the lowest rates of internet access (Kentucky, Minnesota, West Virginia and Arkansas) all bucked the trend and had suffered a 53 per cent increase in sexual crimes over the period studied, while the states with the best internet access (Alaska, Colorado, New Jersey and Washington) showed a 27 per cent decrease.

While this correlation does not definitively prove the influence of porn on its viewers one way or another, it's important to flag that many governments (especially right-wing ones) have attempted to prove that porn makes rapists but have been unable to. Rapists definitely use porn, but then so does everybody else. It's an area that needs more study. Ideally, I'd be given five hundred or so sets of identical twins and two islands, where the boys will be separated and have indistinguishable upbringings, with one difference: island A has internet access; island B has no wifi, just board games and knitting patterns. After fifty years I'll tell you the crime stats. Thank you for not telling Amnesty on me.

Concern Two: Porn makes men disrespect women.

Too easy for me to believe. Before I started researching this book, I'd have sworn on my life that porn was to blame for much of modern sexism. Here are some hot opinions from past Sara: for a straight man, the abundance of porn reinforces that women are all for his sexual consumption. Our worth depends on whether he considers us fuckable or not. He cannot take women seriously because he has seen too many with spunk on their face.

So, there *is* evidence that porn use influences young men's attitudes. In a study from 2014 conducted by Gert Martin Held from the University of Copenhagen, random participants were approached by mail, asked to watch a thirty-minute violent pornography film and then to fill out a questionnaire about how much porn they'd seen before, how much they enjoyed the porn they'd just been shown, and then some leading questions about how realistic they found porn to be and others relating to the treatment of women. The study found that men with a higher past porn use were more likely to support violence against women, more likely to believe it was occasionally justified. Even more relevant, those reporting higher arousal from the porn they'd just watched were more likely to agree that giving women a thump now and then was okay. The study concludes that men may learn a sexual script from watching porn that they believe applies in the real world, which is cause for concern. This study only comprised two hundred people though, which is pretty small.

For comparison, twenty-eight thousand people completed the University of Chicago's General Social Survey between 1974 and 2010, and they found no connection between porn use and sexism. The difficulty with extrapolating from these results – calm down, guys, there's nothing to panic about – is that they only asked if participants had seen one or more porn videos in the past year – so there is no way to discern between a heavy porn user and someone who saw one at a hotel they worked at and then it was 9/11. I guess we can be reassured that watching one porn movie doesn't turn people into raging sexists.

I am very interested in a study by Australian academic Alan McKee. He interviewed a hundred men, asking things like 'Should women be allowed to hold powerful positions? Should they be able to work outside the home? Can they have abortions?' and the results showed that being provincial, right-wing and middle-aged were far stronger predictors of sexist attitudes than the amount of porn watched. Lucky that ain't the majority of our politicians, right, guys?

Concern Three: Porn encourages paedophilia.

I'm gonna be honest with you, paedophilia is where my attempts at liberalism and 'let's examine the evidence, not our emotions' goes out the window. Some people film children being raped, some people pay to watch it. All of those people are breaking the law and I hope they die in prison. I am not considering paedophilia as part of the pornographic genre, because it is criminality. I know there is much to explore in this area of human depravity but that is not for this book.

I'm sticking to the legal parts of filmed sex but, bearing this in mind . . . if porn can make you get a semi for an old boot, does watching porn make men attracted to younger women?

Whether porn encourages it or not, the attraction is there. There's an abundance of youth-intimating categories on tube sites. Looking at YouPorn now, both 'teen' and 'college' are offered on the homepage, with over a hundred thousand videos grouped within each category.

In every age bracket, from teenage boys to octogenarians, 'babysitter porn' is one of the most viewed categories. This tells us something about human sexuality – not that young-looking girls are fanciable, we know that already, they're fertile, we're over it. What interests me here is the power dynamic. Babysitter porn is the story of a young woman, vulnerable, in the house of an adult man – a dubious fantasy. Unless some of the films are about babysitters fucking the teenage boys they're looking after? Either way there is an imbalance in power, and what has surprised me, from my position of naivety, is how often porn works like this. It seems no one is interested in sex between equals, it's all teacher and student, stepmom and son, drug smuggler and customs officer. There's something about dominating and being dominated inherent in sexual interplay. This makes me reflect differently on Angela Carter's notion of all sex being an exchange of power. There is clearly huge sexual potential in power imbalance, something that may be fun in fantasy but can be problematic in real life.

An argument for how persuasive porn can be in influencing sexual tastes involves pubic hair. There are a lot of bald fannies in porn, and that's weird, huh? Pubic hair is a signifier of adolescence. It shows that a person is reaching fertility. Why would there be a fashion for women to emulate being pre-fertile? Why would men find pubelessness sexy? You should be aware that the trend for bald fannies has spread into the real world; lots of women choose to have most or all of their pubes waxed or shaved. Does this mean that we can't help but want to be what we see on our screens? Is it proof that women are so entrenched in being attractive to men that they'll spend time and endure pain to look a certain way? If a man has a preference for women with no pubes, does it mean he is attracted to pre-pubescent girls?

There are stories of young men growing up and then being 'surprised' when they discovered real-life women had pubic hair, but I've not been able to find anyone who actually experienced this. The truth is that while there are plenty of hairless pussies, there is a rainforest of unshavens and anyone who is watching porn regularly has seen everything. Some interesting evidence *against* the influence of porn on young people is that all recent surveys have reported that up to 90 per cent of men prefer their partner to have pubic hair. I'm sure that the pubic hair thing is a trend, like with eyebrows. Bushy one decade, over-plucked the next. People like to deviate from the norm until we've all deviated into conformity and back we go. Now that grandmas are getting Hollywoods, of course granddaughters are rebelling with the natural look.

On the question of male attraction to children on the cusp of puberty, this is called hebephilia and is much more common than paedophilia. The evolutionary theory about hebephilia is that it relates to sperm competition and paternity certainty. A man might be attracted to a girl who has not yet reached sexual maturity because he knows she is not pregnant, she cannot be cuckolding him. If he can form a pair bond with a younger mate and then guard her, he might effectively ensure his paternity certainty when she does reach fertility. It's an ugly theory for our modern sensibility, but younger women are usually smaller and easier to dominate. It used to be traditional all over the world for girls to be married at eleven or twelve. In tens of countries it still is.

Just to be clear, I am not supporting or excusing this. I think the majority of men who feel these types of feelings would not act upon them, would actually feel very guilty. In 2008 sex researcher Ray Blanchard attached phallometric testing devices to 881 penises and measured their arousal in response to their owners viewing photographs of naked people. He found that in both gay and straight men, while they might verbally deny attraction, hebephilia was relatively common. The majority of these men claimed not to be attracted to younger people, yet had a physiological reaction to their photos.

This is where socialisation is important. We learn what is 'right' and 'wrong' from the people around us. We police ourselves, even in private.

One of the worries I expressed earlier was whether porn was a slippery slope – you begin watching loving couples respectfully pleasuring each other and from there you slide unavoidably, watching increasingly violent stuff, until you can only get it up for the most brutal sex. The received wisdom is that porn is becoming alarmingly aggressive because easily bored consumers are demanding it. If this concerns you, the study 'Harder and Harder' published by the *Journal of Sex Research* in 2018 might put your mind at rest. Sociologists from McGill University in Canada studied the most popular videos on Pornhub, assessed the aggressive content in a random selection and found it wasn't true that viewers preferred aggressive content, or that the content was becoming more aggressive over time. They actually found, when measuring the length of time spent on visible aggression (biting, slapping, choking, etc.) in these videos, that violence was a declining trend. And films where the female performer seemed to be enjoying herself were far more popular (in views and 'likes') than any in which women simulated or experienced distress.

We can't help but worry.* Even when I read a study like this one, I am still anxious about the people who do like the choking. Even if it's a small proportion of young people wanting to try extreme sex acts or play out violent sexual scripts, I worry about the ramifications for them if it goes

---

* I got my mum to proofread a draft of this and she said, 'Just because they haven't proved it yet doesn't mean it's not having a terrible effect.' That's something many people can't help but believe.

wrong. The study uses words like 'habituation' – people get used to seeing violence and it becomes normalised. That does worry me, and it appears difficult to quantify. There is a multitude of studies examining how watching hardcore porn might change how the viewer interacts with the real world, but unfortunately there are so many other factors in somebody's life, it's impossible to say definitively what causes an opinion or a behaviour. Until I get my porn-island twin study off the ground, that is.

I have been seeking a study about empathy and sexual arousal. I want a clear answer to my question from right at the beginning: does being turned on make someone care a bit less? Something I have experienced personally from sex with men is that when they are very aroused, they are also very motivated to orgasm. Motivated is a polite term, but it's why stopping just before or during sex can be difficult to orchestrate. There are all sorts of reasons that someone might want sex to stop, from feeling nauseous to being in pain or any number of psychological reasons. When I was much younger, a teenager, I used to have a game I played where, to check if a guy was 'good', I'd pretend to be dead during sex to see if he stopped.

Stop judging me. There was logic to this at the time. I believed that when a man was sensitive enough to worry – 'she's gone limp, she's not moving, I'll check if she's alright' – then I would know he was worth my time. But no one ever stopped, so I quit doing it. It was a horrid feeling, but I recognised a psychopathy in aroused males. A line was crossed where I mattered less than their orgasm. I don't think I'm alone in this experience, feeling like someone is using your body to masturbate rather than having sex with you. And

I know for a fact some men don't believe they should be expected to 'stop' past a certain point, because there are Reddit threads thousands of posts long that *should* be titled 'How to Be a Rapist and Not Even Know It'.

Extending this outward, this is my theory for what happens with porn. I believe/hope that most non-aroused individuals would tell you they believe all porn performers should work safely, in supportive environments; that they should be able to choose what the job entails; their willingness and happiness should be of the utmost concern; they should be well remunerated. But I think once they've got a hard-on, the boner wants what it wants. The masturbator is not so concerned about ethics and workers' rights. I've looked for proof of this and the study that comes closest is called 'The Heat of the Moment: The Effect of Sexual Arousal on Sexual Decision Making'.

Professors Dan Ariely and George Loewenstein assembled a group of men, got half of them to masturbate and then compared the groups' answers to questions like 'Would you encourage a date to drink?' and 'How attractive is this sixty-year-old man?' The experimenters were focusing on three areas: 1) openness to sexual exploration, 2) willingness to coerce or manipulate to get sex, and 3) willingness to have 'unsafe' sex.

Numbers 2 and 3, while morally reprehensible/illegal and stupid, actually make good evolutionary sense. The paper states that 'most appetite systems in the brain, including hunger and thirst, are designed to increase motivation during times of opportunity'.

It's harder not to eat a doughnut when a doughnut's in front of you. I get it. Pretty terrifying when another person's body is the doughnut though, eh? I'm reminded of a section of tosspot's bragfest dating manual *The Game* by Neil Strauss. A Pick-Up Artist (PUA) is informing a group of men that they should never lie to a woman in order to seduce her, that lying is cheating. The only two acceptable lies, he goes on, are 'I'll only rub it around your ass' and 'I promise I won't finish in your mouth.' I don't know if you've ever had someone insert their penis or ejaculate where you don't want them to, but I have, and it's pretty fucking horrible. Not just the sensation, which might be painful or sickening, but the disregard. Have you ever had something stolen, a wallet, a laptop, and felt an outrage – BUT THAT WAS MINE? It's like that, but with your body.

The Game was published nearly fifteen years ago, and I wonder if it would receive the same reception now. I wonder if that line would be found as funny? Or if I am very much the wrong crowd?

The theory of the sexual decision-making study was that when aroused, participants would be more likely to behave in ways which would increase their chances of having sex, which makes complete sense. You'd be most ready for dinner after laying the table too, I expect. The results of their questionnaires found that the masturbating men did show more interest in sexual variety and frustration with 'just kissing'. They also showed a higher likelihood of finding a twelve-year-old attractive and of contemplating having sex with an animal. When it came to the morally questionable behaviours, the aroused men said they would be more likely to pretend they loved a woman to get sex and to keep trying to have sex after a woman had said no. The last question was about drugging a woman to have sex with her WHICH IS

THE INCORRECT WORDING THAT IS NOT SEX
IT IS RAPE and the aroused men were five times more
likely to say they would do that. So let's all throw humanity
in the bin, shall we? What, there's more study? Oh good. The
last section, about using condoms, found that the turned-on
men were less likely to, so it's lucky no one is ever aroused
when making that decision, isn't it?

I think this study is fascinating, but it's also incredibly
limited as it only measured the responses of thirty-five men.
This area of human psychology needs a lot more focus. This
is important stuff! The experimenters themselves note that
'self-insight' is vital. If men know that they are less likely
to use contraception or more likely to drug someone, then
they can make sure they always have condoms on them or
take themselves straight to prison just in case. If men knew
they might make less empathetic decisions when aroused,
couldn't that help them check themselves: 'How will I feel
about this tomorrow?'

Addicted to Porn

Concern Four: Porn is addictive.

Here's an interesting fact for ya: men ejaculate more sperm, and better-quality sperm, when they are watching porn than when they are using their imagination. That's why fertility clinics give men stuff to masturbate to, because it improves the potency of the orgasm. Porn tricks the male body into thinking it is *really* trying to get someone pregnant. The power of visual images changes how the body responds. A small study in 2015 also tested the Coolidge effect and found that new porn stars, those not previously seen by the participants, resulted in larger ejaculate volume, higher motility and a quicker ejaculation. The male body is practising sperm competition, even when all by itself.

Another experiment on male ejaculate, which I found so interesting, showed that male masturbatory orgasms trigger only a quarter of the prolactin that is released during copulation. So an orgasm with someone else will make a man feel sleepier than one he has alone. Why has nature done this? We talked earlier of the theory that men get sleepy after sex to stop them inhibiting the female, so she can leave and have sex again – can it really be that?! What interests me is that without the prolactin, masturbatory orgasms will be less satisfying. And perhaps this explains why often people report feeling dissatisfied by masturbating to porn, or a bit empty, or low afterwards. They were expecting a more satisfying hormonal hit, and didn't get it.

Prolactin is not the addictive element of sex and orgasms, although it affects the pleasant satiation feeling we get afterwards. Addiction is always related to dopamine – the neurotransmitter we discussed earlier. We already know how it helps us achieve goals that aid survival, so of course it's integral to sex. The moment a person looks at an erotic image, the reward system in their brain switches on. This circuit includes the ventral striatum and orbitofrontal cortex, both of which help elicit the good feelings you get when you do something rewarding. People's brains learn, over time, that porn is a reliable way to seek good feelings. But while someone will get a satisfying hit of dopamine when watching porn for the first time, they will need something novel, newer, harder, stranger to get the same effect again. Like a drug addict seeking a bigger and bigger hit. The porn watcher might not realise that they're bored with the kind of porn they've seen before because it's no longer stimulating the reward circuitry in their brain.

People don't tend to watch the same porn over and over again for this reason. It wouldn't get you off in the same way. With some people this pushes them to watch all kinds of things they wouldn't normally – things they wouldn't identify as their sexual preference. It could be amputees or very young or old people, or, you know, horrific violence and aggression. I worry, along with the penis size thing, about what this is doing to the inner life of men. Do they feel shame if they cannot share what they watch with their loved ones? They can't announce to the family WhatsApp group that they've started wanking to bestiality.

Mum has left the conversation

And the really interesting thing, or if not interesting, very relevant, is that the worse someone feels about porn, the more they do it. The trouble with behaviours that stimulate dopamine response is that when someone tries to cut down, tells themselves they shouldn't, they become more obsessed, fixate upon it, end up doing it more. This is why Jesus's advice about not thinking lusty thoughts was so unhelpful.

This is also the problem we have with educating young people about the effects of porn – if we simply pump them full of shame, they won't be able to have a healthy relationship with masturbation and they might be even more isolated within their habits.

I've been interviewing people about their relationship with pornography to help me understand it, and my friend Matt told me the best story. When he was thirteen he knew his dad kept porn magazines in the boot of his car. One day when Matt had a friend over, they snuck into the garage and stole some. Matt loved the women and their bodies, and he decorated his bedroom with posters and centrefolds. Fully naked women, arching and curving and holding their vulvas open to be viewed. Matt felt adamant that when his parents came home, he'd defend his new wallpaper. This was how he wanted his room to look; he would insist on his right to enjoy these beautiful sexy women. He knew his mum would flip out, but when she got back she didn't react. She looked at his room quietly for a bit, then told him, 'I'm so glad you've done this.' She said, 'Before you and your brother were born I used to have pictures of penises up everywhere, I really loved to look at them – but I was worried that it would make you guys uncomfortable. But now that you've put your pictures up, I can put my penis pictures up again.' His mum went downstairs, and Matt hurriedly took the posters down because he didn't want his friends coming over and seeing penises everywhere and thinking that his mum loved dicks.

This story made me so happy, I thought that was such incredible parenting. Matt's mum didn't make him feel bad that he enjoyed looking at women's bodies, she used an empathy exercise to make him realise why the reverse would make him uncomfortable. She didn't give him a guilt complex, she made him consider other people's feelings.

I asked Matt if he and his mum had discussed this as adults. When he reminded her of it, she told him she had walked downstairs worrying, 'Where the heck am I going to find loads of penis pictures?'

It makes me think a lot about how I handled the situation with Nicholas. When he told me that he got more excitement or more satisfaction from pornography, I didn't know about dopamine in the brain, I didn't know about reward centres and novelty. And actually I don't know that it would've helped if I had, but he did promise to stop watching porn and then he failed and felt worse, and I did too. If porn is creating a problem in a person's life or in their relationship and making them feel bad, what should we do?

Gary Wilson is one of the most famous anti-porn educators and his TED talks have had millions of views. He has a website, yourbrainonporn.com, if you would like to investigate his work. Wilson explores issues like male anxiety about penis size and body shape, but also how porn may desensitise sexual responses and lead to men becoming less aroused by their real-life partners.

Much has been made of the relationship between porn use and erectile dysfunction, and we must be sceptical of some of the science. I read on an anti-fap website that internet porn has caused a 3,000 per cent rise in impotence, which is hugely shocking, the kind of stat that makes the villagers want to storm the castle with burning crucifixes. But I read elsewhere that the huge rise can largely be attributed to a change in how they asked the question, the difference between 'Do you have difficulty achieving an erection?' and 'Have you *ever* experienced difficulty getting an erection?'

Several studies have only found weak links between porn use and erectile dysfunction, but that doesn't mean that watching a lot of porn has no effect on a man's sexual responses. I am not denying that quitting porn like the NoFappers might have a wonderful array of side effects. For example, the dopamine circuitry ceases to be hijacked and perhaps men can live more in the moment. I interviewed two men who considered themselves to have been 'sex addicts', who said excessive porn use had been part of their 'problem'. They were both evangelical about getting porn out of their lives and credited this with feeling more 'present' and having healthy (very sexy) relationships. Just as in other forms of addiction, some bodies, some personality types fall prey to certain stimuli more than others. How much porn is too much differs from man to man. One thing that really struck me about both of my interviewees was that watching hours of porn every day was isolating them from absolutely everybody in their life. They were alone.

While I worry about the damage to men's relationships and their self-esteem, let us jump to Concern Five: Porn makes men sad about their penis size.

Penis Power

There's a very wide representation of female bodies in mainstream porn, but all male porn stars have massive dicks. This is an important detail. It is non-negotiable, it is what the men are there for.

What do we read into this? Firstly, as we have already ascertained that across all cultures it is mainly men watching the porn – these big dicks are there for them. While most straight men might not consciously acknowledge it, might not admit aloud on a stag do, 'I much prefer watching a large-phallused dude going at it,' the videos they buy and click on confirm that preference.

The most famous male porn stars have always been the most generously endowed, like the previously ~~celebrated~~ mentioned Ron Jeremy (nine and three-quarter inches) and John Holmes (he never confirmed a measurement but was estimated at twelve or thirteen inches). The average penis in porn is between eleven and twelve inches long, which is considerably bigger than average – in fact it's double. If everyone we saw on TV was ten feet tall, perhaps we would be discussing why we all have insecurity about our height . . . but the reason we don't is because—

Humans aren't ten feet tall.

Okay, seven feet tall then. Basketball players are much taller than the average person, because being tall is of benefit to them – it makes it easier to score baskets. It doesn't make all men wish they were seven foot. With porn, being well hung is *believed* to make men better at sex. But while this might add to male insecurity, it is the result of our species' obsession with penis size rather than the cause of it.

There are many olden references to the importance of a big peen, pre-dating internet porn by hundreds of years. Leonardo da Vinci claimed that 'the woman likes the penis as large as possible, while the man desires the opposite of the woman's womb. Neither gets their wish,' and this brings us to another Conundrum of Heterosexuality™. Unlike Tiresias we cannot experience intercourse in a different body, so we guess. Men say that they enjoy a better sexual sensation from a tighter orifice, which makes sense physiologically: tightness can provide more stimulation.

There are also the important connotations of a small vagina: virginity, youth, sexual inexperience. As we have already explored, choosing sexual inexperience or virginity in a mate is a way to ensure paternity certainty. Doesn't this explain the prevalence of 'tight'-orientated dirty talk in porn? Alongside the 'you're so deep' tropes relating back to sperm competition, it's very common for women to offer 'my pussy is so tight' or a penetrating man to groan in appreciation about how 'small and tight' a woman feels. This has to do with sperm competition too.

The opposite, a large, non-tight vagina, is mostly a myth. The vagina is an elastic organ, it stretches then resumes its original shape. A woman may give birth to a baby and then, a few months later, find it as tricky as ever to insert her tampon. But despite this, an insult for women is to be called 'baggy' or 'loose', with the mistaken idea that this physical state is synonymous with experience.

Let's think about Donald Trump's penis again. In 2018 Stormy Daniels described the president's dick as a little mushroom. She said it looked like the toadstool character from Mario Kart (not pictured, can't afford it). People who dislike Trump rejoiced. The immature rejoiced. The most powerful man in the world emasculated by a porn star. Because I am a boring old fart, I did not enjoy this. This humiliation of a human based not on his (misogynist, racist) politics but on his private parts. PRIVATE. Not tell-the-news-about-them. What do things like this teach young men? It doesn't matter who you are, or what you achieve, just don't have a risotto ingredient for a penis. I don't worry about President Trump's feelings per se, but I do worry about men's anxiety about their own genitals.

And what about the backlash? It was insinuated by political sources and explicitly by Trump supporters that the problem was not the presidential phallus but the gaping, flapping-in-the-wind vagina of Ms Daniels.

There is a stigma around women who have enjoyed many partners, as we've explored when thinking about cuckolding. The men who sleep with them have no paternity certainty, and while this should not concern us in the modern 'contraceptives are available' world, if there are evolutionary reasons for some men to be attracted to newly pubescent partners (hebephilia), then those same men may be subconsciously turned off by sexual experience.

Maybe these things are related. Maybe a tight orifice offers enjoyable sensations and reinforces the idea of being the first or only sexual partner. But a mistake that men make about their female counterparts is that we seek to be 'filled'. That there are parts of our internal organs only a big cock can reach. That we are unsatisfied by small willies. I'm not saying this to be nice, it's not true. I have a vagina, I have been having sex for over twenty years with many* different-shaped and -sized penises, and my enjoyment of the sex was never, ever about their girth or length. With a bigger penis I have to be very aroused to accommodate it or I cannot be penetrated without pain. Pain turns me off – it's horrible. Some positions are impossible with a bigger penis for the same reasons.

But I don't think men want to hear this. I do not think they believe it. Which results in bad sex and an unnecessary preoccupation with their own erection. Penis size anxiety is less about satisfying sexual partners and is much more about impressing other men.**

An internet survey of over fifty thousand people found that while 85 per cent of women were satisfied by their partner's penis size, only 55 per cent of men were satisfied with their own and 45 per cent wished to be larger. There's a gap, isn't there, between the happy partners and the men who don't care if she's satisfied, they wish it was larger anyway.

Men who go for penis enlargement surgery or complain of low confidence on message boards often cite wanting to satisfy sexual partners as the reason for wanting to be larger. With the huge irony, LISTEN TO ME PLEASE I KNOW WHAT I'M TALKING ABOUT, that *turning a woman on more* is what will make sex more enjoyable for her. More

---

* So many.
** With gay men these are the same people, so as you would expect, there is great fetishisation of penis size and aesthetics in the gay community. They are the connoisseurs, being both owners and appreciative of others.

engorgement of vulva and vagina, more lubrication of the genitals results in increased sensation. Being very aroused makes the act of penetration far more exciting. Being only slightly aroused means that having a penis in you, no matter what size, is quite blah. You can pump and pump away and it all goes a bit numb.

This is all part of the Conundrum of Heterosexuality™. Why all these spam emails about penis enlargement to make your lover scream? Those emails should all be about fingering and licking – free stuff you can do more of, for longer, and which will drastically improve any female partner's pleasure. Teasing: why don't men understand the great sexual delight of making someone desire something they can't have rather than shoving their dick in as soon as it will be accommodated?

My theory is that that stuff is not physically enjoyable for the man, so it's of less interest. It's easier to blame your dick than spend an extra ten minutes going down. We have seen the gender discrepancy in porn consumption, and a contributory factor must be that the majority of the sex depicted is not necessarily the sort of sex a female body would best respond to. Nothing wrong with a good hard shag, of course, but as you'll remember, all the same nerve endings that a penis has are condensed in our little clitoris. Imagine if all porn ignored the penis? That is what non-clitoral heterosexual sex looks like to us. It's male fantasy, it's impractical and please improve. Thank you.

Men are conscious of penis size, and they blame it on wanting to impress women because it's embarrassing to admit they care about other men. In our society men are nude at the gym, they wee in front of each other and are quite aware of how they rank among their friends. The study mentioned above found that men who believed they were bigger than average (22 per cent of respondents) also rated their looks more favourably, which suggests that feeling confident about their penis creates confidence about other aspects of their appearance.

Perhaps this applies to self-worth in general? In the book *Manhood: The Bare Reality* Laura Dodsworth interviews men about their genitals. One of them admits, 'Whenever I'm somewhere where men are naked I'm always looking at other dicks,' which is exactly the same as how I feel in changing rooms, surreptitiously looking at other women's bodies and feeling inadequate. The anonymous man continues, 'I put myself in a pecking order of men and their dicks and I believe that there is an importance to the size of my dick and that if it's not big enough then . . . I don't know, I think it probably comes straight back to, will I be loved?'

That makes sense, doesn't it? We understand the illogical way that self-confidence works. How we feel about ourselves dictates how we think we look to others. It's worth noting too that it is not the actual penis size that matters, but the perception. Surveys of clinics show the men who go for consultations about enlargement are well within the average. Like with women who have dysmorphia about their weight or attractiveness, the same irrationality is undermining men. Here is the pity of having a culture that equates a large penis with masculinity – it affects male self-esteem. Their sense of self and worth is connected to what's in their pants. This is what incidents like the one with Stormy Daniels and Donald Trump reinforce: bad men have small dicks, small-dicked men are insufficient, a small-dicked man has less worth.

Where does this penis concern originate from, if it's not women complaining, 'I can't feel it, is it in?' There is a theory that because boys growing up see their father's penis and are aware of its larger, post-pubescent size, they associate this with strength, authority and adulthood, which is Freudian, but logical for once.

I wondered earlier why the human male's large penis evolved, as we know it does not physically aid the chances of conception. But it would be relevant if a large penis enabled its owner to better dominate other men and/or impress possible mates. Is a large penis a reliable signifier of high testosterone? Short answer is no. The hormone rises and triggers penis development during adolescence but does not reflect a higher T level in adulthood; the size is determined by genes rather than hormones. Taking steroids, which are androgens, will in fact shrivel your D and Bs.

Okay, what about this: could the larger penis have been selected for by female partners' preferences? There is a study which seems to confirm this. Researchers at the University of California and University of New Mexico offered seventy-five women a range of synthetic phalluses and asked them to choose one for their 'ideal' partner. Interestingly, they found that women chose a slightly bigger example than average, 6.4 inches, for a one-off partner, and 6.3 inches for a relationship. I mean, this falls inside our range of average, although maybe slightly higher than the six inches we bandy around as bang in the middle. But, can you hear me, this is an ideal-world preference. Picked only for length and girth, and puny compared to what you've been watching in porn.

An interesting fact of evolution is that penises may have been prevented from growing proportionally even larger by the vaginas of our female ancestors. Males with too-large penises would have ~~had them bitten off~~ been selected against, as sex would have been more painful, more likely to cause injury. When the hyperbole of porn is taken away, there are many men who will tell you that being too big has created problems in their love life. The world's reportedly largest penis (over thirteen inches when erect) belongs to Jonah Falcon, and he describes light-headedness when he manages an erection due to the amount of blood needed to fill it. He is not able to fully insert it in anyone because of the pain it causes them and has not had a lasting, long-term romantic relationship. While this hypersexual signalling gains much interest from people, it does not lead to a more satisfying sex life, more a kind of freakhood.

The penis is so fascinating as it can be a source of power and vulnerability. I'm convinced that this relates to both sperm competition and male status. There is also its potential for violence. Pull it out at the urinals, nothing. Pull it out at the bus stop or the children's playground – pandemonium. The penis is an organ of possibility.

Many of the #MeToo complaints involve being flashed at. It's probably the most common of the sexual transgressions committed by men. We had an assembly on it at school because so many girls were getting flashed on the way home. There was a repeat offender who lurked by the lake in the park, and another one who waited in the underpass near the library. We knew they were different men because underpass man tried to ejaculate on you. Lucy from my class got it on her skirt and bag and became a school celebrity. In assembly they told us not to worry because flashers never raped anyone. They told us that these men liked to get a reaction, so the best thing to do if you saw an adult man exposing himself was to point directly at his penis and laugh. These penis-waving men *wanted* us to run away and cry. Empowerment was standing our ground and shouting, 'Look at that stupid little willy!'

As an adult I've been flashed twice and both times failed to suppress my fear. I think if I was prepared, if I knew it was about to happen, I could be assertive. But both times it was unexpected, and I froze. Where is my strident, groin-kicking past self when I need her? Why does my body not believe that these men aren't dangerous?

What's this got to do with porn?

I think it relates to the sex differences in the consumption of it. Whereas you would presume that straight women would have evolved to find nothing sexier than a rock-hard dick, there are qualifiers.

There are things to assess. Mate potential and safety, for example. And what about all this dick pic sending now? Surely that proves my point – men like sending them FAR MORE than women like receiving them. Women are very polite. It is one of the first lessons in heterosexuality, complimenting a man on his penis. Like a child with a finger painting. 'Well done, that is so good, did you do that by yourself? Let's pop it on the fridge.' Men like to watch their penis in sex too, they like to watch their penis thrusting. What is that telling them about their own masculinity?

This brings us back to our original question. Is the large human penis naturally selected, sexually selected or a by-product? It may have been slightly sexually selected for, although there is no evidence that smaller than average men have less sex (in evolutionary terms that would equate to fewer offspring). And if it is a by-product, of what? All evidence suggests that it is men who associate respect and masculinity with a larger penis. If being well endowed improved a male's status in his tribe, that would have led to better food, less conflict, more sexual partners. This in turn would have led women to prefer a largish penis because they subconsciously desired the same status for their own sons.

It is worth us revisiting Pompeii now, the phalluses – and especially the cartoonishly large ones – depicted in the artworks and considered pornographic by the Victorians. Analysis of these paintings, murals and statues reveals an interesting detail. Many of these sexual scenarios had an agenda that was not about titillation but about power. The language of the phallus was to denigrate, to lessen. A politician on his knees with a penis in his mouth was not an illustration of giving/receiving joy but one of debasement. Such a portrayal was comedic and satirical – a high-status person demeaned. Copulation in this ancient Roman art exhibited status; the penetrator was powerful and the penetrated was reduced. This reminds me of the connotations of the language around anal sex when I was a teenager: 'doing it up the arse', 'taking it up the shitter' spoke not of pleasure but of subjugation and disrespect.

So too, I'm sure you're already aware, with the language of porn. A huge amount of it suggests not only a power dynamic but diminishment and punishment. Let's consider a few of the titles as I tell you about a petition I couldn't sign.

Shame Waving

I cried when I read Gail Dines's book *Pornland*. Dines described the porn she found within one minute of opening her computer, and I'd never heard of anything so horrific. Torture – not consensual *Shades of Grey* S&M, but acts of hatred upon the female body. In my ignorance that is what I was expecting all porn to be. And it isn't. All I've found in my own research is middle ground. And that's reassuring – there is loads and loads of middle ground, with extremes at either end.

One extreme is the artists and anarchists, the people who are exploring gender, race, sexuality, disability and power dynamics through filming sex. There is a list of anthologies from these porn makers at the end of this book if you want to find out more. There are also the feminists, people like Erica Lust, Anna Arrowsmith and Cindy Gallop, to name a few, who are sex-positively creating porn that explores female sexuality. They are fighting the misogyny they see in mainstream porn not by attempting to shout it down, but by creating an alternative.

The other extreme is described below on a petition I was sent by a woman I respect and admire. She asked me to sign and retweet it. She wanted more people to see it – could I help her out? I read the petition.

Ann Summers has teamed up with Pornhub for a 'fun range of sex toys'. But Pornhub, the world's largest porn site, is simply a portal for abuse since a staggering 90% or more of pornography now shows women being sexually assaulted.

This includes violent sex in every orifice often by gangs of men, while they spit on, strangle, hit and humiliate the young women they are abusing. It is about millions of teenage girls crying, sobbing and screaming in pain and fear while they are abused on a daily basis. Or worse.

If there were no camera, the men doing this would be jailed for GBH, assault and rape.

The titles of the videos on Pornhub alone speak for themselves:

'Unwanted Painful Anal' (3.9 million views)

'Noose around her Neck, Real Hanging' (118,000 views)

'No Daddy Stop. I'm not Mummy' (2.5 million views)

'Human Toilet Girl gets a Stomach full of Fresh Urine' (71,000 views)

'Anal Tears' (1.5 million views)

'Extreme Brutal Gagging' (472,000 views)

'How to Sexually Harass Your Secretary Properly' (10.6 million views)

When Ann Summers suggests 'Ways to Spice up the Night', 'Bring the Glam' or 'Romance is What You Make it' . . . is this what they mean? Tell Ann Summers to Dump Pornhub. Sign the petition today.

But I didn't. I wrote and deleted thirty-nine replies about why I felt unable to sign and share. I couldn't clarify my thoughts, so I guess I am working through them here instead.

That very first statistic – 90 per cent of pornography shows women being sexually assaulted – is impossible. Firstly, we found out earlier that Pornhub uploaded fifty-four years' worth of porn in 2016 alone. Who watched all of that and documented what it contained? Seriously. Fifty-four years means no one has watched 100 per cent of it. You can't complete Pornhub.

I've been doing my own research into porn for over a year, I have watched videos on all of the tube sites, and I have to admit something – titles like the ones listed on the Ann Summers/Pornhub petition haven't come up. There is an algorithm, right? And in what it has suggested to me, there is no puking or anal tearing or Daddy-I'm-not-Mummying. There are a lot of stepsisters and stepmothers, and there is this fake taxi guy who seems so happy to accept sex instead of a fare that it's no wonder Uber is sending them out of business.

Compiling statistics about porn requires extrapolation. Someone might study twenty-four hours' worth of content, noting what percentage they consider 'abusive', and then report that percentage as representative of a whole site. But who is deciding what is sexual assault? The people running the study, and isn't that a subjective judgement? The reason I quoted the 'Harder and Harder' study earlier is because I agreed with how they were defining aggression. There were other studies that used too wide a range of criteria: 'assault is aggressive physical contact', 'assault is domineering physicality or language', 'assault is any contact that could leave a mark or cause physical pain or both'.

This makes spanking assault; this construes many acts that may well be consensual as an attack on a woman's body. The difference between assault and foreplay is context. Who is deciding that, or rather, can a person viewing porn decide that without asking any of the performers involved?

Spanking can cause pain. What about hair-pulling? Bites? I mean, I'm turning myself on here. Yet those things must have been logged as aggressions on the female body to have arrived at the '90 per cent is assault' figure. What about choking? Choking is a violent way of killing someone, it can be a deadly assault . . . but it's also an enjoyable, playful part of many Tories' sex lives.

So your problem was the statistic?

My problem is with exaggeration, the hyperbole intended to create shock. Like we saw with the *Time* magazine cover, I think anti-porn propaganda catastrophises, and that prevents a reasoned and reasonable conversation. There are massive discrepancies in reports of how much porn is violent, from as low as 2 per cent up to 90 per cent. This reflects how bias might change what is logged as violent, but also the difficulty of assessment when there's so much material being produced every year. Hollywood releases about six hundred films per annum, so if you wanted to find out how many of those are violent (answer: loads) at least you could watch them all.

Good luck getting this book into the feminist section.

Another problem I have is with describing the male porn performers as 'gangs of men'. This suggests that they are criminals, that they have broken down the door and started raping everyone, rather than actors pretending, and I know it's not *really* pretending because they *are* doing those

things, but I don't think the male performers should be vilified. It's not their idea. These male performers arrive, are
briefed, are told what to do, are paid. Exactly the same as
their female co-workers. I'm not denying that there is assault
and manipulation and rape and battery and all those awful
things we wish people didn't do to each other, but to make it
sound as if the men are doing this for their own enjoyment
is irresponsible. If the women are victims of coercion, then
surely the men are too? Or does having a penis make you an
automatic oppressor?

This petition denies autonomy to the women who work in
porn. The adjective 'young' is needlessly used to make them
seem more vulnerable. You only need to read one interview
with someone like Sasha Grey to realise that what might
look like a person having a horrifically horrible time might
not be a person having a horrifically horrible time.

Shouldn't any conversation about porn reflect the variety
of the industry? The titles above were selected to shock and
worry us. The language is emotive. The words suggest pain,
force, humiliation, as well as paedophilia. When I read those
titles, unwanted images appear in my mind. I feel sick. They
work on me, those words, I'm not immune.

Sex and violence are connected. The reason that there is
violent porn is because violence is a mate-guarding technique
in our species – it is how males dominate, depress their partner's confidence and sex drive, and ensure paternity certainty.
I'm not trying to make monsters of men or say that domestic
violence is natural. I'm just acknowledging the presence of
dominance behaviour. Think about rape in male prisons. It is
a place where status and hierarchy are incredibly important
for a person's safety, survival and access to resources. With

no women to subjugate, men subjugate each other. The sex is not about sexual satisfaction, although there might be some. The rapists are often men who would not identify as homosexual. It is a dominance behaviour. Similarly in war: men, women and children are brutalised by enemy soldiers. It is a way of destroying, desecrating.

'Pleasure' is derived from domination; it rewards a person with dopamine. Domination is a survival tactic like sex and eating. The racism and racial stereotypes in porn contain so many echoes of colonisation. White men punish and disrespect women of every other race with their bodies. Black men are employed to role-play white men's fear. There is an episode of the *Hot Girl Wanted* series, where an African American male porn star is directed to throttle a white woman and to 'go harder'. In the interview afterwards he talks about his softness, how the sex he acts in porn is not the kind of sex he has. He is aware he is performing a racist trope.

An interesting detail is that women apparently search for violent porn more often than men do. The statistics analysed by Seth Stephens-Davidowitz in his book *Everybody Lies* showed that women are twice as likely as men to look for porn involving pain and humiliation, which feature in 25 per cent of their searches, with 5 per cent looking for rape or forced sex (which is banned on Pornhub). Is the female fascination coming from a place of fear? Or because it is more arousing?*

I imagine if you watch a lot of porn you become desensitised to the language, and the content too. I imagine those

---

* I explore this baffling area of female sexuality in *Animal*, if you want to find out more.

words lose some of the meaning they have for me, because the viewer has become habituated. When I read 'extreme brutal' or 'unwanted painful' I wince. 'Anal tears', 'real hanging' – these are not things I want people to have to experience. I would ban it, arrest everyone, but what if the people are choosing to do that, in exchange for money, because it is their job? Mary knows she is going to be a toilet, Leonie knows she has a rough anal scene – just because I don't like it, do I have a right to stop them?

If you decide the answer is yes, then please make me prime minister because I will. Leonie and Mary will live in my house, where I can keep an eye on them and make sure no one goes to the toilet on them, and everyone will say, 'That's imprisonment and kidnapping, you can't control people,' and I'll say, 'Make your mind up.'

We live in a free society where, no matter our personal feelings or morality, we do not have the right to limit the behaviour or earning potential of another human. Unless it's hurting someone. People can use their bodies how they like, even if they choose to do painful things.

But even as I express that I am aware that sometimes those choices are not black and white. I have been learning about how 'gonzo' porn is sometimes made with women who have just auditioned. They are given a small fee – no boundaries are discussed. Puking is real, crying and pleading is real. The women ask to stop and are told they won't get paid. And that is illegal; anyone who does that should be in prison. The women should feel they'd be supported if they reported what happened, they would be believed – but the stigma against the industry and the women who choose to work in it means they don't. Their assault, their rape is on tape, and people wank to it and – here is the crux – how do you support and protect vulnerable people without inhibiting the rights of others?

I think paying for all porn would legitimise it, and make it easier to police. Why is there not a Netflix for porn? You could pay seven or eight quid a month and know that all the performers were being paid for their appearances, but also that there were some ethical codes being upheld among all the porn makers. I sent out a questionnaire to my mailing list asking if people would watch less porn if they had to pay, and everyone said yes! Is that because of shame and guilt? Why do people think it is morally justified to steal porn? Is that because even those who use it every day are unsettled by the idea of people getting rich from having sex?

I understand that. We have to admit to subconscious judgement and prejudice.

When I watched the original *Hot Girls Wanted* documentary, I really listened hard to what the women were saying. I was surprised how low the money was: they were getting a couple of hundred dollars for sex. And they were explaining they would rather have sex a couple of times a week and get $500 than work all week in a mall. We've all hated jobs. I really, really hated working in a shop. Her sentiments made sense to me, IT FEELS LIKE DEATH, THE DAY LASTS A MILLION YEARS.

The documentary noted how 'extra' money was earned by doing certain scenes; the girls did a job that involved gagging and being sick on a penis. I didn't know that was a thing, that there are specialist websites. They specialise in new girls, who get interviewed and then obviously have to deep-throat or whatever. Their eyes stream with tears and they look so scared, and it is very hard to watch. Although some people clearly do, on purpose. It's as alien to me as someone who would cum watching people having a car crash or having a piano dropped on them. Intellectually I comprehend all the biology behind it, but emotionally I'm sure nature has got her wiring wrong.

The women said that the male performer was nice beforehand, they got a bit of extra money, they knew they had to look like it was hurting them. I will never get those images out of my mind, I feel scarred by them and how sad they made me. My subjectivity does get in the way because I do not want to do that and I do not want other women to have to do that. I want to give them all the money that scene would pay so they don't have to do it.

Up to a point I can understand that porn is a form of acting, that sex can be faked through – or that some people can enjoy novel sex with a stranger while being filmed. But only up to a point, and I can't help my bias.

I am trying to treat having sex like any other job, even if only as a thought exercise – but when the sex becomes aggressive, I can't feel, 'That's a bad day at work, like when I used to work in Tesco's.' I couldn't sign that petition, but I also can't simply sign off on 'sex work is work', even if for some people it is. It is not so simple as sex for money, because of the imbalance of power.

Sex
Power
Money
Money
Money

The Oldest Discussion

Two years ago I was walking to the station after a gig. I had my guitar in its case on my back because I was going through a phase of pretending I could play. My headphones were in as I listened back to my terrible comedy. A man coming in the opposite direction spoke to me, gestured for me to stop. I removed an earbud grumpily. As I said before, I don't want to talk to men on dark roads.

'Are you working?' said the man.

In my experience of being a woman, certain men will use any excuse to speak to you. Any banal question, any stupid pretext. This has slowed down as I've aged, and I'm grateful for it. In my teens and twenties I tried not to read in public because an open book was a creep magnet. Over to the bus stop or cafe table the man would saunter: 'What ya reading?' 'Fuck off,' I would think while having to engage in unwanted small talk. What did these men think was going to happen? That I'd get so aroused explaining the plot of *Lord of the Flies* that I'd be like, 'Forget the bus, let's screw in an alley!'? It should be against the law to interrupt a person who is engrossed in a book. All books should be titled *Leave Me Alone*, so that anyone asking what you're reading will get the message. GOD, I should have called this book *Leave Me Alone*, I've really missed a trick . . . I wonder if it's too late to change it? 'Yes, it is,' says Laura, my editor, in an email that would have been friendlier if I hadn't missed my deadline by six months.

'Are you working?' the man repeated. He wasn't that much older than me, white-skinned, stubbly. 'I've finished work,' I told him, contempt underlining my words. Maybe he recognises me, I thought, he's asking if I'm on my way to a gig – I should be nicer.

'Can't we go somewhere now?' He looked around him for 'somewhere' and I realised that, far from being keen on comedy, he'd misidentified me as someone selling sex. That's what the 'work' meant – 'working' girl, sex 'work'.

'I'm going home.' I started walking away. I was embarrassed by what he was asking of me and angry with him.

'Can I come with you?'

I put my headphones in. He followed me for a couple of minutes, baffled by my rejection. He kept talking to me. I didn't turn my head, strode widely until I reached a busier street, then lost him. On the tube home, I looked down at my outfit to see what he saw. Skirt and thick tights, winter uniform. Knee-length black boots. Sure, in cliché-land boots might signify a streetwalker but they're ubiquitous in cold weather. Knee-length boots are a rare combination of warm and flattering, there should be parades in their honour every October. My coat – oh dear, here was my mistake. It was fake fur in leopard print. I'd covered the breast with brooches, because my friend Katie said no one wore *one* brooch any more. I had seven brooches, they were all fake pearls and peeling gold paint and had belonged to Nanny Babs. I loved the jacket, I'd defended it – rowed with my boyfriend when he'd described it as too 'vampy' to go to the pub in. But now it had spoken to a stranger, telling him I was sexually available.

I felt insulted by this man. I'd grown up being called whore, slag, tart, only in insulting terms. Being called a prostitute in the playground was intended to belittle and humiliate. If anyone at school called your *mother* a prostitute, that meant you had to fight them, teacher or not. You had to, for her honour. So a man treating me as if I sold sex – I felt it was abusive, offensive. How dare he look at me in my normal boots and vampy coat and make a judgement about what I would do for money? Did I look poor? Did I look desperate, did I look like I needed drugs? 'Where was his logic?' I thought – I had a guitar. I'd sell that for crack before touching an ugly man's ugly penis.

This reaction, *my* reaction, to his mistake illustrates my shameful judgements against sex workers and prostituted women. My hurt feelings are the result of conscious and unconscious bias. I've formed stereotypes about the people who work in the sex trade, about why they're there, what they look like. I am not the only person to discriminate in this way. A brief search of newspaper headlines using the words 'murder' and 'prostitute' will demonstrate how frequently we're all absorbing the message that people who have sex for money become 'other', are defined by it. If you work in admin, a report of your death wouldn't differentiate you from fellow victims. Sexual behaviour in any form commands a disproportionate amount of human attention, and newspapers reflect this. In 2006, as police searched for a serial killer in East Anglia, the victims were described by *The Times* as 'prostitutes and other young women'.

OTHER young women.

The distinction is significant – some young women are young women and others have graduated, not via the ageing process but with their first 'trick', to being prostitutes. Some young women are young women and others are defined by their jobs. Imagine if this distinction happened in any other way – 'young women and Geminis', 'young women and blondes', 'young women and dog lovers'. But star sign, hair colour and pet preference don't fascinate and repulse the public the way sex for cash does.

When police were hunting the Yorkshire Ripper in the 1970s they differentiated between the people he attacked, using the chilling phrase 'prostitutes and innocent victims'. Describing some of the women as 'innocent' insinuates that some were not. The suggestion is that in choosing (or being compelled) to sell sex, some of those attacked by Peter Sutcliffe were complicit. That by willingly getting into his car or negotiating a price they had done something to deserve being hit with a hammer and stabbed with a screwdriver. I'm thinking back to that man propositioning me in the street. If he'd been a murderer – and let's face it, he definitely was – my death would have been reported differently depending on whether I'd ever sold sex. If so, my tragedy would be tabloid: 'Call Girl Dumped in River', 'Hooker Stuffed in Bin Bag', 'Whore Killer Strikes Again'. The end of my life reduced to sex and violence to titillate and dehumanise.*

Even if it was my first time . . . if I had followed him willingly to my demise, the language that reported it to others would have blamed me. I would've been a dead thing rather than a deceased person. This sort of language reflects ignorance and cultural morality and it serves to devalue certain people's lives. This is doubly relevant as those same people, those who work in the sex industry, are far more likely to be the victims of violent crimes than women in the general

* See also any reporting about 'rent boys'.

population. They are eight times more likely to be murdered.

There are evolutionary and cultural forces that combine to create stigma around sex work as well as making sex workers extremely vulnerable. For people who do not *choose* sex work but are forced or compelled into it, being prostituted, pimped or raped for money is a crime against them in itself. There is also a wide spectrum between the two. It is not as simple as some people choosing and some being forced.

I don't know if you've ever heard of George Ryley Scott, I hope he's not your great-grandad or something. He wrote a history of prostitution called *A History of Prostitution*, which was published in 1936, back in history itself. Most of the book annoyed me, so I wouldn't recommend you add it to your Audible wish list. The introduction contains this assertion: 'Every woman is a potential prostitute, just as every man is a potential consorter with prostitutes. It is mainly a question of price.'

When I read that I threw his book across the room, but my initial reaction may not be correct. Now I am rolling that statement around in my head, it's like a bottle of water in the boot of the car, annoying but vital. There is an argument that all sex is transactional, that all human interaction is giving and receiving. It is not enough to throw away sentiments (and books) because I disagree emotionally. We must deconstruct this as logically as we can.

For instance, when the ~~murderer~~ man approached me in the street I was affronted, partly because I found comparison with a sex worker hurtful, but also because I resent being presumed sexually available *at all*. I resent being considered 'for sale'. To be a woman is to occasionally feel, thanks to a few men, as if you are a shop – a department store with orifices on every level. It can feel like persecution. You're trying to check a bus timetable or call your mum, while simultaneously advertising sex without meaning to. I've gone on about this already with the ex-looking-at-teen-in-shorts incident, but it's worth repeating that when men approach women uninvited, when they shout 'Show us yer tits' from cars or ' Give us a smile' from building sites, they are asserting what they feel is a right: to be sexually entertained by women. So this 'every woman is a potential prostitute' statement is problematic for me because the assumption that an entire gender is purchasable effectively removes real choice, autonomy, humanity from women. It is the extreme end of male sex entitlement. How could anyone respect someone they consider to be fundamentally bartering for the right price? It's this kind of thinking that has led to the rudeness and resentment of rejected men, the insanity of incels and the film *Indecent Proposal*.

Indecent Proposal

The strapline for *Indecent Proposal* was 'What Would You Do for a Million Dollars?', which is misleading. It should really be 'Who Would You Do for a Million Dollars (and Is It Robert Redford)?' 'What Would You Do' pretends the film is giving you options, but it isn't. You can't offer to wash his car for a year or name one of your children after him. This proposal is *indecent*. When the film came out there was a common joke. A woman in middle age would say, 'A million quid to shag Robert Redford? I'd do it for free!' Then everyone in the pub would laugh because the idea that a movie star would pay for sex with Audrey the pigeon-toed school teacher was absolute bants. This joke was responsible for 25 per cent of all humour in 1993. The other 75 per cent of jokes were provided by quoting *Robin Hood: Men in Tights*. Like if someone said, 'Lend me your ears,' you would pretend to throw your ears at them, and if you had a facial mole, you'd move it to a different place for every scene.

The 'I'd do it for free' sentiment is integral to *Indecent Proposal* remaining within the genre of 'romantic comedy'. The film's premise is a gushy 'imagine if someone you were willing to have sex with made you a millionaire', rather than 'imagine a world where poor people are unable to refuse the whims of the rich'. *Indecent Proposal* could also be considered a dystopian horror: 'imagine if billionaires could rape anyone they wanted as long as they paid husbands generous compensation'. So maybe that's enough with the jokes, Audrey.

You really can take the fun out of everything.

Yep. Picture us in the cinema together. I'm yabbering on, telling you my theories and opinions, analysing subtexts, having memories, googling facts I've forgotten – generally embarrassing you to the point of fury. But I bought the tickets, your Snickers ice cream and the popcorn – should you politely ignore my unreasonable and antisocial behaviour just because I paid? Can my money buy your compliance? What a great analogy. START THE FILM.

Indecent Proposal begins with a happy white couple called Diana and David Murphy. They have a cute back-and-forth catchphrase and have been together since school. This detail is important – stressing that they're long-term creates more tension when a strange man suggests he can buy the missus. If these guys had met three weeks ago on Plenty of Fish there would be far less at stake. ALSO, this plot point portrays the female character as sexually inexperienced. Her husband may be her only sexual partner ever. Her innocence and fidelity are crucial. If the couple were swingers or she was Samantha from *Sex and the City* the central dilemma would be far less important. Some billionaire offers a sweet mil for your wife, and you're like, 'Sure, as soon as she's finished banging the gardener.'

These two *are* sexy, though. There's an early scene where they argue about clothes. He's messy and she's picking up his shorts and being so furious that she throws a knife at him. In Hollywood, this kind of violent behaviour is a sign of passion. One minute you're attempting to shank your lover, the next he's bending you over the laundry basket. In real life (where we live), missiles, violence – these are signs of deep psychological instability and/or abusive relationships.

After the knife throwing, David and Diana bone on the floor. They are unrealistically attracted to each other for a long-term couple, they are too keen even for people hooking up on Grindr or having an affair. But I get it – this is fantasy. No one's entertained by the grim reality of living with someone who leaves their dirty pants on the floor. You ignore them for a couple of days, thinking, 'She'll notice eventually,' but she doesn't. You concentrate on pretending you can't see them, walking around them sighing at the exertion, until you've had enough – five days! You shouldn't have to live like this, you're a man, not a pig. 'Why doesn't she respect me?' you think. 'Why doesn't she respect *herself*?' you think even louder, seething with resentment, yet when she's woken by the grinding of your teeth and asks what's wrong you say, 'I'm FINE,' to clarify that you're furious but will never speak of it to someone you cannot bear yet cannot leave because you share a mortgage.

David and Diana also have a mortgage and they cannot keep up the payments. David's an architect, he's built another house and doesn't have money for that one either. The couple talk sadly about the economic downturn. This gives David a great opportunity to say something cool like 'I can't duck this recession like I did your knife', but he doesn't. We realise as an audience that the economy is the real enemy. Diana is scared: 'What are we going to do?' David reassures her that they will survive. He will drive a cab, wait tables. And this is ~~exactly what he does~~ not interesting enough as a plot. This is not a film about a couple who behave sensibly when confronted with financial issues, this is a film about twerps. David borrows 5K off his dad and takes Diana to Las Vegas, not to sensibly work as cab drivers but to gamble their money.

Here's the thing: if you have a small amount of cash you can swap it for no cash via a roulette wheel or pack of cards. And this is David's plan. David is an architect, yes, of his own demise.

At the casino it's all going great to start with. Diana steals some chocolates and finds a dress she likes in a boutique. She holds it up to her body but gasps at the price. A creepy guy strolls over and offers to buy it for her: 'I've enjoyed watching you, you've earned it.' Diana doesn't have a knife handy to throw so she whips out some sass instead: 'The dress is for sale, I'm not.' This is called 'foreshadowing'. We know what the film is about, it's only David and Diana who don't. They start gambling with some dice and win some money, then even more money. The creepy guy creepily watches them winning and kissing each other. Then it's bedtime. David and Diana have $25,000 in cash. They are really thrilled and ~~go home to pay their mortgage~~ have sex on the money.

In the morning David and Diana head back to the gambling games. They are trying to double their cash into $50,000 by winning but instead divide it down to $5,000 by losing. Then they go to a sad cafe, which is my favourite scene. They are talking about how they promised they wouldn't go below the five grand they arrived with. This would be a good time for David to say something cool like 'This is my dad's money, I should respect that and not chuck it down the toilet', but he doesn't. Instead they decide to risk everything, because what could be worse than only having $5,000? Having no dollars. The waitress who is serving them coffee rolls her eyes like she's seen it a million times. I'd like to see *her* backstory: when the recession hit she reassured her family, 'I'll do whatever it takes, I'll wait tables or drive a cab.' Then she actually *did* that. Her film is called *Minimum Wage in Exchange for Labour Proposal* and it ends with her driving the yellow taxi back to a house she still owns, then having sex with her husband on the few dollars she made in tips.

Surprise surprise, David and Diana lose all the money. This is where the waitress would come in to gloat if she wasn't a one-scene character. Now, despite having no cash left and no reason to be there, the couple continue to hang around the casino waiting for plot to happen. They don't have to wait long. As they wander around the tables of gamblers they see Robert Redford. They're told his name is John Gage and that he is a BILLIONAIRE. David and Diana don't ever forget and accidentally call him Robert Redford, and I think this is very professional of them. Robert Redford is playing with chips that are worth $10,000 each, and he is throwing them around the table like they're just little coloured bits of plastic.

I still don't understand why D&D haven't gone home. Maybe they think this rich man will leave money lying around they can have sex on? Or do they want some of the free refreshments I've heard casinos offer? Either way, I'm annoyed. John Gage spots them and asks David, 'Would you mind lending me your wife?' Not for sex (yet) but for luck. The man asks the other man if he can 'borrow' a woman, as if she were ketchup or an iPhone charger. David rightly points out that his wife is not an object and should be asked herself. She says yes, I don't know why. I DON'T KNOW. She can't believe she *IS* lucky, she just lost twenty-five grand in an afternoon. What is she up to?

Anyway, she kisses his dice. It's all very charged and dramatic. The billionaire bets a million dollars and then wins another million dollars for free when the dice roll correctly. Gage doesn't punch the air or cry with joy, as he already has a thousand million, that's what a billionaire is. This new million will simply join the others in an overcrowded bank account offshore somewhere.*

Gage *must* be happy, because he arranges a room for David and Diana and says to help themselves to whatever they want, all on his tab. Neither of them exclaims, 'That's a bit weird, we just met you,' or 'Must be off, we have to go get jobs as waiters.' Perhaps they're in shock, I'll allow that. Being poor, but more especially battling with debt – it can lead to terrible decision-making. It certainly did in my experience. After university I had two student overdrafts and two student credit cards that were charging me more in fines than my small income. I hated myself because it was my fault. Having bills, bank charges and loans hanging over you is a constant cloud; the worry shadows every thought. It felt like an unsolvable problem so I focused instead on forgetting, drinking or drugs, or stupid men. I would go to sleep hoping I wouldn't wake up. I became unable to make sensible choices because I thought I'd fucked things up so badly that they were unfixable. So I'll extend this out to David and Diana. Perhaps they are also experiencing that awful anxious madness.

David and Diana go to their new room and a box is delivered, it's the dress that Diana was ogling in the foyer downstairs. David doesn't freak out like I would if someone sent

---

* The film doesn't make it explicit that John Gage is taking advantage of tax loopholes, but I can tell he banks offshore from his haircut. I can always tell.

my boyfriend a dress. Cut to a party. David and Diana dance, looking lovingly at one another. John Gage watches them, and we watch *him*, waiting to see how he'll instigate the money-for-sex situation we've been promised. The men have a manly dad chat: 'Where do you see yourself in ten years?' David replies that he would like to be a billionaire one day. I laugh at him but he can't hear me. Diana pointedly says that there are limits to what money can buy. I throw my shoes at the screen, yelling, 'People who tell you money has no value are always the first to ask you for money!' This is what my mum used to shout about my dad. 'Money won't make you happy,' my dad said when my mum asked him to pay child maintenance, as is the law. It was school dinners she was trying to buy, not happiness, but that was ages ago and now we're all ~~friends~~ still related.

'Some things aren't for sale,' Diana explains in a dress that was. 'You can't buy people.' I agree with her on this. The buying and selling of people used to be called slavery. Nowadays it's referred to as trafficking and is illegal. It continues to happen, just like murder and other violent infringements of human rights. Restricting a person's freedom, enforced labour or, in the case of sex trafficking, pimping someone to be raped for money are some of the worst crimes imaginable. Diana doesn't mention this in her argument, probably because she doesn't want to ruin the vibe of the party. Gage calls Diana's response 'naive', a fun way of letting her know he doesn't consider her an equal. Then he explains that the cliché 'you can't buy love' is, in fact, a cliché.

'It's true,' says Diana.

'I agree,' says David.

Now that everyone is likeminded that clichés are clichés

but also true, it is time . . . the moment we've all been waiting for, the INDECENT PROPOSAL:

GAGE

Let's test the cliché. Suppose . . . I were to offer you a million dollars . . . for one night with your wife?

As with the earlier 'borrowing for luck', Diana is not addressed. She is talked about, not to. Gage's indecent proposal is to David, not Diana. Let's imagine this was a direct exchange. Would the effect be different if the billionaire asked, 'Diana, would you sleep with me if I pay you a million dollars?'

Diana would now be empowered to respond, positively or negatively, rather than having to prompt her husband to answer on her behalf. Simply by asking her the same question she would be gifted autonomy over herself. This is basic manners, isn't it? If you want to pay someone for sex, please ensure you ask them personally. These 'man-to-man' conversations in the film subtly reinforce the idea that men own female sexuality; it is the male to whom a man owes respect and from whom he requests permission. In real life we see this with the practice of asking a father's permission to marry his daughter. I know everyone loves tradition – and I know that you hate me for even bringing this up – but it's ridiculous. You going cap in hand to her daddy: 'Can I have it?' 'Yes,' says Daddy, 'I'll walk it down the aisle and drop it off for you.'

Some religions include gradients of belief that take patriarchal ownership literally. If you would like some chat to ruin any party's vibe, research dowry deaths and bride burning. Thousands of women are murdered every year because the father who 'owns' them does not pay enough to their new keeper. Then there are irreligious heathens who simply enjoy doing 'what is done' and see no harm in it. But even while we're playing, even when 'permission' is not given and taken in a *real* way, the game is still that a woman's decisions are not her own, that they can be halted by a male relative if he desires. When freedoms for (some) women have been so hard won, why are we still performing and ENJOYING the role-play of subjugation?

I started this chapter describing a man who approached me for transactional sex. What's different about his request and John Gage's? Is it just the amount? In both instances a woman who has never had sex for money was asked if she would have sex for money please (to be fair to the murderer, at least he asked me directly). Gage doesn't know the couple, he has made guests of them in order to manipulate this situation. Yet audiences have not interpreted his behaviour as predatory or even recognised his 'indecent proposal' as sex work. Perhaps it's the size of the sum that creates a non-seedy atmosphere. Is it true that while I am insulted by an offer of £30 or £40 for intercourse, no one would be insulted when offered a million?

A billionaire makes this story otherworldly, a fairy tale. A million dollars makes this conversation surreal. I'd compare it to a tourist experience in Morocco or Tunisia, a family holiday interrupted by a local man, dusty and smiling, offering camels for a female relative. I don't know if these guys are real or if they're actors paid by Lonely Planet, but they are a vital part of the atmosphere. My mum had such a story, we all laughed about it. 'I was tempted!' her boyfriend said. 'Five camels!' But if camel is your currency it's the same thing. We wouldn't laugh if men offered money. It's the ridiculousness of the mammal that makes that proposal silly rather than indecent.

Huge discrepancy in wealth creates as much of a cultural divide as, well, culture. If Gage had offered a more usual $300 for the night we'd judge his character far more harshly, we'd be able to see his intentions unobscured by the hyperbolic figure. The million also means that Gage is not taken seriously at first.

> DAVID
> I'd assume you're kidding.

> GAGE
> Let's pretend I'm not. What would you say then?

> DIANA
> He'd tell you to go to hell.

David is embarrassingly slow here, letting his wife answer for him when it was supposed to be the other way around.

Later, in bed, the couple can't sleep. Diana worries that David wants her to accept Gage's offer. She suggests that she *would* do it . . . for *him*. Love this technique, we've all been there. Getting your own way by pretending to believe it's your partner's most secret desire. 'I thought you *wanted* me to leave the bins rotting in the kitchen,' we say innocently, and the age-old 'I got sacked from work *for you*.' If Diana were self-interested, if she exclaimed, 'I need the money, mate, so I'm gonna do it,' audiences would not like her, they would judge her on her willingness to have sex for money. Even worse if she admitted sexual motivation, told her husband, 'I fancy him, he looks like Robert Redford!'

Instead Diana considers the proposal (outwardly at least) as a wifely duty. For Diana to be likeable yet sympathetic, she must balance between not *actively* wanting to shag the man and not being completely coerced against her will. This is the sweet spot: she isn't keen, but neither is she traumatised. Diana is under financial pressure but not starving, this isn't *Les Misérables*. This middle-class couple are in difficulty but have options like driving a cab, waiting tables or going back in time and putting that cash in the bank rather than underneath their rutting bodies. If this film began a year later in Diana and David's narrative, when they're homeless beggars; if John Gage stopped his car to offer a visibly destitute woman money for sex, would Audrey still quip, 'I'd do him for free?'

So how desperate does a person have to be for sex work to become survival sex?

Survival Sex

Some people maintain that sex is labour like any other. 'Sex work is work,' they insist, it's a job. For those people, someone like me asking about 'economic coercion' or whether a person selling sex has 'real' alternatives is equivalent to me walking round Sainsbury's checking whether staff have been trafficked from home and FORCED into stacking shelves. If we assume that no one works at Sainsbury's for fun, that they only do so because Sainsbury's pay them – isn't that the same as someone who wouldn't have sex with you unless you gave them money? In both instances, the worker does not undertake the labour for its own sake; they do not expect it to bring them pleasure, only cash. If you consider the physical undertaking of sex to be a labour just like stacking shelves, you might argue that the only difference between prostitution and Sainsbury's is an orange and maroon uniform.

Examples of survival sex in the modern world are seen in instances like 'sex for rent', when people of low or no income are given shelter in exchange for sex. This is a very upsetting idea to most people. We would call this 'taking advantage' or abusing somebody rather than a fair exchange. The difficulty of treating sex as labour with value is that logic changes. Sex ceases to be something you should never, ever be coerced or forced into and instead becomes your last line of credit when your wallet is empty.

When there's no financial exchange, the coercive nature of survival sex is much clearer. I mentioned earlier that I spent a day observing porn workshops with schoolboys. The workshops were created by the Great Men Initiative and aimed to educate eleven-to-fourteen-year-olds. The first exercise involved them putting together a porn storyboard starring their favourite celebrity. The kids chose Taylor Swift, Rihanna, Katy Perry. The stories involved the celebrity babysitting or coming to their school or being their mum's friend . . . and then sex. One group chose Mila Kunis. The story they presented was that Mila was in Superdrug shoplifting make-up. The security guard caught her and called the cops. A policeman arrived and took Mila out to his van. She was in handcuffs and crying, begging to be let go. The policeman said he wouldn't arrest her if she had sex with him. Mila agreed and then performed a series of ambitious sexual acts and positions.

The kids all laughed at each other's stories, then the men leading the workshop analysed their ideas.

'Do you think Mila had a choice?'

'Yes,' some of the boys answered straight away, 'if she doesn't want to have sex she can just get arrested.' 'She shouldn't have been stealing,' someone added.

'Should policemen be having sex with people in their van instead of arresting them?'

A beat, then a long, resigned 'noooooooo' in unison. Then an ardent discussion ensued about willingness, what consent means and the complications of power dynamics. The Mila character was analysed – did she want to have sex with the policeman anyway? Does that change things? The boys knew that sex should not be a punishment and that making someone who is afraid and crying have sex is wrong.

'Rape is when people who don't want to have sex are made to have sex.'* The boys all knew that, assented and were then pushed to consider, 'So is this pornography about rape?'

A short silence. A lone voice offered, 'Yes, it is,' but the others were unsure. In the scene they had created, Mila was not physically forced, she was active. Because this was porn, she was sexually enthusiastic. They were confused. They agreed with some statements along the way – the policeman *is* behaving wrongly, Mila *might* be afraid – but they couldn't conclude that this was non-consensual sex. This did not look like rape to them.

What if this were real life and not teenagers' fantasy? In 2018 in New York an eighteen-year-old called Anna Chambers was driving with some male friends when they were pulled over by police. The car was searched and a small bag of weed was found. The friends were told to go. The two policemen didn't take Anna to the station, nor was she arrested or charged. Instead they kept her in the back of their van, restrained by handcuffs, while they performed twenty sex acts upon her. When released, Anna attended hospital for her injuries and told a nurse what had happened. Swabs and tests found the DNA of both men via the semen they had left inside and on her body. When the case got to court, the cops claimed the sex was consensual. I wonder what the boys would have made of this, if it would have filled them with the fury it does me?

It's not *impossible* that an arrested person might willingly desire sex with a police officer. Perhaps they have an intense

* This was a student's definition of rape, not mine.

uniform fetish, maybe being told off makes them horny? People are weird and varied and we can't ever say THAT WILL NEVER HAPPEN when it comes to human behaviour. But it's also clear that when the powerful and powerless intersect, the person on the 'less' side is vulnerable. A person in authority can be terrifying or manipulative or both. Guards with prisoners, teachers with students, presidents with interns – there is a reason that sex breaching a massive discrepancy of power is unsettling.

This is an instance where I don't think anyone could prove that sex is a labour undertaken like any other. If I rewrote the pornography storyboard (sorry boys) so that Mila Kunis was given a choice, arrest or an unpaid shift at Superdrug, would anyone feel that proposal was immoral? Would we be disturbed by a stint of shelf-stacking as punitive retribution? It doesn't seem excessive, it wouldn't harm Mila Kunis, no matter how bored and annoyed she was. The punishment seems entirely reasonable and sensible until I remember we've just given a proven thief access to a storeroom full of nail varnish and dry shampoo. Swapping this around, a common trope in American sitcoms is a character eating in a restaurant who then can't pay. The manager is angry; the character is made to go and wash dishes in the kitchen. But what if the manager was angry and wanted a blow job? Can we replace dishwashing with oral sex? They are both things you do with your body, they are both things the character doesn't want to do, but he is forced to as recompense for a dinner he can't pay for.

I think it's reasonable to consider a forced sex act as something that will hurt and harm someone, while washing dishes or stacking shelves for a few hours will not. Is that fair?

A male* comic told me, while we shared a long late-night train journey, that lots of straight men were 'actually bi'. That he knew men – some of them outwardly homophobic – with girlfriends and wives, who let him suck them off for fifty euros. 'They pretend it's for the money because then they can pretend they're not enjoying it,' Stewart told me. 'They call me up and say, "I'm a bit skint, can I come over?" when actually they're just horny.'

It's so interesting what we assume about the inner lives and intentions of others. When I imagine these men texting 'I'm skint,' I believe they're skint. I imagine that for these young men, fifty euros is a lot of money. Could be the difference between making rent, getting Mum a birthday present, being able to go out next weekend. 'Afterwards they act disgusted and can't even look at me,' Stewart says, 'because they can't admit they find me attractive as that means they're gay.'

'Maybe they don't want to do it but they have to because they need money?' I ask. That's my assumption.

'No, they want to do it. The cash is an excuse.' That's his.

Stewart is a real-life John Gage. He's not forcing anyone to have sex with him. He's merely offering the money, making the proposal. The decision to exchange sexual favours for cash is up to them. John Gage isn't dragging Diana into bed, he's leaving a million dollars on the nightstand and waiting for her to hop in of her own accord. This is choice, isn't it? Diana and the dollars, lads and the euros. And it's the 'choice' that means real-life Stewart and all the other real-life Johns can defend their behaviour because the people they pay for sex are doing so of their own volition. 'If they didn't want

---

* I had to say 'male' in case you presumed all comedians are women.

to do it they wouldn't,' they rationalise. 'No one is making them.'

Let us agree that *Indecent Proposal* is a film about sex work. What Gage is offering is no different to a man bidding for a geisha's virginity or a woman leaning through a car window to negotiate her services and fee. Money exchanged for erotic labour = transactional sex, no matter the amount or habitat. Interestingly, such behaviour has been observed in non-human species. Some argue that transactional sex is part of nature, a strategic form of mating that can aid evolutionary success.

Nature's Hookers

I first heard this from a BBC News headline: 'Prostitute Penguins', the web page declared, and away ran my imagination; cards in phone boxes depicting black-and-white curves, little wings at angles, beak agape. Little puffin pimps with hats and drug problems. A dimly lit suburban street, the silhouette of a scantily clad sea bird smoking. I chastised my imagination for flippancy and got back to serious research. 'Adélie penguins in the Antarctic . . . ' the article began. *The Secret Diary of a Cold Girl*, I thought, then high-fived myself.

'Adélie penguins in the Antarctic are turning to prostitution. But instead of doing it for money, dolly-birds are turning tricks to get rocks off their menfolk.'

This is journalism for idiots. I don't think the BBC needed to point out that penguins don't recognise human currency. I've looked up the study and it's far less salacious, as truth usually is. Dr Fiona Hunter spent five years observing the mating patterns of penguins. This particular species, the Adélie, are obsessed with rocks because they are so necessary for their offspring's survival. The male starts building a nest to attract a female, and when they have pair-bonded they collect rocks to add to the nest together. All this can be enjoyed in the documentary film *Happy Feet*, which I haven't seen because I'm busy.

Hunter's study found that penguins sometimes steal rocks from each other, and if caught are attacked. But in a few instances, females were observed in extrapair copulations, after which they'd take a rock or two back to their own nest and the male wouldn't attack. It seemed to the human observers that there was a tacit understanding, a deal. They theorised about the advantages of this practice (for the male, genetic fitness of offspring due to mate diversity; for the female, an investment into potential offspring's survival) but were not sure whether copulation was in direct exchange for a stone or was to avoid conflict. Dr Hunter said she believed 'what they are doing is having copulation for another reason and just taking the stones as well. We don't know exactly why, but they are using the males.' The human equivalent of this would be a hook-up based on attraction (which is always about procreation at an unconscious level), and then she helps herself to fifty quid from your wallet afterwards. You're cool with it, it's non-typical behaviour, but it's a way of investing in the future of any off-spring created. I feel like you'd be less likely to prevent some-one taking cash from your wallet *after* sex than before . . . I'll try this with my boyfriend later and let you know.*

Dr Hunter speculated that for an Adélie female this ~~steamy affair~~ extrapair mating could be a way of bonding with a new male in case her current partner dies, but that the male engages 'purely for sexual satisfaction'. It seems that even when anthropomorphising we project our sexist dou-ble standards onto animals. We are all conditioned to believe males want/need/enjoy sex and that's enough, but a female must have a *reason*. She couldn't possibly just want to get her

---

* He only had £4 and kept asking what I wanted it for. I wasn't expecting resistance and had to create a credible fiction about topping up a parking meter, with the additional lies of car ownership and 'Yes, I CAN drive, I just don't do it in front of people.'

rocks off. That is not a pun, don't lose respect for me.

Here's the thing. Dr Hunter observed very few of these sex/rock exchanges – she estimates 'only a few per cent' in the total interactions studied – which leaves me with many more questions. If such a practice was beneficial to survival surely it would be more widespread. What differentiated the females who partook in extra-pair mating? Were their nests particularly devoid of rocks? Were their mates rubbish at providing? Ha ha, we've caught me projecting *my* bias onto the penguins – she *must* be desperate or needy. Perhaps *The Secret Diary of a Cold Girl* begins in exactly the same way as her human equivalent's, looking down the lens and flirtily asserting, 'I love sex and I love pebbles – and I know you don't believe that I enjoy the sex, but I do.' Either way, this behaviour is not effectively understood so I wouldn't go around quoting it as evidence of transactional sex in nature.

A more illuminating study was conducted by a biology professor called Larry Wolf in 1975. His paper is about purple-throated Carib hummingbirds and how he observed the females using sex to get food. Hummingbirds have incredibly fast metabolisms as they expend a great deal of energy flapping their silly wings. They eat flower nectar, pollen, insects and tree sap – and they need a lot, consuming about half their body weight every day to survive. That's like me eating five stone of doughnuts daily and still looking like a shiny fairy with a beak, what a life! The birds are also incredibly territorial, each one claiming a small area of plants and shrubbery for itself. But nature can be very sexist; male hummingbirds are bigger and stronger than females, and they want the best territories with the loveliest, most sugary flowers. You may be thinking, 'Male hummingbirds are well girly,' so let me tell you that they guard their flowers fiercely and fight off any interloper birds. The puny females must either make do with a less nutritious habitat or form a pair bond with a male who will share his bounty. Or there's a third option: a female may exchange sex for temporary access. In times of drought a female will quickly starve and die if she relies on her sub-par garden. If she enters a male's territory he'll fight her UNLESS she 'flirts' with him. Then he'll permit her to drink delicious nectar in the lead-up to mating, after which he reasserts dominance and chases her away. In human terms this would be like visiting a male neighbour who'd punch you if you started raiding the cupboards, but if you're wearing a low-cut top, laughing at his jokes and touching him on the arm, then he'll watch you eating ham from the fridge quite peacefully. Maybe you'll even slurp some soup during the sex itself, but when it's over he'll kick you out without breakfast. This would be your neighbour knowing that you're starving but not helping unless you sleep with him. This is survival sex.

It might be relevant to know that the behaviour observed in these birds wasn't a mating strategy, or at least did not appear to have a reproductive incentive. The mating season had not yet begun when the study was conducted, and in specimens collected by Wolf the males' testes were not yet enlarged and the females weren't ready to lay eggs. I am trying to work out how Wolf could have known these details without cutting open the birds, and the answer is he couldn't. He's a murderer and I've called the police.

While we wait for the feds, let's investigate a further instance of animals paying for sex. Capuchin monkeys are closer to our own species than penguins and hummingbirds but still separated by several million years of divergent evolution. They are small, leapy guys, full of personality – you'll recognise them from TV and showbiz. Ross from *Friends* had a capuchin called Marcel who also appeared in *30 Rock* and numerous movies, which is cruel because I'd like to have appeared in those things. I think if casting directors saw how cute I look eating mango I'd get more work.

The capuchin experiment took place at Yale University in 2006. Keith Chen gave the monkeys silver tokens, then taught them to exchange those tokens for snacks. The study ascertained that the monkeys could obey certain economic principles, e.g. if peanut butter goes up in 'price', buy cheap grapes instead, and vice versa. All very interesting in terms of cute lil' primates grasping the concepts of inflation and relative value. Maybe if they are so skilled and intelligent we should stop doing experiments on them? I'd read in articles online that as soon as the capuchins had an 'economy' they used this 'money' to buy sex and porn. I read in a book called *Porn Panic!* that Chen had 'invented the monkey brothel'. I read in a science journal that the females mating for tokens were proving that transactional sex is hardwired into monkey behaviour. Then I read the original study, which doesn't mention anything about sex at all. BORING.

I googled 'monkey brothel', had an existential crisis, and eventually found the details I wanted in a *New Yorker* article titled 'Monkey Business'. One day during the study, a capuchin had escaped his cage, grabbed the tray containing tokens and lobbed them to his friends. This was annoying for the experimenters; flooding the market with new currency will always lead to devaluation. This monkey was the Bank of England printing money to bail out the bankers. So now you have this Wolf of Wall Street situation going on in the capuchin lab. The monkeys are newly rich with tokens, jumping around and demanding snacks, while Chen describes seeing 'out of the corner of his eye' a mating, followed by the male giving a token to the female, which she promptly exchanged with the experimenter for a grape.

I think Chen's 'brothel' is going to be poorly reviewed on PunterNet.

There's too much assumption in seeing a token changing hands after mating and saying it *must* be 'payment' for sex. Especially as Chen only observed this once, and from the corner of his eye – the least reliable part of vision. The experimenter states that he took 'measures' to ensure this never happened again. I wonder what he did? The anti-prostitution lobby would love to know!

There's a whole theory about transactional sex in primates which has been misconstrued and misrepresented. The pop science book *Mismatch* states: 'Male chimpanzees and macaques have been shown to give meat to ovulating females, with the idea that they will be able to copulate with them in return for this. This is called the "meat-for sex theory" in scientific speak.'*

---

* The full title of the book, by Ronald Giphart and Mark van Vugt, is *Mismatch: How Our Stone Age Brain Deceives Us Every Day and What We Can Do About It*. It was recommended to me by a professor of anthropology called Gil Greengross and it does have lots of interesting ideas in it, but it also oversimplifies or exaggerates the results of certain studies and makes a lot of sweeping statements and conclusions. Like this one from page 114: 'You could even argue that the large number of stand-up comedians who are "physically challenged" suggests that humour is an alternative mating strategy for men who would not get a look-in on account of their appearance or status.' It turns out that by virtue of my job not only am I a man, I'm an ugly one.

The meat-for-sex theory suggests that male chimpanzees swap bits of dead animal carcass (meat) for sexual access to females (sex), but studies have NOT proved that anything like a direct trade takes place. Yes, they have seen male chimps giving meat to ovulating females, but not exclusively. Over months of observation it was found that fertile periods in females did not encourage more hunting in males, nor were ovulating females given more meat than their non-fertile ~~friends colleagues~~ other chimps.

The quote above is misleading. It makes a copulation-for-resources trade sound like a human business deal when it is a far more generalised behaviour. *Science* magazine made the same mistake. Underneath a photo of a chimpanzee holding some bone and gristle they published the caption: 'Meat for a mate. A male chimp offers meat in exchange for sex with a female.' Again, this gives the impression that there is a literal transaction taking place – 'Here's your pork chop, Stephanie, now take your knickers off' – when that isn't the case at all. Studies on chimps in the Ngogo and Gombe communities both found that meat sharing didn't give males any immediate mating advantages. What they did find was that over a much longer time (three years) females were more likely to mate with males who had periodically shared protein with them in the past. So rather than being directly transactional (pork-chop-bend-over, in scientific speak) this appears to be about bonds, familiarity and the attractiveness of a male as a proven provider. The better hunters had more meat to share and so shared more often. These males were also of higher social status due to the size and strength that enabled their superior hunting, and those attributes combined to make them desirable to females. Even I think they sound sexy and I'm vegan.

The relationship between food provision and sex in *our* species is complicated. We have a considerable body dimorphism between the sexes. Just as male hummingbirds are larger than females, just as male chimpanzees are bigger, faster and stronger than their mothers and daughters, humans are also unequally sized. This size discrepancy has ramifications: the potential for violence, the possibility of provision and protection.

How would male strength and fitness have affected the women of pre-agricultural times? If the men of the tribe hunted more successfully than her, she may have been reliant on them for a portion of her sustenance. When she got pregnant, an increased need for nutrition combined with a decrease in physical agility made her even more dependent on the generosity of others. This continued after the birth and through the several years of breastfeeding.

We've gone through this already.

And I've no doubt all this is in Diana's mind as she lies in bed debating the merits of fee-paying cuckoldry with her husband.

More Indecent Proposal

Debating her survival sex Diana dabbles in philosophy to assert that the 'self' and 'physical self' are separate and distinct:

DIANA

It wouldn't mean anything. It's just my body. It's not my mind, it's not my heart.

She argues that the parts of herself which do mean something, the parts which she owes to her husband, are metaphysical, emotional. That perhaps flesh can be rented without any loss to self or love. Diana doesn't phrase it as poetically as me but I've probably thought about this longer than she has. Years ago my uncle cheated on my aunt. It was unfortunate that we all knew about it, but my family never stops gossiping and enjoying each other's misfortunes and tribulations. So we all knew he cheated and then we all knew that she'd forgiven him. She had to legitimise it to all of us. 'It's only sex, not love,' she defended her defence of him. But years later she told me, drunk, that it felt like everything and nothing depending on how she looked at it. 'It's only bodies and touching and a few minutes of animal and then over.' My aunt was right, it was meaningless. 'Except it's everything.' She was right twice and caught in contradictory truths. I think of this when I turn over 'sex work is work' in my mind, because it is, and then it isn't. Sex and meaning can be pulled apart but reunite quickly. Isn't that what we

are struggling with? Even when we are conscious and intellectual and reasonable, our physiological responses might be
more basic – which David from *Indecent Proposal* is going to
demonstrate for us beautifully.

The film leaps out of bed and into a legal office. A rotund
lawyer takes a call from David. Does he know who John
Gage is? Of course he does, 'he's a billionaire and a major
poon hound'. Awkward pause. Does David wish to sell
his wife via a lawyer who speaks more respectfully about
women? Or does he want the man buying his wife to be less
of a player? We'll never know. The silence is over. David
explains how they met Gage and what the deal is. 'How
could you do this?' asks the circular lawyer – we assume the
guy is an uptight monogamist who thinks you shouldn't rent
your wife out – 'I could have got you TWO million.' It's
a misdirect, hahaha, this film is a comedy. Now the lawyer
says he has to ask about 'the moral issue' . . . his fee, another
misdirect, hahaha. The lawyer wants 5 per cent of the million. David is the pimp and the lawyer is the pimp's pimp and
we're all chuckling away in the nineties.

The scene transitions, taking the lawyer with it. Now he
is sitting opposite John Gage and going through the stipula-
tions of the sex contract. We can see it's very professional and
above board because there is a fountain pen. The men have a
fun chat discussing what happens if Gage is impotent (he still
pays) or dies in the act (he still pays*). Finally, all the men are
happy with the deal and they leave the office to collect the
person who has been sold. Diana looks pale and worried as
her husband and lawyer leave. Demi Moore is doing some

* Via his ghost? Not specified.

delicate acting, a wobbly 'holding back tears' face. John Gage tells Diana not to worry, he doesn't bite. How reassuring to know that the person paying to have intercourse with you won't use their teeth.

David is having a celebratory snack with his ~~sphere~~ lawyer, who tells him, 'I couldn't have got five hundred for my girlfriend. Not that I'd do that. But it's okay that you did.' It's a rollercoaster of a sentence that manages to reinforce that women have a monetary value, insult his own partner, whom he appears to think he owns, and then assert moral respectability. He adds, 'For a million bucks *I'd* sleep with him.'

HEY THAT'S AUDREY'S JOKE.

Also, it's not a million bucks, it's a million bucks minus 5 per cent, which is $950,000. The lawyer of all people should know that. David checks his watch and realises what time it is: time to change his mind! He runs through the hotel looking for John Gage's room, he is sweating and rolling his eyes. He catches an elevator – I don't think he's been in one before, he's bashing his fists on the walls rather than pressing the buttons or doing a wee. John Gage's apartment is empty apart from a Hispanic cleaner. 'Up, up,' she gestures, and points in a way I thought was crudely sexual until I realised she meant THE ROOF.

David arrives on the top floor as a helicopter takes off with Diana in it. She's not driving because she's not being played by Tom Cruise. David's hair spreads out in all directions, flailing in the wind. I know it's just air displaced by the helicopter but it looks like really emotional hair acting.

John tells Diana that she's in charge, but she wasn't driving the helicopter and she's not driving this. People who hire the services of sex workers repeatedly reassure themselves of 'choice' as an antidote to the fact that they're paying someone to do something they don't want to.

But that's all employment—

Is this pragmatism? Okay.

The film hides the sex between Diana and Gage, we are left to imagine it. We do not know if it was work or pleasure. Diana reappears at the hotel in the morning. David is exhausted from running around and punching lifts. He smears her lipstick and then they smooch passionately. The film does not allow us to do a scientific examination of David's sperm load the next time he ejaculates but we must presume it would have high motility due to sperm competition. John Gage's too, actually.

Perhaps David could write 'How to Sell Your Wife to a Billionaire' for Literotica?

The film is half over, indecency has been proposed and consummated. David and Diana go to the bank and find that the house David was building has been purchased by somebody else, bummer.

Diana tends to ripe tomatoes on a sunny day, but David wants to talk about when she had sex with Gage. 'Was it good?' he asks. David thought he could get over it, but he can't. Being a human being, a conscious animal, means that we often have a split between what we think and what our body *feels*. Our intellect and our wife may remind us 'it meant nothing, it was just sex', but natural selection has built us to be jealous. David is battling this even though he was sculpted by a scriptwriter rather than evolution. He is rooting through Diana's bag for clues, shouting and throwing stuff – I bet Professor Takahashi would love to slip David into an fMRI and see what his fictional amygdala is up to.

The couple split up. It turns out John Gage bought their new house. Diana confronts Gage, which seems to turn him on. He romances Diana by getting her to be an estate agent for him. He tells her a sad story about being stood up, buys some dogs and she is won over. Meanwhile, David rips up photographs, buys zero dogs and tries to punch John Gage but misses, falling on the floor. Having reached rock bottom (the pavement) he now decides to get a job, NOW. Casino cafe waitress would be rolling her eyes, like 'Some people', except she's not in it any more.

When he is back on his feet, both figuratively and literally, David turns up to speak to Diana at work. He is sorry: 'I was afraid that you wanted him, I was afraid he was the better man.' The only thing Gage had more of was money. Status and money are connected, it's really shitty, but they are.

With both Diana and David now working for a living, you might be wondering what happened to all that money. We find out as the posh new couple Diana and John enjoy a zoo fundraiser hosted by excellent comedian Billy Connolly. It's so nice to see the American rich protecting African wildlife without a gun in their hand and a lion under their foot. Billy Connolly announces the next animal, it's an ugly wet one, the hippopotamus. David rushes in, trying to impress Diana. 'One million dollars!' he shouts. He has saved the zoo and seemingly forgotten his lawyer's commission. He will now need to raise 50K to pay for this hippo. With no wife who will he pimp?

Luckily, he regains ownership of his wife a bit later. John Gage pretends that he doesn't love her any more and gives her his lucky dollar, which is a massive pay cut but she doesn't mind. 'She never would have looked at me the way she looked at him,' Gage explains to his driver. They drive off and Diana gets a coach to a pier, where David is coincidentally sitting sadly, and it's all going to be okay because the zoo is saved.

I hope you enjoyed my describing the film as much as I enjoyed watching it five times. Now, let's consider how sex and money intersects in *all* of our lives.

The Economics of Dating

Indecent Proposal is an extreme and fictional example, but we all experience romantic interactions with others where money changes hands. When you consider buying drinks and the other expenditures of dating, it's apparent that money and choice underwrite each other, although we are often oblivious. Breaking it down—

You're not going to rap again?

You wish. In 2015, back when people wrote blogs, a woman called Lauren Crouch used hers to moan about a guy she'd met through dating site Tinder.* She'd had a date with him in Costa Coffee but declined to go back to his house for dinner because she didn't know him. They messaged and he invited her round the next day. Lauren said no, presumably because she doesn't enjoy getting murdered, and he then asked her to refund him the cost of her coffee.

It's funny, isn't it? All the newspapers picked it up because this was back before the Trump presidency and they had a lot of pages to fill. They printed Lauren's description of the date, with the guy saying he had an Ocado delivery coming and had to hurry back. They printed screengrabs of the messages between them, with her saying no thank you to meeting up again, she hadn't felt a 'spark', and his reply: 'OK, fair

* 3nder for people who only do one at a time.

enough. Can you pay me back for your coffee? I don't like wasting money. Prefer to use it on a date with someone else.'

The amount he wanted refunded was £3.50. I did some investigative ~~procrastination~~ journalism to find out what the hell you order in Costa that costs £3.50, and the only coffee of that price is called a 'creamy cooler', which sounds deliciously revolting. These creamy coolers are the coffee-shop equivalent of ordering lobster and champagne. 'A creamy cooler to go,' is what Kanye West would say if he popped into Costa on his way to a concert. Rappers would rap about creamy coolers if their music was set in cafes and not da club.

NO—

I wasn't. We can all enjoy judging this guy – sure, he'll splash out on Ocado for himself but the beverage he bought Lauren was a loan on the understanding of . . . what? Putting out? A guaranteed second date? Wanting the money back suggests there's an unspoken deal which she broke. He demands reimbursement like she's a shop that overcharged him or sold him a faulty product. He wants his £3.50 returned so he can 'use it on a date with someone else'. He will replace her with a woman who functions correctly, accompanying him to his home and watching him unpack his upmarket food shopping with the proper appreciation.

In an interview with the *Telegraph** Lauren was asked if she'd repaid the man, and replied, 'I don't come with a money back guarantee. Dates aren't commodities.' But her situation demonstrates that they are to some people – to at least *one*

---

* There was NO NEWS in 2015. It was before all those celebrities died to avoid Brexit.

man, or he wouldn't have asked for the £3.50 back. The difficulty with unspoken deals is—

You can't hear them.

Of course, if they are silent and assumed, we can find ourselves at cross purposes in intimate situations. We can't read each other's invisible rule books. The *Telegraph* had a survey at the bottom of the article:

SHOULD HE HAVE ASKED FOR HIS MONEY BACK?
☐ Yes, she wasted his money.
☐ No, it's a little bit stingy.

After voting you get the stats: 78 per cent of people agreed with me, 'No'. Which means that 22 per cent of *Telegraph* readers had clicked 'Yes'. Money spent on someone you don't see again is a WASTE, apparently. Money is supposed to buy you things, and he got NOTHING. For those 22 per cent, if you have no intention of becoming romantically involved with someone or are as yet undecided, you shouldn't let them pay for any drinks or snacks as they may feel resentful when you don't want to see them again. And you know what, that's fine. That is entirely reasonable.

So why did 78 per cent say he was *unreasonable*? Is it the quibbley small amount that made him 'a little bit stingy'? Would we have felt differently if he'd spent hundreds of pounds on Lauren's meal? Or is it that 78 per cent of *Telegraph* readers accept a bizarre status quo where men of any income are automatically expected to pay for women on dates?

Yes.

I disagree. I took Lauren's side against Ocado Man until I read her saying, 'I always offer to pay anyway and women should always offer to pay.'

Listen up, Lauren, 'offering to pay' is not the same as paying. Offering to pay is a gesture, paying is equality. 'Women should always offer to pay' strongly suggests that no man will ever let them. That by 'offering' you've excused yourself. To me women should always *insist* on paying, because we're reinforcing our own infantilisation when we don't.

APPARENTLY it is 'traditional' for men to pay on dinner dates, and I say 'traditional' while rolling my eyes like a teenager listening to their stepdad. I was unaware of this 'tradition' because I've never dated, I'm too busy, there's no time for sustenance – 'You're not hungry, get upstairs.' I became enlightened via the reality TV show *First Dates*, a charming programme where supposedly well-matched people make small talk about previous relationships, dead parents and career goals. I like it: except for one thing, the show fetishises men in heterosexual couples paying the bill. Whenever a receipt hits the table, there is a tracking close-up creating tension: 'Oooh, what's going to happen?' Then the camera zooms in on a man's face, who's often had quite a terrible time, and he's juddering under the weight of expectation and sweeps the paper in a saucer towards him. 'Don't worry, I'll get it.' Then a woman puts up the least resistance you've EVER SEEN. 'You sure,' she intones with no upward inflection. Without waiting for a reply she turns to watch a couple on another table. Yes, Lauren, she is *offering*, but without intention or insistence.

What is this silliness? I know that people pay for each other – 'I'll get this one,' we proffer, 'my treat,' we assert to our friends, family and partner – but the idea that a man is expected, *obliged* to pay on a first date just because he is the *man* is shocking.

Maybe I've been doing feminism too long. I thought we were all working towards a society where there aren't expectations prescribed by gender? Surely women are contradicting ourselves as we list our demands: 'What do we want? Equality! Respect! Lasagne, green beans and small potatoes!'

There's an episode of *First Dates* where the man doesn't offer to pay, he insists on splitting the bill, and everyone reacts like he shat on the table. The waitresses bitch about him in the corner. His date cries down the lens in her post-dinner interview: 'I had to buy my own pie!' The man is depicted as disrespectful, the woman grossly insulted. It plays out like a scene from Jane Austen, everyone talking about manners and gentlemanly conduct.

If I was a man, I'd be angry about these kinds of double standards, but when men do reject 'tradition' or try to address the sexism of it they're perceived as unmanly. This is how a sexist state of affairs is maintained – by reinforcing that it is 'the norm', with any deviation punished. This has always happened with feminists. When passionate and furious they're dismissed as 'mad'; when solidly reasonable – 'Please don't pat my bottom, sir' – they're overreacting about something harmless and need to 'lighten up'. Men who question their prescribed roles are either vilified the way feminists always have been, or told it's not a problem, it's a little thing, don't worry about it, men are winning, you can't complain.

And lots of men don't. Just recently there was a *First Dates* episode where a young woman called Cecilia insisted on paying for herself, and the *Sun* ran it as a story* with the headline '*First Dates* girl accused of "emasculating" date by refusing to let him pay the bill'. Accused? But by whom? Oh, the *Sun*, who printed ~~educated opinions~~ tweets from people insisting that '*First Dates* girl' should've allowed the guy to 'be a gentleman'. I like Cecilia. She asked her date, 'Give me one rational reason why you should? There's no rational reason why a woman shouldn't pay.' CECILIA, get over here and write my book for me. I agree with this queen, there is no *rational* reason for this type of gendered behaviour – but human beings are quite irrational, if you haven't noticed. Some of the irrationality has a biological basis, some of it is cultural.

Taking the latter first, I've a friend who dates a lot and I asked her, 'When you go out with a man for the first time, do you expect him to pay for you?' She replied slowly, abashed, 'It's not *ideal*. I know what you're getting at, it's not ideeeeeal. But it's just . . .' – she stared into space, then returned her eyes to me, pupils large – '. . . *romantic!*' What is romantic about being treated like an invalid? Oh, it was *sooooo* romantic, he spooned soup into my mouth and helped me go to the bathroom.

Why are romantic stories always about men rescuing women? As children we're fed tales of princes saving thin, pale wenches from towers, ogres or long sleeps. As adults we read romance books that repeat the same man-saves-woman narrative, but this time with thrusting groins and glistening pudendas. Economic disparity is the crux of romance – female characters are never CEOs or Olympians, they are

---

* No excuse for this, there's loads of news now.

servants and slaves while the men are royalty or nobility. The importance of male status and female prettiness, beauty and the best, is repeatedly reinforced.

One of the most famous and admired romantic stories is *Pride and Prejudice* by Jane Austen. The name 'Mr Darcy' is synonymous with chivalry, desirability, the ultimate gentleman. His union with Elizabeth Bennet is the happiest ending in literature until you examine it more closely . . .

Once upon a time Mr Bennet has five daughters, none of whom can inherit their family home because they've neglected to be sons. Property in the Regency period passes to the nearest male relative, in this case Mr Collins, an idiot vicar cousin. Mrs Bennet is desperate to marry off her daughters before her husband dies and they are made homeless. This is not a whimsical urge – during this time women had the legal status of children, charges of their fathers until marriage, when custodianship was passed to their husband. These women were not well educated and did not, could not, work. The Bennet sisters are appendages that need to be fed, clothed and supported by men. Luckily, they manage to meet some very rich people with big houses, and three of the five become betrothed despite their poverty. Jane seduces Mr Bingley by being beautiful, incredibly quiet, patient and blushing. Lizzy seduces Mr Darcy by taking long walks and being able to keep a secret. Lydia runs away with soldier Mr Wickham on the sly and is punished by being sent up north.

Hooray, the family are saved! And while it is the love between Lizzy and Darcy that makes this book so pleasurable, we must not forget that it is MONEY that saves the Bennets. It is a story of economic entrapment, but when women do not have the ability to earn money for themselves, what other option do they have? *Pride and Prejudice* is one of my favourite books, but I still realistically question whether Elizabeth falls in love with Darcy or with Pemberley, his nice big house. I question this sort of romance, because it looks a lot like Stockholm syndrome. Lost in the background of this novel is the Bennets' friend Charlotte, who marries the annoying Mr Collins – not for lust or love but out of necessity. You wouldn't want to share a train carriage with him, let alone your life, your bed. Another *Indecent Proposal*, but while Diana need only sell herself once, Charlotte and all women who marry for financial reasons might be expected to do it repeatedly.

Don't start picking on marriage.

Don't get me started on marriage. Does romance *need* inequality to blossom? Are the sparks of lust and longing strengthened by crossing a chasm of disparity? There was a study reported in the *Daily Mail* in 2014 that suggested equality was a turn-off: 'Doing the housework means men get LESS sex'. I was baited by the intriguing headline. The article went on to wonder whether men performing traditionally womanly tasks like cooking and cleaning meant that no one wanted to shag them any more. Then the study itself was described. An institute in Spain had analysed data from 4,561 middle-aged American couples, a very specific amount of people. 4,561 isn't a study size, it's a PIN number. The couples had been interviewed about their sex lives and it turned out that the ~~monsters~~ men who did no housework at all had sex 1.5 more times a month than men who did their fair share.

At first I got distracted pondering this half sex, the 0.5. Is that a blow job, a lost erection, or when it slips out and you're laughing too much to finish? Then I remembered how averages work, how it's all divided between everyone, and I moved on to more serious thoughts. Why the extra sex? Could it be that some couples find nagging makes them horny? Would a couple who row more about a husband's laziness end up having make-up sex which ups their average? OH, it suddenly strikes me, what if the kind of chauvinist who won't run a hoover round is also pushier, sexually insistent, won't-take-no-for-an-answer with his wife? I don't want to accuse men who don't iron their own shirts of being rapists—

I think you just did.

Whoops. The researchers of the study had the same worry and ruled out coercion by checking that women in those households were as happy and satisfied with their sex lives as the women in the shared-housework homes.

I have another thought: what about the women who do no housework? I don't do any and I've never had a problem getting people to kiss me. Maybe this isn't so much about gender, perhaps people who are covered in crumbs are just sexier? That's why when someone's really sexual we'll say, 'Oooh, she's so dirty, oh yeah, filthy,' stuff like that. That could be a very literal compliment.

The study's researchers did not make that suggestion. Instead they took it to prove, in the words of co-author Julie Brines, that 'men and women have deep-seated ideas about what is masculine and feminine'. *Scientific American* interpreted it like this: 'Displays of masculinity may evoke feminine displays in women, which activates or intensifies sexual charge. Put the man on a rider mower, in other words, and boom – fireworks. Stand him at a sudsy sink, and it's a probable no go.'

I find this so hard to believe. I can't imagine finding mowing man attractive, on his little grass car? No thank you. I do like the sound of dishwash man but I'm biased – I don't have a garden, I do have a sink. For me the idea that housework is emasculating to the point that it dampens passion for your partner is depressing. This gendered perception of housework was oddly repeated by Prime Minister Theresa May when she was interviewed along with her husband on *The One Show* in 2017. She talked about 'boys' jobs' and 'girls' jobs' around the house; apparently he puts the bins out and she puts gender relations back to the 1950s. AND HERE IS THE RELEVANT THING, Theresa May is old. So were the American couples interviewed for this study; they'd all got married in the 1960s and 70s. When it was repeated by Cornell University with younger couples, the data showed that men who did chores had more sex, and more satisfying sex, than men who didn't.

This means attitudes have changed. It means that Julie Brines was wrong with her assertion of 'deep-seated ideas about what is masculine and feminine'. Turns out they weren't deep-seated, just regular-depth ideas that are formed by the society we grow up in and that'll alter and vary as our culture does. Hooray! This isn't merely about who tidies up after whom, this isn't point scoring. It's about healthy relationships where people respect each other's time and input. Freedom from chauvinism benefits everybody. But while household roles appear to be culturally influenced, is the same true of our expectation that men should pay?

Season one, episode five of *Sex and the City* is not *generally* considered an academic resource, but while we're assessing how culture affects and reflects our attitude to masculinity we

~~can watch TV programmes and pretend we're working~~ must engage with and analyse that culture. This episode is very relevant to our deliberations. It revolves around Carrie, she's the main character, an exceptionally thin woman with resplendent hair. She's been on a date with a French guy and slept with him. In the morning, he doesn't go into her flatmate's room and do it with her, like when my friend Michelle had sex with a Frenchman. Instead he leaves an envelope full of dollars next to the bed! Carrie freaks out – oh no, the French guy thought she was a hooker (her word), which is stupid because a professional would've got the money up front. Then Carrie's friends come over to be in *Sex and the City* with her. Samantha, also thin, doesn't know what the problem is: 'What are you getting so uptight about?' Samantha speaks like a cat who is smug but also aroused. 'Money is power. Sex is power. Therefore, getting money for sex is simply an exchange of power.'*

Samantha from *Sex and the City* has articulated her opinion like maths, which is always persuasive and cleversounding. Let's unpack her equation. Sam says, 'Money is power,' and I'd agree with that. On both a macro- and microcosmic level, those with money seem powerful. Rich corporations can exert influence on politicians, rich people can pay

---

* Sometimes while I'm writing I remember that I'll have to say all this out loud in the audio book. I'll have to do my terrible Samantha from *Sex and the City* impression, and I can't wait. I don't know if I'll read that last sentence in the audio book. Or that one. Or indeed this one. Won't it be weird to talk about the audio book inside the audio book? It's *quite* weird to be talking about it here, in the book. Or in the audio book if I've recorded all this and you're listening to me deciding whether you should call the men who took Blanche DuBois away.†
† While we're on this topic, it's worth remembering that Blanche DuBois relied on the kindness of strangers because she had no money of her own.

others to work for them. The richest countries loan money to the poorest and use their indebtedness to deprive them of resources while taking advantage of their citizens for cheap labour. The poorer you are, the fewer choices you have. You may be dependent on a government, a harvest, a person. It's no coincidence that many abusive relationships involve the withholding or control of cards and cash. There is no escape without money. You cannot travel, hide or survive without it. If you think about your own life, your options and freedoms will depend on what you can afford.

'Sex is power,' Samantha asserts next. This sounds a lot like bullshit at first. You don't find women in thongs running the country, no one's ever got her tits out in a meeting to get more respect. Actual sex, the literal act of sex, is an interchangeable exchange of status. Rolling around, taking turns at vulnerability and domination. Even within the most vanilla sex there is back and forth – the stronger person might enjoy having their arms held above their head, the weaker person could sit astride and enjoy feeling dominant. Consensual sex is playful and trusting, permitted dominance and pretend submission, tumbling over and under. That sex is a sharing of power.

When I was a teenager I read in magazines that female sexuality was powerful. It's the kind of thing my mum would say too, she'd tell me that our sexuality gave us power because we could use it to manipulate men – to get what we want. It was not something that seemed true to me. I never watched a cat winding his way round a trousered leg meowing to be fed and thought, 'Look how powerful that kitty is.' Can-opener is power. Opposable thumbs is power. Pussy is owned.

There are many people who'd disagree with me on that.

Erotic Capital

My friend Carla is a stripper. She earns a lot of money. When she talks about stripping being empowering, I listen. It makes her feel physically powerful, because she feels attractive. Her body is strong, and the desire she elicits makes her feel she has power over the men who desire her. She mesmerises. Having another human watch your movements like your body answers every question is a wonderful feeling. Carla is able to make men drunk on wanting her. When she talks, I think I agree that being desired is a form of power – if we didn't live in a capitalist society. In hunter–gatherer times, attractiveness, fertility, beauty were a currency of their own. Like money, you could exchange them for protection or food.

I only found out about 'erotic capital' recently. I was interviewing Kalinda, who works as a dominatrix escort (her description). She said, 'Women who don't take advantage of their erotic capital are doing themselves a disservice,' and I bit my pencil and asked what the hell she was talking about. Kalinda told me she'd written her university dissertation on this topic and would send it to me. We must be so grateful to people who do not treat us like we're stupid; it is the ultimate generosity and the only way we'll learn. I now know that erotic capital is a value that we all possess, calculated on our sexual attractiveness and exchangeable for other forms of capital – money or services or goods. As in all economies, some of us are richer than others. It's not fair.

Kalinda made a fascinating point in her dissertation about the gender pay gap being easily bridged by how much more money men are willing to spend on sexy women than women are willing to spend on sexy men. My friend Carla sells her erotic capital in a strip club and makes more than her equally gorgeous sister who works for an insurance company – the latter being an example, for Kalinda, of someone refusing to capitalise on their sexual attractiveness and thus 'doing themselves a disservice'.

Brain exploding emoji

In capitalism, we're all machine-people selling our time and services. Our value is dependent on skills. Being sexually desirable is a skill, or a service, that most women refuse to sell. Or refuse to admit they are selling even if that is what they're being paid for.

I asked Kalinda how she felt about men paying for dinner. She told me a meal is a wage paid in exchange for her time spent at the table. Things are so clear in her universe, and I'm jealous of that clarity. She has priced everything and is not abashed. 'What if the man hasn't enjoyed himself?' I asked. 'He did,' she replied, winking, and I couldn't think of any more questions.

Afterwards I worried about obligation, expectation. I asked my mailing list some questions on this topic and I got really upset by an email from a girl who'd gone out with a group of friends. A man had bought them some champagne, then another bottle. At the end of the night her friends said one of them would have to go home with him. They all had boyfriends, so it was decided she had to do it. It made me feel sick. Did the man know she felt she was 'paying' for their drinks? Did he care?

I was really angry on her behalf, but having been young myself, I understood that they felt there had been an unspoken deal they couldn't renege on. They had taken too much from him not to offer something in return, a sacrifice.

Obligation is an under-discussed emotion. It can be a strong current tugging our behaviour away from what we want to do and towards what is expected of us, our duty, what we owe to whom. I learned a little lesson about men and money when I was fourteen. I went out with girls I had met through drama club. We looked older (sixteen?), were confident and liked dancing. In Romford there were three nightclubs that DID NOT CARE how old you were. I'd smile to the bouncers and they'd move out of my way. Please note this was a closed-mouth smile which cunningly concealed my braces.

Alright, Ocean's Eleven.

I went out a lot from fourteen, fifteen, sixteen. I didn't have very much money because I was a child, not a hedge fund manager, but I quickly learned that men in pubs and clubs would get us drunk. They would come over and ask me or one of my friends, 'Can I get you a drink?' And we'd say yes because alcohol is the only way to switch off your hateful inner monologue and exist in the moment. 'Yes please, white wine.' But there was always more to this exchange. No one ever bought us a drink and went away. What they offered was a drink, but what they were buying was a chunk of our time, politeness, flirtation – a chance, an in? But *something*. I took these interactions on a case-by-case basis but most went like this:

Man offered alcoholic beverage. Sara said yes as she had no money to buy her own. Sara followed man to the bar, made small chat while he ordered, while they waited if it was busy. 'What's your name? Who are you here with? Do ya live round here? Oh yeah, which road?'

These men seemed old at the time but were probably about twenty-three, which I now consider an embryonic stage of humanity. No one is even born until twenty-seven, and no one should be held responsible for their actions until thirty-nine, nor have children before the age of fifty-two. There is too much to learn.

Sara would try to be entertaining and make a joke, have a laugh at the bar. When the drink arrives, clink the glasses, 'Cheers – thank you,' while making eye contact. Then take a sip, say, 'Have a great night,' turn and walk away. Sometimes I might add an 'I should get back to my friends'. Sometimes the man followed and I'd have to talk to them awkwardly about *Top Gear* or *Gladiators* for fifteen minutes. Sometimes they'd shout at me when I tried to leave: 'What the fuck?! I just bought you a drink.' The walking away was rude, it was not the deal. You weren't supposed to say yes to a drink unless you were interested in the guy, that was the rules, but without money I couldn't afford that system. 'I bought you a drink, bitch, where d'you think you're going?' Sometimes I didn't go through the pretence of gratitude and was called a cunt or a slag. I thought these men were stupid, but they had something I wanted: cash, a credit card, access to the numbing effect of alcohol.

If you're a man who's bought an ungrateful woman a drink, if you've ever felt belittled or tricked when you were simply trying to be friendly or meet someone new, you'll perceive this situation from the opposite perspective. We have things to learn from each other. When I was a young woman receiving attention in bars I never ever considered what it was like to be a straight man. I wanted to screech and play and be free with my friends. Every man who approached was a cloud blocking the sun. I did not know that my youth was enticing because I'd never not been young yet. It never occurred to me that it might take bravery to speak to a stranger, to risk rejection. That the offer of a drink was a socially acceptable way of saying, 'May I enter your life? Might we have fun together?'

Today I'm thinking about how wrong I was to assume that money meant nothing to the men, because they handled it so easily. But it felt unfair to me then, because I had nothing, and life felt like a lottery that other people had already won.

I have money now, and I have never since said yes to a stranger offering me a drink. I have never ever wanted to meet a man who has approached me. I am sorry for men because our culture tells them to introduce themselves to women who in the vast, vast majority don't want to meet them.

Some of them do.

Okay, I am really biased, I think women are incredibly polite because you're bigger than us and we are taught to be polite. We've already seen that in our ancestral past, unknown men were potentially dangerous. For the men outside our tribe we were prey. A woman approached in a bar feels hunted. In the main, we do not want to talk to you. New man, stranger. You might be lovely, but we don't care.

I have money now, I never have to speak to anyone I don't want to, and I love it. What money has bought me is freedom, and I never forget it.

Grid Girls vs Presidents Club

I'd never heard of Grid Girls or the Presidents Club until they were cancelled.

I know now that Grid Girls were attractive women employed as models at Formula 1 events. Once the car whizzes past there isn't much for the crowd to look at, so Lycra-clad ladies were provided. I went on the Grid Girls website and the women were advertised like this:

> Add a touch of glamour to your companies open day, show, exhibition, trade show, private party and race meeting with Grid Girls UK.

There is an email address to write to for a quote and I'm so tempted to see how much it would cost to hire a dozen for my book launch. They're usually quite staid, polite affairs, everyone drinking wine from those tiny 125 ml glasses and pretending they've read your book when they haven't. I'll 'add a touch of glamour' with some hot women. Maybe I'll get them to pose reading the book and that will encourage other, non-gorgeous people to read it? Yes. Grid Girls will find their new vocation is sexing up literature. There'll be a Grid Girl on the front of the *London Review of Books* and sales will skyrocket. I'll design some spandex with Proust quotes on it, get the girls in them and some thick-rimmed glasses, standing behind library counters – suddenly we'll all be bookworms. Let's get these unemployed women back to work and improve the nation's literacy all at once.

It's not your worst idea.

Why did the Grid Girls lose their jobs? Were they rude? Did they forget to smile? Did they age or put on weight and thus fall foul of our society's restrictive beauty ideals? No. They continued to do what they had always done – be beautiful near cars. Their dumping is explained by Sean Bratches, the Managing Director of Commercial Operations at Formula 1, who wears a suit not made of Lycra:

'While the practice of employing grid girls has been a staple of Formula 1 Grands Prix for decades, we feel this custom does not resonate with our brand values and clearly is at odds with modern-day societal norms. We don't believe the practice is appropriate or relevant to Formula 1 and its fans, old and new, across the world.'

Mr Bratches says that Grid Girls are 'at odds with modern-day societal norms'. We know the Grid Girls haven't changed so it's norms that have. They've evolved over the last few decades and all the decades before that. People swish along like a river, generation after generation running past, comprised of many beliefs and behaviours but generally going in a similar direction. Then there are occasional phases of enlightenment where the river becomes conscious and goes 'WHAT THE FUCK ARE WE DOING WORSHIPPING THE SUN/ BURNING PEOPLE AT THE STAKE/KEEPING PEOPLE AS SLAVES?'

In a relatively short period of time, the objectification of women has gone from unnoticed to unfashionable to unconscionable. But within this we have many contradictions – like

Grid Girls. Women who have chosen to pay their mortgage by being looked at are suddenly being told that how they feed themselves and their kids isn't appropriate any more. It is 'at odds'. It is not believed 'appropriate'. Nothing has physically changed about female bodies and the instinctual reasons we like to look at them, but it's now interpreted as damaging, disrespectful, demeaning.

Leaving a pin in that for a second – let's gatecrash the Presidents Club. We can't attend in the proper way because only men get invited and I'm a woman, a bossy one who won't let you go without me.

The invitation to the 2018 Presidents Club dinner had a woman on it, Marilyn Monroe. She is symbolic of sumptuous sexuality even decades after her death. Whenever I see a photo of her I like to remember that she had endometriosis, a condition where cells that should be lining your womb migrate around your body and stick to other organs, causing extreme pain. Marilyn couldn't work when she was on her period because of the agony.

> Saying things like that is why we don't want you at our fun parties.

AHA, in fact there *were* women at the Presidents Club party, 130 'specially hired hostesses'. Women weren't invited to the Presidents Club, they were *provided*.

The rough details of the event were provided by some *Financial Times* journalists who worked there undercover in 2018 and then published an exposé. The 360 guests were 'figures from British business, politics and finance and the entertainment industry'. There was dinner, a show and a raffle, all held in the ballroom at the Dorchester Hotel. I've hosted events there myself, by the way – award ceremonies for PR companies or women's magazines. Comics refer to these types of gigs as 'corporates' and they're very well paid and soul-destroying. The hostesses 'specially hired' for the Presidents Club were paid £150 plus £25 towards a ~~new soul~~ taxi home. They were hired through an agency called Artista, whose website offers 'The Professional Face of Your Event'. To ensure those professional faces are also attractive, potential staff post photographs that can be vetted by clients. The prerequisite for the Presidents Club was that hostesses be 'tall, thin and pretty', which is bullshit, but also fairly typical of this sort of thing and unlikely to get anyone in the papers.

You might be wondering, what is a hostess? On this occasion, the hostesses' job was to bring drinks to tables, which sounds like waitressing, but there's a difference, which I can explain to you because I've done both. With hostessing you have to pretend to enjoy it. You have to smile and laugh at shit jokes and people who speak in clichés. You have to act like it gives you intense personal joy to bring people bottles that cost more than your wages. With bartending and waitressing you just plonk things in front of people and try not to meet their eye. Hostessing needs a bit of personality. They are paying you not simply to move liquid from one place to another without spilling it, but to be sociable, nice, chatty.

I worked for promotional and temp agencies all through my twenties. I've served on boats, I've sat on tables at black-tie events and encouraged millionaires to spend more at auctions, I've perched on casino stools and encouraged gamblers to keep drinking and playing. On paper, the women employed at the Presidents Club were no different.

The job description was getting drinks and being amiable. The thin, pretty women working ad hoc for an agency were students, models, out-of-work actors, skint artists. So far, so quotidian.

The women engaged to work at the Presidents Club were told* that their uniform would be provided on the night: a short black dress with a corset belt. They were instructed to wear high-heeled, sexy black shoes and black underwear and . . . THEY WERE TOLD WHAT COLOUR KNICKERS TO WEAR. Did your work tell you which pants to put on this morning? What a weird feeling that must be, to be a grown adult and get an email from a stranger about your underwear. And why would it matter what colour their underwear was? Because the skirt was so short their knickers would sometimes be visible.

Maybe this was the first test. If you applied for a gig and got a reply about your knicknoks you might feel unsettled and you might cancel. Or you might push on through because you need the money and £150 is a lot for one night's work and it'll probably be fine. So you arrived at the Dorchester at 4 p.m. There were make-up artists and hairdressers provided. You were given a five-page non-disclosure agreement to sign, but no time to read it. Legally you are now prevented from talking about what happens at the Presidents Club, so I'll take it from here.

The hostesses were presented in a ceremony, walking in twos across the ballroom stage and down to their allocated

* The source for this information was a *Financial Times* journalist who went undercover after hearing reports about the previous year's debauchery. You can find the full article online, along with the rest of the internet.

tables, like the animals entering the Ark but with high heels and a Little Mix soundtrack.* The women had been (black) briefed to keep their allocated men happy. They were to drink with guests, which is . . . unorthodox. They were all given a glass of wine before heading out. 'Why are they trying to get me drunk?' they may have wondered. I hope it puts your mind at rest to know that the event's brochure warned guests against 'harassment and unwanted conduct'.

One of the interesting things about being a human being is that we are so utterly subjective. We define things like harassment very differently. Unwanted conduct could include so many things, we're not mind readers – how are we supposed to know who's enjoying a lovely flirt with us and who doesn't want our groin rubbed against them? For this reason, I can't tell you that some of the oligarchs, chief executives and film directors attending the Presidents Club ignored the brochurial request. Perhaps they did not define groping as harassment? Some of these business owners may've believed that hands up skirts was *wanted* conduct. The *Financial Times* reported lewd comments such as 'rip off your knickers and dance on that table', requests for prostitution (their word), cocaine in the toilets, a man exposing his penis, as well as hostesses being 'repeatedly fondled' on bottoms, hips and legs.

There was also lots of completely willing hand-holding, lap-sitting and dancing. I interviewed someone who worked at the ball in 2017. She doesn't want to be quoted because of the non-disclosure agreement she signed, but what she made

* Please remind me to rewrite the Bible for millennials. With a Little Mix soundtrack.

clear is that some of the women working did enjoy themselves. Some hostesses drank and flirted and caught their taxis home. Some of them smoked and took drugs and got paid for sexual favours – and if that was their choice, I don't care, I'm not the police. But other women were mauled, insulted and badly treated. Some women thought the job was a paid, debauched night out and would be keen to do it all again. Others did not know what they were signing up for when they agreed to do it and found the experience traumatic. The woman I interviewed said that she had been told it would be 'fun' but that it wasn't.

I thought that was interesting, because it brings us back to how subjectively we define things, without sarcasm this time. My idea of 'fun' is daytime drinking, then having a hangover and some soup by 8 p.m. My idea of 'fun' is hiding your wallet, and then you can't go home and you're annoyed with me and I'm really laughing. My sister Cheryl's hen do was a surprise arranged by her friend Lyndsey. 'It's gonna be so fun,' she assured me. It cost £46 for front-row seats to see the Dream Boys. There was a very sad buffet and I had to watch my sister being lapdanced by a six-foot-eight muscle man. He laid her on the floor so he could do 'the worm' on her, Cheryl tried to get up and accidentally head-butted him. That was the only fun bit. I left early, feeling lonely. I think we can accept that some people's idea of fun can be someone else's nightmare.

But there's a difference between a night out and a job. If you're at a party and someone keeps groping you, you can complain, tell them to leave you alone, move away. You have the same rights as Gropey – you're both guests, you're equal. If you've had enough and want to escape, you can call your mum or a cab. You can flick the bird and walk away because you're not financially obligated to be at this party. You are free.

The expectations that underwrite employment restrict behaviour. There are financial consequences for disobedience. You are not free. If you are at work and your boss says something that could be a little suggestive, you laugh it off. You pretend to think they're joking and try hard to be polite and seem unbothered. 'Haha, yeah right,' you say, smiling and walking away. People who do not ease the tension of a superior's boundary-crossing become known as difficult. People who complain are told they are misreading the situation or can't take a joke or are accused of lying. Employment creates a power imbalance, and inferiority enables predators. The American comedian Louis CK targeted newer, younger comics. Kevin Spacey didn't manipulate and abuse his co-stars, but youthful drama-school students and aspirants. Harvey Weinstein assaulted, molested and propositioned actresses auditioning for him, because the only person more vulnerable to their boss than a current employee is a potential one.

I WILL NOW DECLARE THAT EVERYTHING IS ALLEGED SO THAT FABER & FABER DO NOT GET SUED BY SEX OFFENDERS* WHO CAN AFFORD EXPENSIVE LAWYERS TO KEEP EVERYBODY QUIET.

It is the imbalance of power that makes the groped person's position difficult. If an inferior puts their hand down your trousers, you get them fired. The workplace demands subservience of workers; to be successfully waged involves

* Alleged sex offenders. The lawyer wants me to remind you that, at the time of publication, Kevin Spacey and Harvey Weinstein are yet to go to trial and states that they are not guilty.

compliance. The workplace puts some people in authority over others. To be paid is to be subjugated.

Alright, Karl Marx.

You have no idea how horrible working in Tesco's was. It doesn't *always* feel bad, we don't always even notice. When you've agreed to work a shift, when you need the money, when your clothes to go home in are locked in a changing room with your phone and debit card and you can't leave . . . though I have to say that Tesco's never sent me any instructions regarding my underpants.

The Grid Girls have not reported allegations like those described at the Presidents Club. They are such different situations. In one of them attractive, thin women got paid a wage for being thin and attractive, saw some race cars, then went home. In the other, thin, attractive women were employed because they were thin and attractive and were then imposed upon, put into a situation where some of them were depersonalised, objectified and vulnerable.

The Grid Girls wanted to work and have been involuntarily deprived of that option because some people feel that if we live in a society where it is acceptable to lustily objectify women, then women will remain vulnerable to predatory males. One group of women are blamed for another group's experience, barely acknowledging the misbehaving rapist men in between. The problem with the Presidents Club as I understand it – and you may of course disagree – isn't that the women sold their evening, agreed to wear short dresses and serve men drinks, it is their treatment while they were there.

Maybe the men were confused as well?

Maybe they were. I think that is the quandary with erotic capital: if some women choose to sell theirs and others don't, can we trust men to be alert enough to the difference? In Leeds there is an area called Holbeck which has a 'legal' red light district, and many women who have nothing to do with the sex trade complain of being propositioned there, men calling at them from cars, following them. Girls on the way home from school have to put up with it, and this isn't the sex workers' fault – it's the Geoffs'.

The behaviour of the men at the Presidents Club, like the men I saw on stag dos in Amsterdam, appears animalistic to me. Is that because men in groups become tribal again? Something awful and ancient happens to them when they're together? There have been studies that found being in all-male groups alters testosterone levels, and especially if groups of men are then joined by one or two women – this creates a competitive environment. However, there was a recent experiment where men on stag dos were separated from the group and asked about their night. The majority of men individually said they weren't enjoying themselves but were doing it for the others! Male pack behaviour relies on complicity from all the males involved, and male safety means going along with the crowd.

If men look to each other for social cues and what is appropriate, and they all see each other leering and groping and saying bawdy things, they are all reassured that their behaviour is correct, so this is a vicious circle. It's also difficult to admonish men for their behaviour at the Presidents Club when the President of the United States has already behaved much worse and been rewarded.

Samantha from *Sex and the City* said, 'Sex is power,' but

I would submit that sex is only power because it can be exchanged for money. It remains money that is power. Sex is exchangeable for money, so it is powerful if you're swapping erotic capital in an environment you control OR where there are exact, stable conditions and a communication of explicit consent and informed agreement.

There is a reason strip clubs have bouncers, big men to protect women from other men, and rules. A whole heap of rules.

Men Should Pay

'Sex is a resource that men desire and women possess' is not my opinion, nor Samantha from *Sex and the City*'s. It's from the 2002 study 'Cultural Suppression of Female Sexuality' by American psychologists Roy Baumeister and Jean Twenge. They continue: 'To obtain sex, men must offer women other denied resources in return, such as money, commitment, security, attention or respect . . . The harder it is for men to obtain sex, the more they will be willing to offer women in return.' They conclude, 'Sexual scarcity improves women's bargaining position . . . suppression of female sexuality reduces the risk that each woman will lose her male lover to another woman.'

Or as 'meninist' Peter Lloyd puts it, 'Life's a marketplace where women are the sellers and men are the buyers. Like eBay but played out in restaurants and nightclubs.'

I don't think that paying for someone's dinner is *explicitly* transactional – buying a homeless person a sandwich doesn't mean you're expecting a hand job in the park later. Your manager pays for lunch at a meeting without expecting you to drop your trousers, your mum cooks you a roast every Sunday with no sexual undertones whatsoever – it's clear people can provide sustenance for each other without tensions and obligations. But where dating is concerned, expectations and implications could be different for the people either side of the table. Alex might believe that Stevie offered to pay because he earns more and was feeling generous, but Stevie might have paid thinking Alex is more likely to sleep with him if he does. That's quite worrying, isn't it?

I have to wonder how men feel about this. How many men feel the sting of financial outlay privately? Does that lead to misogynist anger? I think women who expect men to pay for them are wrong – there we go, I've said it. There is a BBC online article this week where a woman says she lets men pay because of the wage gap, and that is not a sensible way to counteract the undervaluation of women, is it? A middle-class woman necking Chablis while the cleaners, the nurses, the childcare assistants are rinsed by our economic structure. Ditto women taking their husbands' money after divorce – I think it's terrible. Sorry, but if we are not living in *Pride and Prejudice* any more, why this antiquated stealing of income? Sure, if it is for children, childcare, the house they live in, that stuff. But 'keeping her in the lifestyle to which she is accustomed', no way. I am not a meninist. But some of the stuff they bring up is very valid. There are women who use our courts to punish men – oh God, I've read too many incel forums.

If we take gender out of the equation – imbalance isn't there. I asked my friend Suzi what happens with lesbian couples. Is there an unwritten rule, is it the elder of you? The taller? The one who earns the most? She said usually the person who asked the other out will pay, but both will take turns to treat the other. She said when someone pays the response is always 'Thank you, I'll get the next one.' SEE HOW SENSIBLE LESBIANS ARE? And they reliably make each other orgasm.

As I mentioned near the beginning, studies demonstrate that women do care about wealth and income. They find it attractive, it's been scientifically proven, which really pisses me off. Heterosexual men value youth and attractiveness as signals of fertility, and heterosexual women value signs that a man can provide, and it all makes me want to puke.

Psychologists Michael Dunn and Robert Searle at Cardiff University conducted a study where women rated the attractiveness of pictures of men. They found that if they put a man next to an expensive car he was judged more handsome. GROSS. For another study they dressed the same men in either expensive designer clothes or cheap logo-less ones, and again female participants all preferred the richer-looking men. This explains David's worries that Diana prefers Gage – he is aware that wealth might mean something to her on a deeper biological level—

None of those people are real.

They are to me. This clarifies why men feel the pressure to splurge on creamy coolers and champagne as a way of signalling 'I can look out for you, I can provide.' The eHarmony website has a pseudoscientific article telling women that whether a man pays or not is a way to see how invested he is in you. It claims that a man who asks you to go halves isn't interested. 'Saves me so much time waiting for him to text me,' says Linda, an idiot. I find this state of affairs farcical, but it has echoes of evolutionary programming. And it makes sense of how a woman's refusal to let a man pay can be viewed as emasculating. If masculinity is built on social displays of ability to provide, then denying a man the opportunity to 'display' is reducing him. Why does that matter, if we all know masculinity is a construct? Constructs are ideas, concepts, floaty invisible things to be discussed at university and rejected in real life. Western women have legally protected autonomy; do we go through a charade of men paying for us because being taken care of turns us on?

I would equate a man paying for dinner with a woman shaving her legs.

Masculinity is a construct, *sí señor*. It is constructed to convey elements of male behaviour that were of evolutionary benefit. All humans are a mixture of attractive qualities. Some men are muscly and strong, some men are sneaky and clever; both are equally useful in finding food, escaping enemies, providing for their family and tribe. Some straight women will be attracted to bigger men, others to very intelligent men and some greedy ladies to guys that are both. Our species reflects a great range of physical attributes and personalities because it was our variance that allowed us to adapt to every habitat on earth while constantly competing with each other.

Traits considered 'masculine' are varied – strength, protectiveness, being a good provider – but all of them convey status. In turn, status has always allowed men access to resources and made them attractive to mates. Status is also vital to the safety of a male. In evolutionary terms, low status makes you extremely vulnerable – to aggression, attack, not just from strangers and enemies but from your own tribe. The reason modern men freak out when disrespected or disregarded is that the brain chemistry which controls their emotional response is trained by evolution to know that a fall in status is dangerous for them.

So if paying for a meal is a gesture of generosity, wealth, ability to provide; if it is a social demonstration – 'I'm a strong boy who is healthy and successful and everyone should respect and/or fancy me'; if it's the human equivalent of a peacock spreading his sexy blue-green tail . . . then to deny that gesture, to shut it down, is like running in with garden shears and chopping the poor peacock's feathers off.

If reducing a man's masculinity lowers his status, then a rejection of masculine display will bother him. It may feel to him like diminishment. Even if we intellectually understand that there is no reason for a man to pay for a woman's dinner, it may still feel good for him to do it. And hurtful if it's refused. This is like women shaving their legs, because while we know that it is a silly, pointless thing to remove leg hair – it takes hours of our week, costs money – even when we know our partner doesn't care, or when we're single and our legs entwine only with each other nightly, there is something about stubbly or hairy legs that *feels* unattractive. It can make us feel unfeminine. Not everyone, of course; some women don't feel like this and I admire them with all I have. I imagine these women using the time saved to write poetry that hits the heart like lightning. I imagine them being able to meditate for hours without getting bored. I imagine them being friends with Lena Dunham. They are the female equivalent of men who don't care if their wives earn more than them and they are better at equality than the rest of us.

While notions of femininity are culturally constructed in the same way masculinity has been, they are similarly built upon ingrained insecurities. There is this yucky, illogical longing in me to be small, smooth and beautiful because to generations of my ancestors, a woman's youth and fertility were her access to resources, her social safety. Youth and fertility were a woman's strength and status.

These are underlying, animal things for us to consider. I don't think men have to pay for dinner, I don't think women have to shave their legs, but KNOWING that some of us still feel the pull THAT. WE. SHOULD, I'm trying to comprehend why that might be, why it's difficult to throw off. It seems like housework is culturally influenced, men are getting better at doing their own dusting – but it is still men who propose marriage. When women earn more than their husbands, the divorce rate is higher. And while that is seen as a male reaction to emasculation, I think maybe that *is* freedom. Money allows us choices. Leaving is the biggest choice and only women with independent incomes can easily make it.

Everything is really about money, even when we're discussing sex and power.

The UN says that 99 per cent of land and property in the world is owned by men. This has such huge ramifications for all human relationships, romantic, sexual or otherwise. That's what Samantha from *Sex in the City* should be quoting, although I guess stats are more of a Miranda thing. And how can we improve this imbalance if we are absorbing shit that does us harm? On both sides. For every Cinderella story telling little girls they are to be beautiful and helpless and rescued by a man, there is a Cinderella story telling little boys they are supposed to be rich and strong and rescuers.

Some people take the economics of dating and make the implied unambiguous. This may be a student with a sugar daddy, a stripper charging per dance, a masseuse offering a massage with 'a happy ending'. There are people for whom the notion of erotic capital is made literal. 'If you pay me this, I will do this.' There is a huge spectrum of varied ways that people do this. I read adverts from men advertising free rent and board in exchange for sex two or three times a week and one blow job. I read about 'nude cleaners', women who charge slightly more than clothed cleaners and then are alone in the house with a strange man who insists on them bending over to dust things. I cried when I read men writing about how easy it was to 'convince' these women to have sex 'because they need the money so badly'. One of these men bragged that he 'wouldn't go to a real hooker', which is interesting, isn't it? This man doesn't mind paying for sex, but believes there is something 'purer' about coercing and bullying a woman working in his house than a woman offering that service explicitly. I have known people who took on variants of sex work. My friend lived for years in a house with a man who masturbated in her room and 'massaged' her, in exchange for a very low rent. It was all she could afford. My aunty had a man who would loan her money and then release her from debt if she posed naked for him.

There is a great variety of sex work, although most people have a clichéd idea of what it comprises. There's deep-rooted stigma in our society's treatment of people who sell sex, something those people have to fight against for their rights. There are also people who are exploited, and whom many, including feminists, would like to help – to save – to protect. We have a contradictory set of attitudes and ignorances that mean that most do-gooding is running on the spot, most governmental intervention hurts the wrong people and helps no one, while stigma is reinforced. Why are we all stupid about sex work and prostituted people? Why do we not understand them as separate things? Is it possible to prevent sex slavery *and* liberate monetised sexuality?

Sex for Money

We talk so much about consent nowadays. 'My body, my choice,' my niece says when she doesn't want to kiss me. '#METOO HAS GONE TOO FAR,' I roar, but she knows I'm joking.

We are teaching and talking about what consent means, what desire feels like, teaching children how to be sexually respectful adults, but this is all swept away with transactional sex. If we agree that sex work is work, then we're claiming that consent can be bought.

A couple of years ago everyone was sharing this great 'Cup of Tea' analogy.* It was a way of clearly explaining consent, even to very young children. It basically went like this:

> If you offer someone a cup of tea and they say, 'Yes I would bloody love some,' then you know they want a cup of tea.
>
> If they are passed out, don't make them tea. If they can't answer the question 'Do you want tea?' don't make them any. They can't tell you if they want some or not because they're passed out.
>
> If you offer tea and they say, 'I'm not sure, errm, I can't decide,' then you can make tea if you like but you

---

* This analogy was created by the lovely Emmeline May, who kindly gave her permission for me to quote it.

can't force them to drink it.

If the person says, 'No thank you,' to tea, don't make it. Don't get annoyed, they're just not thirsty. There is also a situation where they might say, 'Yes please,' to tea and then, after you've made it, change their mind. You can't make them drink it.

If someone said yes to tea and is now unconscious after you've made it, you can't make them drink the tea. Ditto if they pass out while drinking the tea, you mustn't keep pouring it down their throat.

Is the tea poisoned or something?

If someone said yes to tea another time, that doesn't mean they will always want to drink tea with you, and you can't start turning up and demanding tea. You can't force someone to drink tea because they liked it before.

It's a great analogy and it seems to cover all bases of consent, drunkenness, tiredness, changing your mind, being unsure. But it doesn't cover sex work. Sometimes someone doesn't want tea but you can PAY them to drink it. Sometimes someone is happy to drink tea as a job and that is a choice, and sometimes someone is incredibly desperate and has to drink tea because they are scared, or forced, or poor, or addicted, and you can make them drink tea any way you want because you have money. You can throw the tea in their damn face if you pay them enough and they've agreed first. Sometimes you can pay them to drink tea and then beat them up afterwards, and you feel pretty safe in your violence because no one ever believes people who drink tea for money, because the way our species reproduces, and the inbuilt worth associated with female chastity and lack of worth associated with sexual promiscuity, means people who drink tea for money are simultaneously the most judged, most mistreated and least supported people in our society. In any society.

I could have written a horror story, all the horror stories. I could have told you about the girl murdered on her sixteenth birthday by a 'customer'. The woman who will never have children after a 'customer' repeatedly stabbed her genitals. The teenage boy pimped by the paedophilic father who had abused him. The brothel with bodies buried in the garden of the women who tried to escape or became pregnant. I occasionally get carried away and I'll want to tell you something, not because it's particularly relevant, but because I know about it so you should too.

There are realities of buying sex that make being against it a completely reasonable position. If you read Rachel Moran's book *Paid For* – and I highly recommend it – there are several of her experiences that will never leave you. Moran wants the sex trade ended so that no other underage girl should go through what she did, so that no men feel justified in treating women as things. Things to batter, rape and spit on, because the act of selling sex makes them – what, dehumanised? Lower than people? Or because the aggressor can get away with it? Many serial rapists start with sex workers. Many of the world's most sickening serial killers have preyed upon them, partly because they are vulnerable through the logistics of their work, and also because, as we have seen, some men gain sexual pleasure from sadistic acts.

My personal opinion, which is subjective, biased – to some, discriminatory – is that I wish people didn't have to sell sex. Not because sex is a beautiful, precious thing or any other bullshit, but because I have an inbuilt hatred for the people who buy it. SORRY. Sorry everyone. I am listening to the people who want to sell sex – I think the law should respect their wishes and they should be decriminalised and supported. I think all human beings should be free to use their body however they want . . . unless that involves buying sexual access to another person. Then I think they should have a wank and shut up.

I have never paid for sex. I have felt horny, I have felt lonely. I have never felt like I would pay someone to pretend to be aroused by me or to hold me. So I guess my adventures in understanding another human's point of view end here. I found my line. I really want to empathise but paying for intercourse sounds so much like paid rape that you've lost me. And that's not fair. Rapists are getting off on the fact the person they are violating does not want to be raped. With sex work, that might not be true. As we saw on PunterNet, those deluded fools believe that the women are hypersexual, that they 'enjoy it'.

What I do empathise with is experiencing unwanted sex, and this is what has created the problem for me. Even when the fee is a million dollars (less 50K for the lawyer) I know what unwanted penetration feels like on my own body and while I absolutely understand it is survivable, I do not think there are any circumstances that excuse it.

My mum once told me she believed sex workers should be paid for by the NHS. She said that sex was a human right, that human beings need affectionate and sexual contact with each other, and that there are so many people who are desperate for physical contact who do not have it in their lives – sometimes because of illness or disability – and for whom it should be provided.

My instant reaction was that my mother was very wrong. 'Sex is a human right' seems dangerous to me – surely it's in conflict with the human right NOT to have sex if you don't want it? I thought on the way home about how an NHS service would work. It would have to provide a basic wage and accommodation before any sex work was undertaken, so that the sex workers would still have the ability to say no. You couldn't have a state-supported sex work service unless the basic wage underwrote their survival before they accepted any client. Say £250 a week. And then jobs costed and paid on top of that?

> But then none of them would bother having sex with the people?

That would be proof they were only ever doing it for money and would rather not.

> That's any job, that's all jobs.

Yes, that's any job. *straight-mouthed emoji*

I asked Jane, the first sex worker I interviewed, about this NHS sex worker scheme. She countered with another question. First she said that what my mum meant by 'sex is a human right' was an acceptance and acknowledgement of male sexuality. She told me about a reality TV discussion about sex work and disability. On the front row were a mother and her son. She had been procuring services for him because he 'couldn't get a girlfriend', and now they had set up a brothel in their house. Everyone in the audience laughed and clapped; it was a funny, sex-positive moment. Jane asked me, 'We're very comfortable and familiar with teenage boys' sexual urges, but if fathers were hiring gigolos to finger their quadriplegic daughters, wouldn't people be outraged?'

She's absolutely right. But we've encountered the mismatch in attitudes to expressions of male and female sexuality throughout this book. One more shouldn't surprise us.

Brighton University Students' Union Freshers' Fair ran into controversy in 2018. I wonder what *you'll* think about this? One of the stalls was run by Sex Workers Outreach Project Sussex (SWOP). This is an organisation that offers confidential support to people selling sex, as well as providing condoms and things. Criticism from the mainstream media afterwards was that the Freshers' Fair was 'encouraging students to get into sex work'. Which is a bit of a leap. The organisation isn't called Sex Work Is Fun Take a Condom (SWIFTAC); they are not on a recruitment drive. And in fact, Brighton University made a statement to clarify that 'the University does not promote sex work as an option to students'. But here is the tricky nature of stigma.

When I first heard about the SWOP stall, I absolutely understood why they were there: so that students selling sex to support themselves would know of a qualified resource that could help them. And just as importantly, as a symbol of acceptance, that what they're doing is not shameful or wrong, that it is a profession alongside working in a call centre or a shop.

But I guess why people worry is because if you take the stigma away, if you say, 'Selling sex is a job just like hairdressing,' then more people might be encouraged to do it. Is that why we are not averse to whorephobia? Do we think it's doing a useful job, keeping too many people from selling their bodies to make ends meet? Do we think that being judged and maligned works to put people off? We worry about the permission it gives the people buying sex, that the more legitimate it becomes as a profession, the more men will wander the world like John Gage, thinking all women have a 'price'.

I can comprehend why people get concerned. They imagine a student is walking around the Freshers' Fair, 'Ooh, there's a mixed-gender volleyball team, ooh, there's a debating society; avoid the performing arts lot, they're always harmonising – hang on – SEX WORK. I guess if everyone else is doing it, I should do it too.' And the idea of encouraging or suggesting that people sell sex *is* abhorrent. There was a worrying instance a few years back of Jobcentres advertising for sex chat line workers. There would be nothing wrong with this EXCEPT people on benefits have to accept any job that will have them. If they do not show sufficient willingness to work, they have their financial support stopped. So what we have here is a shitty situation where a person might be told they HAVE to work on a sex chat line. That's wrong, not because there is anything wrong with talking a chap through a wank, but because not everyone wants to do it.

Not everyone wants to work in McDonald's or push trolleys.

I know. But I believe that while certain jobs may be unenjoyable drudgery, they would not impact harmfully on a person's mental health and wellbeing in a way that *enforced* sex work would. And I say that with the qualification of having worked in McDonald's. I hate the system whereby people are made to agree to jobs they don't want, but this instance does clarify that even while 'sex work is work', it cannot be pressed on people. This is why people object to legitimising selling sexual services.

Which is what anti-sex-work campaigners thought about the SWOP stall at Brighton University. What you have on both sides is people wanting to assist students. Anti-sex-work advocates know the dangers that this work entails and want to protect people from it, whereas the support services know the dangers and want to support those who choose to do it, or who feel they have no other choice. And there are a lot more people selling sex while studying than you might think. A study by the University of Swansea of over six thousand students found that one in twenty people had worked in the sex industry, 5 per cent of male respondents and 3.5 per cent of females. Across the country this would add up to tens of thousands of people, people who might need specialised counselling and advice.

What I personally want to know is for how many people the sex industry is the preferred option, and how many feel it is their only option. But even that is too complex. People who sell sex sometimes think differently later about what they felt were free choices at the time. We've all experienced that, reflecting on a younger self with an elder's insight. Seeing coercion and denial years later.

As I stated in my introduction, I fail to understand the people who pay for sex. I also bemoaned that I never get to ~~endure~~ enjoy locker-room chat, but a podcast* with male comedians talking about brothels gave me an insight into both. I have included the quotes below because of their mundanity. I think they represent the derision inherent in mainstream attitudes. These men are being very flippant about sex workers and I was going to change their names, then reminded myself this isn't a secret podcast, fuck 'em:

ELLIOT

. . . so I walked back over to this cash machine and this

---

* It's called *Sloss and Humphries on the Road*. You can find it on iTunes.

woman comes up to me and sort of grabs me and was
sort of like, 'Oh, shall we go down here?' And I'm like,
'Yeah, yeah, yeah, dope,' and then I quickly realised, like
– oh this is a prostitute – this doesn't just happen, like,
I'm not Brad Pitt – women don't come up to me in the
street and just grab me cos they wanna sleep with me,
that doesn't just happen, so then—

JAMALI
Nah, they want some financial exchange.

KAI
She actually said, 'Sucky sucky, ten dollar.'

ALL
Laugh

JAMALI
That should be the giveaway.

ELLIOT
Nah, nah, she was just outside some beach hotel
thing, and so I just thought – I'll enquire, innit, I'll
enquire and I go, 'How much?' and fuck, man, it was
reasonable, like it was reasonable. So . . . so I ended up
going off with this lovely lady and you know, it's always
good to help someone feed their kids and yeah, we sort
of do the deed, you know, and afterwards she goes to
me, 'Ah, would you give me an extra five euro?' And I
said, 'What for?' And she goes, 'I wanna go buy a slice
of pizza.' And I looked at her and I was like – 'If this is
a date we're doing it the wrong way round, like . . .'

JAMALI

Ah mate, Elliot was getting Third World pussy, man –
fucking hell.

KAI

Who takes a prostitute for dinner?

Hey, this is Sara again now. I know that the guys are 'joking'. They are being flippant on purpose to impress and
entertain each other. When Kai is racist and says 'sucky
sucky', that's because he thinks that is funny. An old stereo-
type, to be fair to him; it's the kind of joke you'd have found
in an *Austin Powers* movie two decades ago. Elliot is describing a situation where he was approached as a customer. A
woman offers him sex, he doesn't say what the price was, but
it was very low, and then afterwards she asks him for a small
amount of money for something to eat. The fact that they
find this funny betrays a huge lack of empathy. Everything
they say makes me think they do not consider this woman a
person. She is 'Third World pussy', someone you wouldn't
take for dinner. It's low-level hatred towards the sex worker;
it's not hammering her in the head, just outright derision.

Later in the conversation Elliot gives a defensive speech
about going to brothels:

ELLIOT

. . . it's definitely sleazy, it's definitely – but I think if
you're respectful, I think if you're nice, if you go, you
know, they're sex workers – you're cool about it, then
it's fine, you know, it's – I think in that job if you get a
bunch of coked-up lads at five in the morning who've
come in from Yates who are all fucking demanding . . . I

think like, you know, you've gotta be respectful cos it's a human being at the end of the day. Saying that, I got another prozzie story from last week—

The men who use sex workers do not think THEY are the bad people. They know that some other men are, but they do not identify that their own behaviour might be disgusting or gross to the sex workers. That is why the users of PunterNet are so hung up on women smiling or putting effort in, because otherwise they cannot keep pretending that the women 'want' to do this.

Jamali does not admit to buying sex, but he adds this to the conversation:

JAMALI

Well the thing is, there is that – I mean, prostitution gets put into this category where we think – STREETWALKER and ON HEROIN, when that's not the case. I mean, there's many levels to it – there's, you know, there is obviously a sex slave industry in the way people have been shipped over here and kept, but then there's also people who charge ridiculous amounts of money, do you know what I'm saying? So there is – I think categorising them all as one thing is probably wrong of us.

The class hierarchy that exists in all areas of our society is particularly damaging to the people at the bottom of it. In sex work that means those who work outside, those who are addicted to drugs. The beginning of the film *Pretty Woman* is quite shocking now. I don't know how recently you may have seen it? It opens with police around a bin. A woman has been found amongst the rubbish and bin bags. Julia

Roberts is sad but her best friend tells her not to worry, 'She was just a crack whore.' The film is carefully constructed to reinforce that some hookers deserve \$3,000 and, eventually, love, whereas when others are MURDERED, they deserve it because they had a drug dependency. How many sex buyers also use this kind of reasoning to dehumanise?

Pretty Woman was originally called *3,000* and was about a sex worker paid by a man to stay off crack for a week (\$3,000 was the amount offered by the Richard Gere character for a week of sex work). She manages it, gets paid, he drives off at the end and she goes to get high. That was the first draft, and there are echoes of it still. But now the film reinforces that Julia Roberts's hooker is one of the good guys because she is 'clever' and flosses her teeth and doesn't take drugs. In a pivotal scene, Richard Gere's lawyer attempts to rape the sex worker. She is saved by Richard Gere, who punches him and chucks him out of the apartment. No one discusses calling the police or reporting his crime. It is treated so flippantly, like people who sell sex are less affected by attacks. As if raping someone who sells sex is a theft rather than an assault.

The power–money dynamic is vitally important within sex work, because those with no money have fewer choices. Consider Jane, the sex worker I interviewed earlier. She has a disability that makes work difficult for her. She chooses to undertake sex work rather than sit in agony at her old job in a bank. From two or three sessions a month she can make the same as her old full-time wage. She performs as a dominatrix, which gives her the power to refuse things she doesn't want to do, and is adamant that she enjoys her job sometimes. It's the best option for her – she gets to express her sexuality and she isn't claiming benefits, 'isn't a drain on society' (her words).

When I excitedly tell her about an exit strategy scheme I've heard of, where sex workers in northern Europe are given jobs in old people's homes and they're 'really good at it because they are not grossed out by the human body', Jane replies, 'I find that very patronising.' She says, 'I earn £200 an hour – I don't want to earn minimum wage in an old people's home.'

When I started writing this book I assumed that anyone in sex work or prostitution would want to get out of it at *any* cost. And that is not true. There are people who have options and choices, who opt and choose to sell sex. It is possible to be well-meaning and wrong. This is where feminism has not supported sex workers properly. When some of them have told us, 'This is my choice – please help me to earn my money safely,' our own feelings get in the way – 'I don't want you to do that'; 'you will always be a victim to me.' Kind feelings can create more problems.

Returning to unrealistic media portrayals:

KAI

I like watching that *Diary of a Call Girl* with Billie Piper. Cos there was something she said in that, like, 'I like sex and I like money – so why would I not do both?' – and it's like, ah, she's actually just doing something she enjoys. When you see it from that side it's like, oh that's alright, but when it's like fucking trafficking, like a fucking girl in a window that's fucking misled, that's when it's like, ah, nah.

The Secret Diary of a Call Girl is the epitome of sex-work positive, a TV show that very much cartoonifies the work of an escort but has glimmers of the truth. As Belle goes through her 'rules' at the beginning, she stresses calling Madam when you arrive and making sure people know where you are, but doesn't add 'in case he tries to kill me – I'm eight times more likely to be murdered than you'. There's an episode where Belle and another sex worker are attacked at an orgy, but they escape. The danger is dealt with comedically. I am not judging – I'm not saying every person who made the show is irresponsible. The writer of the 'Belle de Jour' books and blog on which *The Secret Diary of a Call Girl* series was based is Dr Brooke Magnanti. She gets a lot of flak – she writes brilliantly about working in the sex industry and especially hates it when people say she is responsible for glamorising the work.

But one of my friends tried escorting because of that show. She thought she could do it. It made her feel it would be an easy way to earn money. She called a number in the paper and went to a hotel in Basildon, and there were a number of girls who had dressed up like they were going clubbing. The fee was for the whole day, as many customers as asked you – she was the buffet. She had a drink at a table and then a man asked her to his room. They did it once. It was not what she expected at all – he wasn't particularly nasty to her, wasn't spitting in her face or pulling her hair, he was just fucking her from behind and it didn't feel like she thought it was going to, it was much more upsetting, and she left and didn't get paid. What happened there? What if I tell you that she tried to stop, asked to stop? Do you now think it was rape? Or a grey area? What do you think of a man who is asked to stop by someone he thinks is a 'prostitute' and he doesn't stop because he is 'nearly there'?

A survivor of prostitution (her term), Alice Glass, writes, 'One doesn't consent, simply, to prostitution, it is rather an impoverished form of bargaining.' I am not saying that that is all women's experience, but it is for some. And when we allow the successful, the victorious to dictate how we consider the entire industry, we are doing a great disservice to the majority. Glass defines it like this: 'Prostitution, if it is anything, is a choice between homelessness and having men we don't like, do things we hate.' While 'sex work is work' aims to reduce stigma and disrespect for people who sell sex, is anything being done to educate sex buyers as to how some people who sell sex feel about them?

I was listening to a podcast about ethical altruism recently and they were talking about modern slavery. The clothing industry in developing countries pays workers far less than a living wage; there are no days off, no breaks; there are women sitting in nappies because they are not 'allowed' to go to the toilet. Just so Gap and H&M can sell flimsy, shitty clothes. This podcast claimed that boycotting the high street stores who use these factories is no good, as 'for most of these women, the only other option is sex work'.

The idea that treating female workers in this way is in fact RESCUING THEM from much worse indicates that we think sex slavery is less justifiable than the other kinds.

By contrast there is so-called 'high-class' escorting. The money at the 'high end' is sometimes used to legitimise the treatment of the women at the lower end, as if they're all footballers playing the same sport and those in lower divisions are simply less talented. Perhaps sex buyers imagine that these women are rising up the ranks, that there is career progression? The truth is that the richest, most privileged sex workers, the people with the most freedom to set their own rules, can also set a high value on their services. But all people selling sex willingly are being punished by legislation supposedly targeting criminals who imprison, kidnap and sell sexual access to adults and children. This has been most recently demonstrated by the FOSTA-SESTA legislation brought in by the Trump administration in the US. Laws aiming to prevent trafficking have endangered the lives of thousands of sex workers by removing their ability to advertise to customers. (I've included resources to find out more about this in the bibliography.)

There is a difference between people who choose and people who are forced, a distinction that must be more widely understood and appreciated. Trafficking is not one extreme of sex work, it is as separate and opposed as rape is from sex. The same laws should apply to transactional sex as to non-transactional. Without the appropriate consent, any sex act is rape and the perpetrator should be culpable. The onus of responsibility has to be on the sex buyers. It should be the Johns/Jills/Geoffs worrying about whether a worker is over age and selling sex willingly, because it is them who could go to prison.

Money and power ensure a person has choices. The person paying for sex is always in the superior position. The cash that changes hands should not diminish their accountability, it should increase it. While what we feel about people who sell sex might be unhelpfully built on evolved prejudice or antiquated misogyny, how we advocate for them as a society needs to be freed from that old morality. For that to happen, perhaps it's useful to be aware of the illogical biology that has inspired it.

Apocalypse Now

How do you conclude something when you do not feel qualified to proffer ANSWERS?

☐ Another non-quiz, of course.

Reading back over what I've written, my first thought is that I seem much more open-minded about porn than selling sex. Which is odd, because porn *is* a form of selling sex. I guess the difference for me is that with porn all of the performers are being paid to do things to each other, rather than a customer-paying-sex-worker scenario. This is an idyllic view of porn production, where all people are equally enfranchised and there is rolling consent and much discussion of boundaries. While some is like that, some is not. There are awful people who film themselves having abusive sex with women, who do exploit and push boundaries. People who prey on first-time performers and enjoy hurting them.

I believe that people who watch porn should be more discerning, that as consumers they have the power to influence the future, but this will not happen while they remain ashamed and secretive about what arouses them. And it won't happen unless they put their money in. The easiest solution is that people should pay for porn. If the Netflix model of a few quid a month works for blockbuster films and TV shows, then it can definitely work for tiny-budget poolhouse fuck-fests. Would that system be more sophisticated? Could there then be industry standards ensuring that all performers are well looked after and remunerated? There would be an organisation to complain to about any exploitation. There would be legitimacy if someone had a criminal complaint. Driving things underground makes people vulnerable.

Even as I imagine this I remember how difficult fifty-four years' worth of footage would be to police. Then I wonder – maybe instead we could create a sexual democracy? No one is allowed to have private sex any more, we must all share; all bedrooms have compulsory cameras and we can all wank to each other when we need to. We'll just search the addresses that have our favoured kink and . . . what do you mean my political career is over?

I *had* planned to watch extreme porn. I had a Post-it on my computer saying 'Watch the worst ten porn videos', but I chickened out. Perhaps that undermines any argument I make. But I did download feminist and 'artful' stuff, I watched the work of Cindy Gallop on 'Make Love Not Porn', and I watched about two hundred videos on Pornhub and YouPorn. I got used to watching people have sex pretty quickly. I suddenly understood how watching hardcore sex speeds up the masturbation process – there is no room for the jumbly, interrupted digressions of the mind. They are drowned out by the visceral unsubtlety of the acts. 'I have to watch the anal-tearing and young-sluts-punished videos,' I thought, 'or I am not doing justice to the people who make them.' But the fact remained . . . I do not want to see them. I do not want those things seared in my memory. Same as how I am a vegan without watching abattoir videos. I do not know what to do with that anger. I am not the king, I cannot stop people hurting animals and I cannot stop them hurting people either. Especially people who have voluntarily turned up at the slaughterhouse.

I also planned to go and watch women stripping. I wanted to write about the environment of a quotidian club, I wanted to understand the atmosphere – how men behaved – and to compare it to the Dream Boys I saw on my sister's hen do. Women watching men is a scream-fest, it is giggling and silly and a pretence. No one is turned on, it is a satire. The male performers are very tall and muscly, much larger than the women they are dancing for. And the women dance and shout at the men from a crowd, not in individual booths. The 'fun' is in the reversal of a power dynamic. This is play, men gyrating for women, men imitating feminine compliance, while women pretend for an hour that they can objectify as well as men. All of this undermined by the physical reality that if these strippers needed to protect themselves, they wouldn't need a bouncer,* they could crush a skull with their biceps.

I planned to go and watch strippers as a customer. I would take twenties and my notepad and . . . I realised I could not do it. I couldn't pretend I just got off on paying for dances. I realised a safari trip was deeply unfair. Like someone sitting on the front row of one of my gigs not because they enjoyed comedy but to judge my life decisions. I appreciated that I was uncomfortable with paying someone to talk to me in a strip club, that even that transaction was patronising. So I went the other way, and I contacted strippers about observing them at work – and quickly realised that they get writers

* There *was* a bouncer, though, and he told me off for trying to take pictures of the sad buffet.

wanting to shadow them as much as I get journalists asking about 'being a woman in comedy'. 'WHY?' people asked. 'What do you want to say about us?' The friends of friends were very sceptical about my motives, which is utterly understandable. And the ones that weren't said the places the strippers worked would not appreciate my being there in an observational capacity. I asked my stripper friend Carla, and her incredibly reasonable point was that if I was following her around, she would make less money.

So I studied stripping academically. I read some books and articles and found that the industry is a perfect illustration of economics anywhere. When there are many customers and few dancers, then the performers hold the power. They make a lot of money and set their own boundaries for what they are willing to do. When there are slow nights with more dancers than customers, or when a club sees a decline and slump in visitors, then there is pressure on strippers to show more or *do* more to compete with each other. In these situations the people holding the cash have the power, a power that increases in proportion to how much the strippers want the money.

I did a radio show called *My Teenage Diary* and was asked to read excerpts from my own diary for the year 2001, when I was nineteen. There was a period where I was booking in auditions for stripping, and then not going. The *Stage* newspaper had these adverts in the back, for clubs like the Windmill in central London. All you had to do was dance in a thong and then you'd have hundreds of pounds. Hundreds. Of. Pounds. Like a millionaire! The difficulty I had, as documented in my diary, was that nobody would want to watch me dance because I had no tits. I was caught in a vicious circle – I wanted the money from stripping but I couldn't get it until I had a boob job, which would cost a lot of money, which I didn't have. I imagine I would have written a very different book if I had stripped. I would have personal insights into certain male behaviours, I'd have anecdotes. I wonder if I would have been negatively affected by the experience – as many have been. If I'd now consider it demeaning and regrettable. Or if I would be proud, strong. I would know first-hand how to sell erotic capital. How to manipulate men. Perhaps I would be very furious with people like me who want to discuss things they have no first-hand experience of?

I thought about money much more than sex writing this book. It is not as simple as 'some people have bigger houses than others'. Money means that some people have choices and some people survive. I have been poor and in debt, and I have reflected on how differently my mind worked then. Here is an example – something that I only remembered while researching this year. When I was eighteen years old a British woman called Lucie Blackman went missing in Japan. It was all over the news; she was white and very attractive, which is how the news likes its victims. Lucie had been hostessing at a club. Hostessing like at the Presidents Club, drinking and flirting with patrons. The more your customers drank, the more expensive their rounds – the more you earned. As the story played out, Lucie's body was found – she had been raped and drugged and her body cut up. This terrible story inspired me to go to Japan and do hostessing as I thought that was the only way to get out of debt.

I looked into it. You only had to do sex stuff as extras. You got to drink at work. I could earn enough in a few months to afford my rent in London. My *stimulus* was another woman's murder. The only detail from the story that drew my attention was that she was earning £500 a week. It was good for me to remember how that felt. The different potatoes on the menu depending on your budget.

I dedicated this book to another murder victim, Arminda Ventura, because her life encapsulates everything we've been thinking about. She met John Perry in her home country, the Philippines, in 1984, when she was twenty years old. He was much older, divorced and drinking in a bar alone. She smiled at him nicely, they got chatting. They drank together every night. She told him she was sad he was leaving. He proposed. They moved into his house in Wales. After several years the relationship became very unstable and probably abusive. Perry became very jealous of younger men taking an interest in his wife. He claimed she was sleeping with men while he was out at work, that she was staying out all night with other men. Arminda filed for divorce and the court granted her a settlement of £15,000 plus £75 a week in subsistence. The week the first payment was due, in February 1991, Arminda disappeared.

When the police visited John Perry's home to look for her, he told them that Arminda was a prostitute. That she had been unable to 'give it up' and had left. A search of the house found what was left of Arminda's body. Perry had killed and dismembered her, feeding some of her body to his cat, to avoid paying her divorce settlement. In one report, he was quoted as saying that two years into their marriage he had realised that Arminda may not have loved him but had married him to escape the poverty of the Philippines and for a better life.

One of the essential problems with the notion of erotic capital arises when that is all a person has. When that is their only currency. The age gap between John Perry and Arminda Ventura is one inequality, not uncommon, and as we have explored through the fertility-for-resources exchange, an evolutionarily sensible one. Young women will need partners who can provide if the world does not offer them opportunities to provide for themselves. The inequality of wealth is a more difficult one to overcome. It may be difficult for those of us raised in the UK to imagine a situation where you would marry a man you didn't care about as a way of improving your life. But as we explored briefly with *Pride and Prejudice* earlier, our great-great-grandmothers may well have understood this as being their only option.

We haven't explored the sex work known as being a 'mail order bride' but it's a sort of legally binding transactional sex, with added housework. What's that – sounds like sexual slavery? Yes, I agree, mate. A woman so low on prospects in her home country, so desperate to leave that she will risk the unknown quantity of marrying a man she doesn't know. A man who, because he has 'bought' her, will expect certain behaviours. And obedience. Perry himself said he was fed up of western women's assertiveness and independence, as if those things were personality flaws and not freedom.

When we think about the problems of men buying sexual access to women, it's vital to remember that they are choosing to pay so that the women can't say no. John Perry was a man who considered equality 'too free'. His attitude to his wife is explained by the fact he thought he owned her. We have the jealousy we've explored, fear of cuckolding, his abusive behaviour as a kind of mate guarding – whether her infidelities were real or imagined – when Arminda gained the resources to leave him via the divorce settlement, Perry would rather she were dead than at liberty.

In court his defence was provocation by infidelity. I found this shocking. Up until ten years ago, British courts might excuse murder if a man had been driven to it by his wife's sexual freedom. Although he was found guilty, two of the jurors agreed that Arminda's behaviour had been provocation. To be killed, cut up and fed to a cat. She drove him to it.

The reason so many people struggle with sex work and selling sexual services, and with using erotic capital, is that they may be reinforcing ancient behaviours that are much older than sexism. Domineering, gorilla-like oppression of partners was a mating strategy for some male *Homo sapiens* and we must fight, with all the nurture we have, to socialise men out of it. But this cannot be at the cost of the autonomy of those who *choose* to sell sex. A conversation about what constitutes choice and what constitutes financial coercion might continue for a long time, and for this we must listen to sex workers themselves. This book is about me and my thoughts and interests; I am not attempting to speak on behalf of others. I've included a list of resources and books at the end that might interest you.

I started my journey into this book seeking answers in biology, and there are many things about which I still want concrete evidence. I want to know what exactly is happening in the brain and bloodstream of a person committing violence. I want to know if/how porn has affected the brains of children now growing up with it. The things I have learned – about bonding, arousal, jealousy and desire – make me hopeful that there are many more glimpses into the human animal to come. The experiments on sperm motility tell us about who we might have been millions of years ago, but we are processing that meaning through who we are now. A contradictory creature. One that can reflect on its mating behaviour, one that recognises another's 'rights'.

Being a human being means caring deeply for the people closest to you and then failing to care enough about the people further away. We were built by our successful tribes to be social and work together. Togetherness within the tribe has involved shutting others out. The oxytocin that facilitates bonding simultaneously stimulates aggressive behaviours (in voles). To love is to protect, to love is to compete to provide. Our vested interest in personal and familial success means making losers of others. A raised social position involves domination.

That results in massive inequality between humans, and I don't know how we overcome that. Do we attempt to re-teach ourselves several times a day that sometimes our instincts – who we like, who we want to employ, who we are attracted to, who we are angrily tweeting – are those of an animal? We are underpinned by beastly behaviours and a created narrative of consciousness.

I began wanting to write a book about sex, but what I kept learning was that everything is connected to money. Alongside the built-in distrust and contempt, the 'otherness' towards people who sell sex and sexual behaviours, the rich can't help but believe they deserve it. By rich I don't mean castles and diamonds, I mean any of us with food and roofs and choices. We have to believe that the people who don't have those things have done something wrong, that it is their fault.

I began from a point of wanting to understand sexual psychopaths, the modern-day Marquis de Sades who are unaffected by compassion. De Sade believed that other people's pain didn't matter because he couldn't feel it. He thought that encroaching on others was freedom. He imprisoned, raped and assaulted girls, then paid their families off to excuse himself. He was a person of supreme privilege, which permitted his transgressions. What I have realised through writing this book is that instincts and basic drives matter a lot less than what society tells us we can get away with. There are millions of sadists alive today who pair up neatly with masochists to enjoy infliction and subjection alike. The Marquis's legacy is in fact continued by figures like Donald Trump who do not disguise their cruelty and lack of empathy but rather utilise it to seem more powerful. There is an ape in us, which means that many Americans cannot help but respect him and want to be led by him.

The injustice of the deep-rooted expectations we have of men is that we cannot deal with male victims. They suffer from a stigma and societal blindness just as sex workers do. When I was eighteen, on a night bus home with a group of friends, one of the boys was mugged without any of us seeing. A man on the seat behind him poked a knife in his back and whispered an order to give him his wallet. My friend handed it over, the thief rang the bell and got off the bus. Shane told us, 'I've been mugged.' And everyone was disbelieving: 'How?' 'Why didn't you say anything?' The other boys were telling him, 'You should have shouted and punched him.' 'Why didn't you stop him getting off the bus?' The impossibility of the situation was that Shane had not reacted how he thought he would've in that situation.

Fear takes over the body as an instinctual survival response. Your voice and body will be frozen if your brain has assessed a situation as so dangerous that staying still and quiet will be the most likely way to survive. Many rape victims know this and yet it continues to be misunderstood by juries and the law. My friend Shane suffered terribly after the mugging. Without bruises and a beating nobody understood why he gave up his wallet; he did not understand himself. The emasculation of the crime is what caused his suffering. For all my stuff about being scared of men, all my own demons and bias, I feel our culture doesn't know how to be kind to men, and many of them don't know how to be kind to themselves.

Over 80 per cent of homeless people in the UK are men. The fact that there is anyone living on our streets is unjustifiable. The size of the safety net and the amount of human support needed to provide shelter to the dispossessed is currently considered impossible. We have all drunk the well water. It's too hard to support people with mental health difficulties, we claim. It's not too hard, it requires time, resources, investment; the help should be there for those who need it. It's impossible to help addicts, we say. That is not true. But we have built our society around money, because it represents everything that nature could once give us. It defends us from our ancestral past, the short brutal life of a human who gathered. The power that we evolved to respect and desire has transformed into a literal currency system and now we subconsciously assess 'worth', and the tribe sprawls out so widely we find it difficult to care about those at the edges.

In my fear of men, I have found it hard to be gentle and forgiving of them. I know that you are not a separate species.

I know that men are being fed contradictory messages by culture. Toughness but no roughness. A list of expectations with no room for failure. You know the stats on male suicide – something is killing you, and it's you. It's time we discussed and supported men without anger, being aware of the influence of biology while knowing it is no instruction manual. We are none of us defined or determined by our sex

The reason there are fewer homeless women is arguably because they are even more vulnerable than men. Both genders experience sexual assault, physical attacks and verbal abuse, and for obvious reasons women are in even more danger. The reason there are fewer women sleeping rough isn't because they have more money, it is often because they engage in survival sex, sex for rent. When you consider this, how do you perceive it? Do you feel sorry for men that they have fewer people willing to buy the services of their body? Do you worry about a reality where someone will see a desperate or vulnerable person as a sexual opportunity?

I watched *Apocalypse Now* with my ex-boyfriend John and I hated it so much I rowed with him about it and blamed him. In the 'Redux' version there is a scene with Playboy Bunnies. They're flown into an army compound to entertain the soldiers going crazy in Vietnam, and when they come to leave, they find they have run out of helicopter fuel. There is a war going on, a battle ensues around them and the women need to escape. A bargain is made that the soldiers will give them petrol in exchange for sex.

The scene is obviously constructed to portray depravity, but it also pretends that the Playboy Bunnies 'choose' the sex. Over what? Death? Living in the Vietnam jungle? Having their bodies ravaged by the soldiers by force rather than coercion? I'm still too angry with the film. It makes selling sex for petrol look easy for the Bunnies, because they're already trading on erotic capital. And it makes that situation seem like a fair exchange. I think the monied and powerful who buy sexual services feel that they are entitled, and that it is fair, simply because sex is something they want, whether they are travelling to pay to rape children in other countries under the misnomer of 'sex tourism', or Oxfam workers paying victims of a natural disaster for sex in Haiti, or John Perry marrying Arminda Ventura. If sexual transactions are taking place in a context of too great an inequality, then there is no sex work, there is only exploitation. How do we make the Geoffs and the Marquis de Sades care?

So, who is doing this, who should we punish?

☐ I don't know
☐ I don't know, do you?

The exploiters, the traffickers, slave owners, pimps, rapists and even murderers . . . They were born babies. Fed milk, wrapped in soft blankets. Their brains grew quickly and in response to their environment. People asked, 'What is it?' and they weren't asking about the star sign or whether it was the son of God again. We think that the word 'boy' or the word 'girl' says something about who a person is, who they will be. But that difference is much less dictated by the body they're born in than created by what we expect of them, and how we treat each other.

My money shot is love, all over your face, whoever you are.

X

Cleaning the Money Shot
Away with a Flannel

Wipe it off your eyes . . .

This book is in no way exhaustive, something I wanted to say right at the beginning, except it's a terrible way to start a book: 'Have a read of this, guys, it's very incomplete.' For some further reading I would recommend:

Revolting Prostitutes: The Fight for Sex Workers' Rights by Juno Mac and Molly Smith: this book is so clear on labour laws and human rights as well as detailing the overlap between sex work and migration and/or drug use, showing the ramifications of criminalising behaviours and how they increase individuals' vulnerability. If you want to be informed about the laws around selling sex and if you want to listen to sex workers, please read it.

A Mind of Its Own by David M. Friedman: a brilliant cultural history of the penis.

Manhood: The Bare Reality by Laura Dodsworth: photographs and short biographies of people and their genitals.

Why Is the Penis Shaped Like That? by Jesse Bering is brilliant, funny, full of facts and science and, of course, dicks and sperm. I'd really recommend his book *Perv* too.

Scars Across Humanity by Elaine Storkey: this book covers a huge range of abuse against women, including child marriage, honour killings, domestic violence and prostitution. The evolutionary, animal aspect of humanity is always considered alongside economic pressures.

King Kong Theory by Virginie Despentes: I folded down every corner of this book because each page had something crucial I wanted to remember and repeat to people. Despentes discusses rape, selling sex, porn, ugliness and anarchy, and it's like reading lightning. Her experiences and point of view are vital.

A Natural History of Rape by Randy Thornhill and Craig T. Palmer: this looks at assault and coercion from an evolutionary perspective, with an awareness of how deeply problematic that is.

The Trauma Cleaner by Sarah Krasnostein: this biography is of an incredible woman, Sandra Pankhurst, and is illuminating in terms of her transition and sex work. Pankhurst was raped and then disbelieved both because she was a sex worker and because the defence argued that as a trans woman, she would have been able to fight off her attacker.

Paid For: My Journey through Prostitution by Rachel Moran: I've mentioned how incredible this book is already. It's an important piece of feminist literature and an excruciating insight into selling sex.

Half the Sky by Nicholas D. Kristof and Sheryl WuDunn: this book explores the nightmare that is sex trafficking, but is also balanced in portraying what a small part of the sex industry this crime is. What I found particularly interesting was not only the role of westerners exploiting people from impoverished countries, but also how ineffective attempts to 'save' victims can be, e.g. buying girls from brothels and taking them home, when there is much stigma about what has happened to them and they have no way of supporting themselves.

Pimp State: Sex, Money and the Future of Equality by Kat Banyard: this book is so well written and persuasive and wholly anti-sex work. See also Julie Bindel's *The Pimping of Prostitution*: Bindel has seen first-hand the ravages of what sex work does to people, the violence of it, the suffering, even within more permissive societies and decriminalised legal frameworks.

Sex, Lies and Statistics by Dr Brooke Magnanti: Dr Magnanti used to sell sex, writing a blog under the pseudonym Belle de Jour, which became the TV series *Secret Diary of a Call Girl*, so is probably the best-known pro-sex-work campaigner. This book is her myth-buster and is an important read alongside anti-sex-work polemics like those by Bindel and Banyard, for balance. See also *Playing the Whore* by Melissa Gira Grant: a brilliant book that will make you question your assumptions.

White Chrysanthemum by Mary Lynn Bracht: this is FICTIONAL but based on the true stories of girls and women of Korea kidnapped during war and raped in Japanese brothels. With this, as with so much, I can't understand the men, the faceless men, who queued up to do this to women who were imprisoned.

On the Front Line with the Women Who Fight Back by Stacey Dooley: through her documentaries Dooley has met and interviewed a variety of people selling sex to survive, from mothers in war zones trying to feed their kids to trans women in tourist hotspots. She also explores child trafficking and sexualisation.

Slavery Inc by Lydia Cacho: details international sex trafficking and is an important read.

Coming Out Like a Porn Star, edited by Jiz Lee: a collection of essays that are anarchic and confrontational and the missing voice in debates about porn. See also *The Feminist Porn Book: The Politics of Producing Pleasure*, edited by Tristan Taormino and Mireille Miller-Young.

Pornography Feminism by Rich Moreland: an extensive analysis of recent sex-positivity and moments within the movement. See also *After Pornified* by Anne G. Sabo.

For a different perspective, *Pornland: How Porn Has Hijacked Our Sexuality* by Gail Dines is a world of horror but an equally important part of this discussion.

The Erotic Engine by Patchen Barss: a great history of porn and technology. See also *Beaver Street: A History of Modern Pornography* by Robert Rosen: a broad, jaunty overview from someone with a lot of experience in the industry.

Jenna Jameson's autobiography *How to Make Love Like a Porn Star* is fun and comic and yet still gives space to discussion of consent, power, assault and the painful injuries that can result from stripping. See also *Girlvert* by Oriana Small.

Stripped by Jennifer Hayashi Danns, with Sandrine Lévêque, is a really insightful and interesting look at exotic dancing.

Some more science-orientated books include *Testosterone Rex* by Cordelia Fine, which argues that gender dynamics are created by hormones, environment, evolution and culture, rather than a 'sex recipe' that instructs behaviour; and *Testosterone: Sex, Power and the Will to Win* by Joe Herbert is fascinating about how the hormone drives competition and desire for power.

The Dangerous Passion by David Buss: yes, the guy from the experiments. This book explores the evolution of jealousy alongside romantic love.

Mismatch by Ronald Giphart and Mark van Vugt: an interesting read that considers how primitive brains process the stimulations of the modern world. See also *The Consuming Instinct* by Gad Saad.

Who Stole My Spear? by Tim Samuels is great on male bodies and evolutionary pressures versus contemporary expectations.

How Pleasure Works by Paul Bloom and *I, Mammal* by Loretta Graziano Breuning are both fantastic, readable books that teach about animal processes in our bodies and how they affect us day to day, from social 'happiness' to why some people enjoy S&M.

On masculinity, *Be a Man* by Chris Hemmings and *Man Up* by Jack Urwin both use personal experience, anecdotal evidence and research to explore maleness in our culture.

Man Alive by Thomas Page McBee: a beautiful and painful autobiography written by a trans man.

Stand by Your Manhood by Peter Lloyd: I mean, some of this book is contrary in a rather hateful way. Some of it is really important and needs wider discussion.

. . . and out of your ears

There are also some brilliant podcasts exploring topics I have touched on:

Episode 13 of *Ear Hustle* is called 'Dirty Water': a survivor interviews a trafficker in prison. This is a very emotional listen, but illuminating and important.

Episode 35 of *Vice Meets*, 'Sex Work Is Work', with Melissa Gira Grant.

The *Intelligence Squared* debate 'Pornography Is Good for Us' from October 2016. It's also worth listening to their debate from September 2018, 'How Tech Has Hijacked Our Brains'.

Episode 220 of *This American Life* explores testosterone really interestingly.

Episode 33 of *MOWE* deals with porn, masturbation and dopamine in an engaging and open-minded way.

Death, Sex and Money has a number of episodes on porn, sex education, morality and cultural values around sex. All very measured and entertaining.

The debate about laws around sex work in the US is brilliantly set out by *Reply All* episode 119, 'No More Safe Harbour', and the 'Shutting Down the Online Marketplace' episode of *Sold in America*. The latter series is completely excellent, and the host, Noor Tagouri, allows people to speak for themselves, something I, writing a book, was unable to do.

For that reason I have also recorded a series of interviews with people who have expertise on some of the issues we've raised to accompany this book, for some further exploration, disagreement and enlightenment. Search for 'Sex Power Money' on any podcast-hosting app.

Acknowledgements

If you interacted with me in any way in the last few years, if we had a brief chat about sex, porn, massage parlours or men paying for dinner, you are part of this book. As I roamed around trying to process how sex and money affect our lives, it was your opinions and your understanding that led mine. There are stories I haven't told: the man in love with a scammer who'll take his money but doesn't want *him*; the woman who has sex with friends for money to buy her kids expensive trainers. This subject is so incredibly broad, a see-saw with some people at the far edges but most of us clotted in the middle. I don't think I will ever stop wanting to understand it.

I am very grateful to the people who have spoken to me about their work and experience. Jane and Robyn, who gave up hours of your time correcting my misconceptions and answering my questions, you both shaped this book, as I imagined you reading it and did not want to disappoint you. Charlie Rose, thank you for educating me about the laws regarding sex work in our country and the various legal situations for sex workers abroad. Alex Feis-Bryce, thank you so much for sharing your knowledge about everything and letting me get drunk in a political establishment. There are several other sources that I have disguised in order to protect their privacy. If you recognise something you have shared with me – thank you. You have expanded my understanding of people.

As I began researching my book, especially after I mentioned it on *Woman's Hour* on BBC Radio 4, numerous kind souls got in touch to lend a hand. This is not an exhaustive list but a reminder that any author regularly relies on the kindness of strangers: Rebecca Collins from the Great Men Initiative, Hubert O'Hearn,

Sarah Trotman, Faye Blackwell, Hamilton Young and Leah Jewett, thank you for helping me. Thank you to Matt H. for telling me about your mum and Marcus B for sharing his past so openly, David H for his patience with my prying and Suzi R for explaining lesbian dating.

Thank you to my friends Mona Chalabi and Professor Sophie Scott for your assistance. Thank you so much, Gil Greengross, for showing an interest and then helping me access academic materials. Thank you to Robin Ince, who put me in touch with Professor Matthew Cobb, who in turn prevented me from including salacious but unfounded theories and focused my study. Thank you to Jenny Bede for transcription, thank you to Dean Burnett and the amazing Anne Miller for fact-checking, and to power-brained Eleanor Rees for correcting all the words I used thinking they meant something else.

Thank you to my mum, who once again has allowed me to write about her private life and only laughs at my rude ingratitude.

Thank you to the exes, who I hope don't read this.

Thank you to my dog Mouse, who ate two corners of the second draft.

Thank you, Steen Raskopoulos, for existing. I love you.

Thank you, everyone at Faber, for sticking with me, especially my editors Laura Hassan and Rowan Cope, and good old Julian, who got the ball rolling. Thank you, Dawn Sedgwick, who made this life of mine possible.

Thank YOU, reader, the most. But please don't think you need to tag me in your middling online review. *winky face emoji*

X